Running With Wolves

Tales from the gold and black country

by
Peter Lansley

Thomas Publications

First published in Great Britain in August, 2004, by
Thomas Publications, PO Box 17, Newport,
Shropshire, England, TF10 7WT

ISBN 0 9512051 9 6

Printed and bound by Cromwell Press, Trowbridge

Contents

Acknowledgements

To Jacqui, Tom and Joe – my first team.

To Dad, for the concept for the cover and all the subsequent work; to Mum, for proofing and grammar; to Simon, for timely encouragement, and to Mark and Dave, for humouring us.

To Wirksworth Wanderers, for allowing me to play centre midfield, and to the indefatigable Dossers United, still going, if not strong, after 20 years.

To the players and characters of Brassington Primary School and Wirksworth Colts, for a reminder of what it is like to learn the beautiful game.

To Keith Blackmore, David Chappell, Jeremy Griffin, Russell Kempson, Keith Pike, Nick Szczepanik, Richard Whitehead and a whole array of peerless colleagues at The Times. I promise not to offer any more articles on Wolves for at least the next week.

To the many football reporters out there who can make visiting even The Hawthorns feel like fun, not least David Anderson, Jon Culley, Dominic Fifield, Trevor Haylett, Tony Leighton, Phil Shaw, Martin Smith, Nick Spencer, Nick Harling, Ged Scott and the Midlands mafia.

To Dave Jones and his team, and to their predecessors. To all of the players in the following pages, for their coffee, biscuits and confidence.

To Tim Nash (at the Express & Star), John Hendley, Catherine Preece, Lorraine Hennessy (at Wolves) and Charles Ross. If it were not for A Load of Bull, I would not be here now.

To Peter Harrington, Marc Aspland and The Times, Newsteam, Nigel Bond, Birmingham Post & Mail, Associated Newspapers, Leicester Mercury and Nottingham Evening Post for their photographs. And to the various publications, headed by the Express & Star, whose cuttings have been a valuable source of research and artefacts.

To Cary's wine-bar in Ashbourne, for allowing me to sit writing for hours over one cappuccino, and for playing The Liquidator.

To Tessa Pellow, for design help above and beyond the price of a pint of Marston's Pedigree.

To Liz and David Instone, for helping me bring out the Wolves book inside. Maybe I can get on with my life now.

Introduction

June 11, 2003: Brassington, Derbyshire

D on't smoke, myself. Otherwise, on this sunny summer morning, I would light a seriously big cigar. As England prepare to play Slovakia at Middlesbrough tonight, I've just heard season tickets are on sale at Molineux. On Friday, the new all black away kit will be unveiled. Who knows, maybe it will have a round collar.

Wolves are going into the Barclaycard Premiership, back into the big time, and a knot is tightening in my stomach. The old season will slither to a halt this evening, yet I can't stop the adrenaline rushing at the prospect of the new one. It's sad, I know, but there you are. We have waited two decades for this. Men with middle-age spreads, mortgages and children have been following Wolverhampton Wanderers for the best - if that word is not inappropriate - part of their lives and not been to a top-flight match; at least not in the sense of supporting their team. Wolves have spent 19 years among the also-rans, sometimes they haven't even been that good, and are stepping into the unknown. Those fans feel as if they've been struck by a very bright light on the road from Blundell Park to Villa Park. They hope it is not a brief encounter.

Personally, I know what life at the top is like. For a decade at the start of my football life, Wolves were a big club. They won cups, played in Europe, smashed the British transfer record and boasted international players. An aura of greatness still surrounded them, the echo of a truly great era sounded. Where Billy Wright, Stan Cullis, Peter Broadbent and Bert Williams had won championships and FA Cups, so we believed Mike Bailey, Frank Munro, Ken Hibbitt and John Richards could follow. Even when they were relegated, it was for only one season. Going straight back up underlined the conviction that Wolves remained within sniffing distance of glory.

The addiction over which I'm salivating in the middle of this glorious summer (not an imminent fixture against Liverpool, but an announcement next week of *when* Wolves will again visit Anfield) was contracted during those formative years. As I count down the days to when the Premiership fixtures are published - it's eight, by the by - I spend the odd free evening watching the DVD of Wolves' Wembley victories. Adolescence revisited. I am staggered by how good Hibbitt, Munro and Bailey are in the 1974 League Cup final against Manchester City. Richards, my boyhood icon, has a mediocre game, to be truthful, yet Brian Moore, the commentator, seems to conspire with my favourable prejudices and keeps finding excuses to talk him up. Just as Dennis

From keepy-uppy

THE flag hanging down from the South Stand said it all: 19 years, 13 days, 22 hours and 20 minutes. Without an abacus or a *Rothmans*, I cannot guarantee the accuracy of the statistic that Truls Mansson has kept running on his website since Wolverhampton Wanderers were last members of the elite, but the sentiment is spot on.

Whether it has been 19 years of pain, or of frustration, or of bad luck, it has felt like quite some sentence. All that was wiped away yesterday.

Chris, from York, is not a miserable chap, but he does sum up the Wolves psyche. He put £300 on Sheffield United to win at evens as

"emotional insurance". Lose and at least he had his weekend paid for. Win and, well, that is nirvana for a Wolves fan. We are Premiership. At last. At long blooming last.

With 12 minutes to go of yesterday's exorcism, with Wolves three goals to the good and promotion all but secured, the big screen showed Sir Jack Hayward sitting, relatively peacefully. The Wolves owner looked up, saw himself and smiled, almost reluctantly. I am not taking anything for granted, his reticence suggested. Then he dared to put up two thumbs to the camera.

Hayward loved it so much yesterday that, two hours before kick-off, he had his car

Going up: Lescott shows his delight after Wolves' victory at the Millennium Stadium

Westcott's four-goal festive salvo had set my Dad believing it could happen every time he walked to Molineux, it was Richards' scoring feats that inspired me in my first season as a regular fan.

We have, with ample reason, been fed a steady stream of yarns of the old gold heroes of the 1950s. Yet more than a generation of Wolves fans have continued to worship at the altar that is Molineux with scant recognition of the characters and teams that have had to go to Hull and back even to anticipate seeing their team introduced by Des Lynam on a Saturday night. The last time Wolves were on *Match of the Day* for a league game, Jimmy Hill had just grown a beard. Do I hear: who's Jimmy Hill?

It is the very ignominy of having watched Wolves slip to 17th place in the Fourth Division, in the slipstream of an initiation with the good times, that makes me fully appreciate Dave Jones' team dipping their toes in the lake of gold and honey that's the Premiership. It is not quite true that what you have never had, you never miss: Simon, my younger brother, weeping at the Millennium Stadium as he realised he would finally see Wolves in the top flight, brought that home. But, having experienced the highs and lows, I'm relishing a bit of the high life. It is time to be a smaller fish in the bigger sea again. Then, maybe, just maybe, a slightly bigger fish.

When an approach came my way to write a book about Wolves' 1950s glories, the realisation struck that such an era was outside my knowledge. Those seasons were merely the backdrop to this particular lifetime of following one of the greatest clubs in English football (to those who think the game began with the Premier League's inception, I say: three titles, four FA Cups, historic floodlit European nights). Heroes are what make football go round. They are what keep David Beckham on the back pages throughout a 2003 summer with no football. For the young fan - unaware of the concept of one-club allegiance (good job Wolves went up, not Derby County, or Tom and Joe might have been lost), blissfully ignorant of commerce and hooliganism, still

to going-uppy on our golden day

Lifelong Wolves fan **Peter Lansley** relishes the moment in Cardiff

driven through the Wolves masses in Wood Street and back round the block for a second look. A 5,000-strong game of keepy-uppy was going on just outside Spar, where a queue snaked back towards the stadium for those purchasing their liquid sustenance. To the tune of *Yellow Submarine*, chants of "Albion going down like a big lead balloon", or something fairly adjacent, rang out.

Mike, 41, from Dudley, had promised his workforce a day off if West Bromwich Albion

went down and Wolves went up. Hard taskmaster or what. With his team's propensity for messing it up over the years, he might have thought he was safe. As he hugged Lewis, his seven-year-old son, and Abigail, 10, at half-time, his firm's finances were the last thing on his mind.

Grown men were crying. And that was Dad by 3.45pm. My young brother's premonition that Wolves would go 2-0 up, withstand a barrage of pressure and then nick a third at the end had prepared me

for the best-case scenario. I just didn't know that Si had meant by half-time.

Premiership fans tell me that Mark Kennedy is a big-time Charlie. He certainly responded to the big time yesterday: what a screaming finish, before he followed his Maradona crazy-face-to-camera celebration by working for the team for the rest of the match. Nathan Blake, in his home city, also put a shift in, on top of his goal. Kenny Miller, all deftness of touch, rounded off the dream opening period. When Matt Murray saved Michael Brown's penalty, I wondered just how many heroes Wolves could manage in one game.

The truth is, there were at least 11 on the pitch, with Paul Ince, Colin Cameron and Paul Butler pushing Murray hard for the man-of-the-match honours, and 34,000 in the stands. Dave Jones is a manager vindicated this morning, his response to last season's heartaches as measured as it was inspirational and Hayward, bless his cotton socks, sees his team promoted just before his 80th birthday.

Apologies to Tom, Joe and Jacqui for sending them off to Lanzarote on their own yesterday and I will see you tonight. Apologies, too, to Wolves for booking the family holiday to coincide with the play-offs final. How could I have doubted you?

developing tactical awareness - heroes light up the game. That is why I opted against detailing every match of every title year Wolves played in a decade before I was born.

That is why I have decided that the best way for me to tell a Wolves story - the tales from the gold and black country - is through Molineux heroes of the past 35 years; my heroes. Yes, Dave Wagstaffe was a better player than Steve Daley but, when I was 13, I longed to be Steve Daley. He was the costliest player in England for five minutes and the most maligned for the next five years. When I set out on this labour of love, I wanted to know how that felt, for a Wolves player, from a Wolves perspective.

My inclusion of the likes of Campbell Chapman, Robbie Keane and Kenny Miller are not down to longevity of service but to their ability to send hope emanating from Molineux. Optimism was short when Chapman played in the deep darkness of the Bhatti era and history shows us that his career was modest in the extreme. But to me, fresh out of school and seeking hope, he was a hero.

Wagstaffe, Mike Bailey, Derek Parkin, Mel Eves, Jon Purdie, Andy Thompson, Keith Downing, Mark Venus, Mick Gooding, Mike Stowell and Neil Emblen are all worthy characters I agonised over before omitting from my 'squad.' But there had to be a cut-off, a criterion, so I went for complete subjectivity; I trust you will disagree vehemently with some of my selections but sympathise rather more with the emotions they led us through. Supporting Wolverhampton Wanderers, after all, has never been a straightforward business.

This book is dedicated to Mum and Dad.
Thanks for all your love and support.

Tim Flowers

AN UPWARD CURVE AND A SUNNY PERSONALITY

May 4, 2003: The press room, Molineux

It was already a day for celebration, what with guarantees in place for both Leicester City's promotion from the Nationwide League First Division and Wolves' entry into the play-offs, but as Tim Flowers warmed up during the latter stages of the teams' 1-1 draw at Molineux, the occasion became imbued with an added significance.

As he undertook his humble duties, jogging up and down the touchline in front of the Billy Wright Stand with 25 minutes to go, the South Bank regulars recognised the veteran goalkeeper, back at the ground where his career had begun 19 years previously. Four months earlier, in an FA Cup fourth-round tie, he had been greeted fondly when named among the reserves for Leicester's trip to Molineux. Gradually, on this sunny May afternoon, the odd wave became the odd cheer; the home support threw out a claim to test whether they were applauding one of their own. By the time the crowd were singing 'Flowers is a Wolves fan,' the former Southampton, Blackburn Rovers and England custodian was laughing his acquiescence.

The 36-year-old was allowed a brief run-out, going on as a sentimental substitute 12 minutes from the end for Ian Walker, himself back in the England squad. Dave Jones joked afterwards that there must have been 12 men in the defensive wall when Wolves were awarded a free-kick 20 yards from goal, so eager were Leicester's players to ensure their popular team-mate kept a clean sheet in his last-ever professional appearance.

It was a fitting way for Flowers to bow out. His job was done, Leicester had long since regained their place in the Barclaycard Premiership and would be building a bigger and better squad. Where better for Flowers to take his leave than on the field

Debut day: Tim Flowers, half hidden by team-mate Derek Ryan, turns anxiously towards the referee as Kevin Arnott goes crashing under a tackle by John Humphrey in Wolves' 2-2 Molineux draw with Sheffield United on the opening day of the 1984-85 season.

where it had all started, back in the summer of 1984, against Sheffield United, in the old Second Division. Molineux had undergone an implausible transformation in the intervening years, from the decrepit home for cockroaches and uninitiated teenagers to a platform fit for the Premiership and its multi-million-pound stars. But it was the ideal stage for Flowers to take his final curtain call - and supporters from Wolverhampton and Leicester alike took the opportunity to bid the retiring goalkeeper an emotional farewell.

Little did Tim Flowers know, on August 25, 1984, when Alan Dodd and Tommy Langley scored in a 2-2 draw with Sheffield, that he was playing in the first league game of what was about to become Wolves' 19-year sentence outside the top flight. There was a pleasing symmetry that he should also be involved in the last league game of that stretch. As Flowers hung up his gloves, so Wolves' imprisonment was about to come to an end.

Afterwards, taking an informal seat in the press room that overlooks Waterloo Road, Flowers was clearly on a high from his send-off. Having played little more than a bit part at Leicester in the last couple of seasons, he welcomed his brief restoration to centre stage. Preparing for life as Leicester's goalkeeping coach, this was his final call for an interview as a player. On the buzz of playing for his last club back at the home of his first, he was in scintillating form.

He recalled an illustrious yet varied career shared with Alan Shearer and Campbell Chapman, one in which he had played under Kenny Dalglish, Martin O'Neill and Tommy Docherty. For all his amusing anecdotes and self-deprecation, Flowers did not have a bad word to say about anyone. He had played in front of 2,222 in the icy isolation of an away defeat against Newport County just before Christmas 1985, and in front of 80,000 in a World Cup finals warm-up win over Morocco in Casablanca 13 years later, keeping a clean sheet on his final international appearance. Being able to look back on such contrasting experiences with complete equanimity, to treat as just the same those two imposters, Triumph and Disaster, showed the value of a career spent on an upward curve and of a sunny personality.

Flowers became England's goalkeeper and won a championship medal with Blackburn yet his career could barely have started in more austere circumstances. Wolves had just gone down from the old First Division - wasn't it with the lowest ever points tally at the time, or the fewest goals scored? - and as Molineux rotted, the club also threatened to fall apart. In the midst of two periods of receivership, Docherty took over a team in severe need of rebuilding - and made it worse. There were some triers in there, some good honest pros, such as Alan Ainscow, Alan Dodd and John Humphrey, but Wolves' fortunes were to go downhill, on a very sharp decline, before they bottomed out.

Flowers still regards John Burridge, the Wolves goalkeeper when he was first coming through the youth ranks at Molineux, as his mentor but, in turn, on this day in May, the man whose playing days had just ended also appreciates the next generation. "Matt Murray had my shirt after the game," he said. "He's a phenomenal-looking lad. He's got all the tools for the job. When I stand next to him, he makes me look like Ronnie Corbett.

"He's only young and he's still learning his trade. He could be a real threat for the England jersey. If he continues to work hard with Bob (Mimms), who I was with at Blackburn, then he has every chance. I rate him highly, as I do Chris Kirkland, at Liverpool, who's had bad luck with injuries. But it's good to think two Midlands boys could be in future England squads because this area has always been a hotbed of goalkeepers, when you look back to Gordon Banks and Peter Shilton. Let's hope the tradition is continued."

September 15, 2003: Belvoir training ground, Leicester

F lowers decided to call time on his career because he required a hip operation. When we reconvene our interview, on the afternoon before Leicester record their first win of the Premiership season, trouncing Leeds United 4-0 in dynamic style, he is still rehabilitating.

He reckons the origins of the deteriorating condition go right back to his schoolboy days at Molineux. "I was a Coventry City fan, still am, but Wolves, as my first club, will always be special to me," he says, when asked whether the Wanderers fans were right when chanting back in May that he was one of them. "I was there from a really early age, about 13, when I used to go training two nights a week at that big gym above Dave Wagstaffe's social club, with the wooden floor. Landing on that is how my hip trouble first started.

"Dad would knock off work early and take me over every Tuesday and Thursday and I wouldn't get to bed until midnight. Then in the school holidays, we'd stay in the barracks if we were training at RAF Cosford, or in digs when we were at Castlecroft. As soon as I left school, I moved away from home to become an apprentice.

"We'd play in the Intermediate League on a Saturday morning, home games at Cosford, and then if the first team were at home, get the bus back to Molineux to help out there. Apprentices still did jobs in those days - unlike today, which is a joke - but we'd do the boots, the toilets, the baths, mop up, sort out the laundry. I was there with the likes of Peewee (Paul) Dougherty, Billy Livingstone, Martin Bayly, Derek Ryan, Graham Rodger, Stuart Watkiss. It was part of our education.

"As a lad, I was greatly influenced by John Burridge. People say he was a character but he was very professional and incredibly hard-working. A lot of the stuff we were doing in training then, I still use today. He'd go and watch midweek games - if Peter Shilton was playing locally, for instance, when Wolves weren't - to educate himself and I learned a lot off him. He'd give me the odd pair of gloves, or a jumper. As a kid, you'd think it was Christmas. Much of how I turned out as a goalkeeper was down to studying him. No matter what your technique is, you've got to put the hard graft in.

"People say he was mad; I'd say he was off the wall. I roomed with him and sometimes, he'd have nothing on but his goalkeeping gloves, jumping this way and that, preparing. He just loved goalkeeping. He once said to me: 'I'm going to make you a goalkeeper, my son.' He used to get his wife Jan to throw him an orange in the middle of the night to test his reflexes.

"Another time, I went round to his place and he was watching a game on television - I think it might have been a video of him playing in a League Cup final - and he had a hot water bottle on his head. He had a cold and wanted to keep the heat in. He was a very funny man. Last I heard of him, he was over in the Oman, training their national goalkeepers. He speaks their language, goes to prayer with them. He was infectious, a real star."

It was when Burridge moved on in 1984, with Wolves starting their slide through the divisions, that Flowers was given his opportunity, at the age of 17. As we drink our tea in the Leicester training ground players' room, he flicks through the old match-day programmes I have brought along, showing this skinny, curly-haired boy. He really was no more than that. "The Doc had no money to replace Budgie, so he signed me on professional terms," Flowers recalls. "He had no other goalkeeper, so he had no option but to play me.

"Docherty was a really funny fella, a character. I remember my debut, 2-2 at home to Sheffield United. I was bricking myself and he came in 20 minutes before kick-off

The youthful style and agility that first thrust Tim Flowers into the spotlight.

and said to me: 'Timmy, I want you to do something today you've never done before.' I said: 'What's that?' and he said: 'Play well'. It was great, everyone was rolling around laughing, I relaxed a bit and I did alright.

"We had a decent start to the season but then went on a horrendous run, couldn't score a goal for about three months, couldn't buy a win, until, finally, we did manage one, at Carlisle. If we'd had a stronger squad, I'd have been whipped out and rested but there wasn't a lot we could do. The club were in decline and there was no money.

"It was sink or swim for me. I could have buckled and melted; but I didn't. Every team had a big 6ft 2in or 6ft 3in centre-forward back then and he'd come piling through me every week. As a 17-year-old up against a Mick Harford or Keith Walwyn every game, I'd get absolutely mullered going for crosses. They'd be pummelling into me and I'd come off the field with bruises everywhere.

"I was the supporters' player of the year that season which said something. I don't know how many goals I let in (72 as it happens, Tim) but it built my character, coming through that whole season and only missing four games. I broke my wrist at Brighton, I remember, saving a penalty from Frank Worthington. He hit it that hard and I punched it up on to the bar - and it had to be retaken because some wally had come into the box! Straightaway, I've said: 'Ref, my hand's hurting,' and the physio's come on but the ref must have thought I was trying to con him. So we wrapped it up, Worthington's bashed the retake into the top corner and, when I went for an x-ray afterwards, I'd broken my scafoid. I was Midlands' player of the year and to get those accolades made something of the season for me. Although we'd been relegated, which was devastating, personally it was good. The fans took to me and could see I was having as good a go as I could. I think they admired me for that and that's why those who are still coming to games give me a shout."

Wolves suffered their second of three successive relegations in 1985 and Flowers shared the goalkeeping duties with Scott Barrett, another young hopeful brought in from non-league football, in the Third Division. "I found the second season really hard," Flowers says. "Midway through, I went on loan to Southampton for five days. I saved a penalty at The Dell in a 3-2 reserves win over Chelsea, and was training with Peter Shilton and learning so much. Then, on the Thursday, I got recalled because Scott got injured and I thought: 'Blow this.' But I went back to Wolves and we won 1-0 at Blackpool and I played ever so well. We had thousands of fans up there, all gone up for a weekend by the sea. Seriously, there must have been 5,000 Wolves fans there (the crowd was 4,563, Tim, but those supporters can have that effect). They were great. I moved to Southampton for £75,000 that summer but that wasn't anywhere near enough to stop the club going back into receivership."

When Flowers had signed on as an apprentice, Wolves were only a couple of years out of Europe, having won the League Cup in 1980, and were promoted in 1983, with Derek Dougan as chairman and Graham Hawkins as manager, back to the First Division. The subsequent decline was staggeringly sharp. "The season when we went straight back down, it still seemed like a big club," Flowers recalls, "and the ground was fine. But then we were heading towards bankruptcy and people wouldn't do any work because they weren't getting paid. The place became a total hole. Paint was peeling off, nothing got so much as patched up. It was falling apart. I was still a very young pro and even though I was playing for the first team, I was still helping out with the kit and cleaning up from 8am with the other youngsters. I played in the FA Youth Cup that first season.

"The seniors would come in about 9.30am but we had to get their kit down from the laundry and I remember we'd open the changing room door, switch the light on and all these cockroaches would scuttle off, across the lino floor and under the benches. They'd get through holes in the heat grids that were knackered. We had to reach under there and sweep out as many of them as possible. Molineux had become a dump. There were weeds growing out of the terraces, numbers and letters falling off the old half-time scoreboard. The club were in serious decline."

Flowers runs through some team-mates of whom, one by one, he speaks very highly - Tommy Langley, Alan Ainscow, Jim Melrose, Mel Eves, John Humphrey, Alan Dodd, David Barnes, John Pender - but recognises that, as a team, with the perilous financial position, Wolves were on an inexorable slide. "Probably none of us would get in the side now, at a club with such a great history, but it was an era when Wolves were struggling. Yet the year after I left, Brian Little did a great job before being controversially sacked. Graham Turner came in and did well, signing Steve Bull and Andy Thompson and the team soon hit a crest of a wave, battering teams in the way that we had been getting battered."

Flowers is conscious of Wolves' place in football's rich domestic tapestry, aware of their heritage. "I remember Bill McGarry coming back and having another brief spell as manager, but you could tell he wouldn't be a part of it. He resigned after about a month. When he'd been there in the 1970s, they were a good, successful club and he'd built a team who were competing for honours and playing in Europe. He had a reputation as a hard taskmaster but he was terrific with me. He just saw the state the club that he loved were getting into and he couldn't bring himself to be involved in the inevitable further decline. You can't blame him."

As a Midlands boy, Flowers had heard about the great teams of the 1950s and was even presumed to be part of the lineage. "I was watching Coventry the other day," he says, laughing, "and some old chap was asking a question about the Wolves. He looked at me and said: 'Ask Ron, he'll know.' When I was breaking into the Wolves team, it was almost assumed that I must be Ron Flowers' son.

"He and Jimmy Mullen, two of the stars of the great championship-winning teams, had sports shops in parallel streets in the centre of Wolverhampton and were good to me. I'd go with a chitty from the club to buy some new boots. If they were £20, it'd show £25 on the receipt and I'd have a fiver for myself. I was on £25 a week as an apprentice, with a £25 monthly West Midlands transport pass. When I turned pro, I was on £100 a week plus £100 appearance bonus, which was fine. I was just delighted to be playing. I lodged with Jack and Olive Carr in Codsall Wood and they were lovely to me. When Wolves were at their lowest point, they'd come down to training at Castlecroft and get a pot of tea on for the boys and buy the biscuits. They were part of the set-up, Wolves fanatics. I still get a Christmas card from Olive, bless her; Jack's passed on.

"The funny thing was when I moved to Southampton, the Doc put me on to an agent and I signed a five-year contract on the same terms. It took me a while to realise I'd been shanked because I was never going to be playing a game for years, with Shilts then Budgie there, so the appearance money was a dubious benefit. But for a lot of kids, they get too much too soon and it kills their ambition. That's why I admire the likes of Roy Keane. You see him and he's desperate to win things still.

"After a while at Southampton, Budgie told me what to ask for, so I went in to see Chris Nicholl, the manager, and he promptly showed me the door. I heard Carlisle United wanted me on loan, so I went back in and said: 'I want to start from the bottom again.' Then Budgie left, so Nicholl said swiftly: 'We've got that new contract we discussed all drawn up.' But I think the best players deserve their money because they are the ones who people pay their entrance fee to watch. It's the average players on big money I don't think deserve their pay."

Flowers went on to play with several who earned every penny. Shortly before joining Blackburn for £2.4m in November, 1993, he saved a penalty on his England debut in a 1-1 draw with Brazil in Washington, winning ten more caps and going to the 1998 World Cup finals as David Seaman's deputy. He keeps his winners' medals - for Blackburn's Premiership title in 1995 and for Leicester's League Cup in 2000 - in a drawer. Home is near Warwick, where he lives with his wife and two daughters.

Alan Shearer is probably his best friend in football and the two best managers he played under were Dalglish and O'Neill. "Kenny ruled by his aura," Flowers says, "by the sheer respect he comanded. He's a World XI player. You speak to anyone who was at Blackburn in those days and they'll tell you that he and Ray Harford, God rest his soul, were just fantastic. Whatever Kenny says, you do it. He says: 'Jump out of a window' and you jump. They were a really good partnership.

"What Martin did here (Tim waves a hand in the air) was sensational. His man-management was unbelievable and you can see why he's so successful. His backroom staff, John Robertson and Steve Walford, were excellent too and I remember us finishing in the top ten, winning the final League Cup at Wembley, playing Red Star Belgrade in Europe. We talk about money but you can't buy those sort of memories, nor those that built me up in my early days with Wolves."

Tim Flowers, England keeper, before one of his 11 senior caps. Picture courtesy of Marc Aspland, The Times.

It was ironic, then, that the final season of Flowers' playing career should be at a club who were encumbered by grave financial problems. Leicester slipped into administration after their 2002 relegation but, instead of spiralling closer to the abyss, as Wolves had done all those years back, they managed to turn it around and win the promotion that solved their predicament. Leicester, their £50m debt reduced by 90 per cent as the administrators did their job, came out of it with a marvellous new stadium and a place once more in the

Premiership. This was opulence compared to Molineux, circa 1985. The players did do their bit, however, Flowers points out.

"They were scary times," he says. "We were having meetings when the depth of the club's problems were really starting to hit home. We'd meet the money people and they'd say, 'The playing staff have got to take a 30 per cent deferral on wages,' and we'd all say: 'Clear off, don't be stupid.' Then we heard that if we didn't, that would tip the club over into liquidation. I've been there before, remember. As a group of lads, you've got no choice, you just can't allow it to happen, you can't allow the club you're playing for to go through the floor like that. But it was all quite heavy at the time. There's no doubt about that."

Leicester had one distinct advantage compared with the Wolves situation Flowers had endured. "The good thing was that the players were winning matches at the time," he says. "Victories hide a multitude of sins. We and Portsmouth were the two best sides in the Nationwide League and we deserved to be promoted automatically. Micky Adams did a fantastic job in difficult circumstances and he has proved what he's made of."

As we pack away the old Wolves programmes, the tea cups and prepare to make our separate ways to the Walkers Stadium for our respective duties, Flowers ponders the clubs' different rebirths in the Premiership. "Win tonight and it's a good-looking start for Leicester," he says, as I wince at a Wolves tally that has had the jokers asking what the difference is between them and a cocktail stick. That's right, the one about the cocktail stick having two points.

"It's early days and there's plenty of time yet," he says. "Plus there's some money at the club and so if necessary they can go out when the transfer window opens and add to what already looks to be a strong squad. I really wouldn't worry too much just yet." Within a fortnight, Sir Jack Hayward will announce that his bountiful munificence is to come to an end and new investment will be required to keep Wolves afloat. As Flowers knows only too well from the book ends that hold up the story of his playing career, the financial vagaries of the game mean there are no certainties in football.

Tim Flowers

Born:	February 3, 1967, in Kenilworth
Signed:	June, 1983
Wolves appearances:	72
Goals:	0
Left:	June, 1986
International recognition:	11 senior England caps

JONES CONFIDENT AS HUNGRY WOLVES EYE PLAY-OFFS

WOLVERHAMPTON WANDERERS (0) **1**
Miller 58

LEICESTER CITY (0) **1**
Benjamin 86 (pen)

Referee: G Laws 7 (rep: A Williams, 32min 3). Attendance: 29,190

★ ★ ★ ★ ★

Lacklustre Leicester fail to dent visiting team's progress

THIS TIME LAST SEASON, chins were on their chests at Molineux. Drawing 2-2 away to Sheffield Wednesday as West Bromwich Albion beat Crystal Palace, Wolverhampton Wanderers limped into the Nationwide League first division play-offs with spirits, form and second place long since lost. At least this year, beaten just twice in 21 games, Dave Jones's team will enter them with their heads held high.

Leicester City, already promoted, were here for the party. Their players must have been tempted to ask for their supporters' beach ball as their attentions turned to the sand and sun after an arduous season. After Ludo Pollet had handled after being rounded by Tommy Wright and Trevor Benjamin scored a penalty, it was the first time Matt Murray, the goalkeeper who was yesterday voted their young player of the year, had been troubled in the second period.

Wolves had led when Kenny Miller scored his 23rd domestic goal of the season, firing in a superb effort as the home side dominated. Tim Flowers, who started his career with Wolves 17 years ago, came on in goal for Leicester, his final appearance of a long and distinguished career. The home crowd afforded him a standing ovation. "They were always great to me," he said, "although there's about 20,000 more of

them now than when I was playing here. I really hope they go on and win promotion now."

So Wolves face Reading in the play-off semi-finals, having traded 1-0 away wins with them this season. "It does not make one iota of difference who we play," Jones, the Wolves manager, said. "It's down to a cup competition now. We felt we'd lost something last year and we were running on empty. So we are in a better frame of mind now."

PETER LANSLEY

Wolverhampton Wanderers (4-4-2): M Murray 7 – D Irwin 6, P Butler 6, L Pollet 6, L Naylor 6 (sub: M Edworthy, 46min 6) – S Newton 5, P Ince 6 (sub: A Rae, 86), C Cameron 6, M Kennedy 6 – K Miller 6 (sub: D Sturridge, 86), N Blake 5. Substitutes not used: M Oakes, G Naish. Booked: Pollet. FORM: DDWWDW.

Leicester City (4-4-2): I Walker 6 (sub: T Flowers, 78) – F Sinclair 6 (sub: N Summerbee, 63 5), M Elliott 5, G Taggart 5, A Impey 4 – J Scowcroft 6, M Jones 5, W McKinlay 5, T Benjamin 5 – T Wright 6, S Deane 5 (sub: T Ferrescu, 73). Substitutes not used: J Ashton, M Heath. Booked: McKinlay, Benjamin. FORM: DDWDW.

Shots on target: (h) 4 (a) 3. Fouls: (h) 5 (a) 6. Offsides: (h) 1, (a) 3.

ALMOST ANYTHING IS A CRIME AGAINST HUMANITY IN TODAY'S ARMY

THE GAME
■ The £15 million play-off

At I
Le
T2

THE 🛡 **TIM**
No 6770

MONDAY MAY 26 2003

Blair's £800m

Bush plans early peace summit after Israel

Frank Munro

A GLOBE-TROTTING DEFENDER FROM DOWN THE ROAD

June 19, 2003: At Frank's, Compton, Wolverhampton

There are no mementoes on the wall of Frank Munro's flat, none framed above the television set nor taking any pride of place. In this modest abode in Compton, ten minutes from Molineux, there is a stark absence of reminders of his previous life as an elegant, accomplished Scotland international defender who intermittently captained Wolverhampton Wanderers in the early 1970s. Instead, there is a 1990 photograph of a prematurely white-haired, good-looking man, before his stroke, with his partner, Naomi. Yet, on the morning the 2003-04 Barclaycard Premiership fixtures are coming out, the name of Wolves figures prominently and Munro, his enthusiasm unmasked behind the laconic drawl, asks: "Who's the first home game against? I'll be going with Dave Wagstaffe. I think we'll do okay with the right signings."

For a man who served the old gold and black with such style for the best part of ten years, it seems paradoxical he should have so little to show for a career with a club he evidently still reveres. His income is from a disability allowance, bolstered by neither the now-traditional PFA pension nor the testimonial benefits he maintains he was due from Wolves. Every day, he misses Australia, where his grandchildren live and whence he returned 13 years earlier after the end of his marriage. He is 55, yet the effects of the stroke, "a bloody big one," make him look much older.

Naomi, whom he endearingly calls his "girlfriend," produces coffee and a bag full of *Sporting Stars* from the early 1970s. Even these token accounts of his time with Wolves, when Bill McGarry's team were regularly knocking on Europe's door and finishing in the top ten of the old First Division, have been lent by a friend. "It has never bothered me," Munro explains, adjusting the yellow shawl over his legs, lighting a cigarette. "I was proud of playing for Wolves, playing professionally, but I don't have any keepsakes. I don't even have any of my caps. I gave them all away."

The friendships and the memories live on, but, otherwise for Munro the Wolves player, it has all been spirited away into the ether. His is an empty trophy cabinet. It was almost like that for the talented Wolves team in which he starred. McGarry, who inherited Munro as a young inside-forward and left a year before the defender's reign at Molineux ended, went on national TV the day after Wolves won the League Cup final in March, 1974. He said that if that cup run had come to nothing, he would have packed it all in. Enough of not quite enough; it was nearly the end of the nearly men.

Munro, 20 and just married, was signed by Ronnie Allen for £60,000 from Aberdeen on January 5, 1968. It was a fruitful spell for Wolves as Derek Parkin also joined, the costliest full-back in England at the time at £80,000 from Huddersfield Town, and Kenny Hibbitt signed from Bradford Park Avenue for £5,000. Munro had scored a hat-trick for Aberdeen - guesting as the Washington Whips - in a tournament in America the previous summer. It came against Wolves, who were playing under the Los Angeles banner, and he was excited at the prospect of moving south. He suggested to Allen his best position was at the back but was told he had too much ability to play there. "To me, that was an advantage," Munro reflects.

By September, 1970, with McGarry having succeeded Allen and established Wolves in the top flight following their promotion three years earlier, Munro and John McAlle, another young centre-half, had established themselves as the fulcrum of the back four. Wolves finished fourth that season and, with Mike Bailey in his pomp as midfield anchor, McGarry had hit upon his best defensive unit. "We had a good camaraderie," Munro says. "The numbers from one to six, from Phil Parkes to John McAlle, hardly changed. John was a very good defender and we made a good partnership." Did they socialise together, this team nucleus that was to remain for much of the next six years? "We used to drink together, I know that much," he recalls with a wry grin.

Bernard Shaw was right-back, with Parkin on the other flank. Hibbitt, just breaking in, and Jim McCalliog played either side of Bailey, with Derek Dougan as the target-man that the popular left-winger, Dave Wagstaffe, aimed for. Hugh Curran and Bobby

Gould were sharing the primary goalscorer's role before John Richards burst on to the scene. It was an exciting team, combining youth with experience, pace with poise, long-ball pragmatism with some of the country's most skilled young players. Finishing fourth, ninth and fifth in successive years, Wolves also embarked on some exhilarating cup runs - to the first UEFA Cup final, the semi-finals of both domestic cups in 1973 and, finally, to glory in the League Cup of 1973-74.

In that final against Manchester City, Munro was simply imperious. The opposition were stuffed full of international flair players, from Denis Law to Rodney Marsh, while Wolves were rather more homespun and workmanlike. Yet Munro, like Bailey and Hibbitt in front of him, seemed to thrive on outwitting such illustrious names. He acknowledges, however, that he should not even have been playing.

Only four weeks before Wolves' first visit to Wembley in 14 years, he was sent off against Stoke City. John Dee, the Wolves correspondent for the *Express & Star*, wrote that his dismissal 'hits hard at Wolves' plans for the final.' He said this 'vital part of their defensive machinery' faced a three-match ban if no appeal was lodged - a penalty that would also mean him missing the league games against Birmingham City and Manchester United. His dismissal followed an incident with Jimmy Robertson. Although few of the 30,128 crowd saw it, referee Harry Hackney immediately pointed to the dressing-rooms, confirming later Munro had been banished for violent conduct.

With the refuge of the passing years, Munro admits he aimed a blow off the ball. "Robertson went off injured and John Ritchie came on and scored the equaliser. To his credit, Robertson went to the hearing at Sheffield, spoke up for me and I got off. I shouldn't have, though. I should have been banned for Wembley."

In the final, the manner in which Munro timed his interceptions and moved out of defence in possession reflected a ball-playing centre-half in his prime. With Parkin and McAlle snapping into tackles like their futures depended on keeping City at bay - "Derek's third tackle on Summerbee was more assault than a foul" - Wolves won the battle at the back before taking control higher up, Hibbitt giving them the lead just before the interval.

After Colin Bell equalised, Munro was booked for fouling

Imperious central defender turns dangerous attacker. Frank Munro gets airborne to leave Tommy Booth grounded, watched by Alan Sunderland (right) and skipper Mike Bailey.

Francis Lee from behind but, otherwise, he barely put a foot wrong in an enthralling game won late on by John Richards' low drive. "Underdogs, people tell me we were," he recalls. "I never felt that. I thought we had better players than them. They had a good forward line - Summerbee, Bell, Lee, Law and Marsh - but we had a good team too."

Munro shrugs off praise of his classy performance and highlights his favourite moment succinctly. "The final whistle," he says. "That and going up to get the cup." Watch the DVD and you see him receiving his tankard while wearing his compatriot Denis Law's shirt. "He'd said: 'Shall we swap strips at the end?' I was over the moon," Munro says. "Then I gave Denis' top to a kid in a wheelchair as we walked off."

That summer, Munro narrowly missed out on going to the World Cup finals. "I was named in the initial 30 but not the final 22," he says. "My most memorable game for Scotland was at Wembley [on May 22, 1971]. Martin Chivers was running amok and scored twice as England led 3-1. So, at half-time, the manager moved Frank McLintock into midfield, Billy Bremner into attack and sent me on for Hugh Curran. I marked Chivers and the score didn't change.

"I also remember facing Dougan at Hampden, against Northern Ireland in the old home internationals. I brought the ball down on the edge of the box and waltzed past him. He chased after me and hacked me down. I said: 'What the bloody hell are you doing? We've got Arsenal on Saturday.' He just growled and said: 'There's no friends in this game.' Doog was playing up front with George Best and scored the winner, or at least that's how it was recorded. Truth is, he swung at the ball with his right foot and

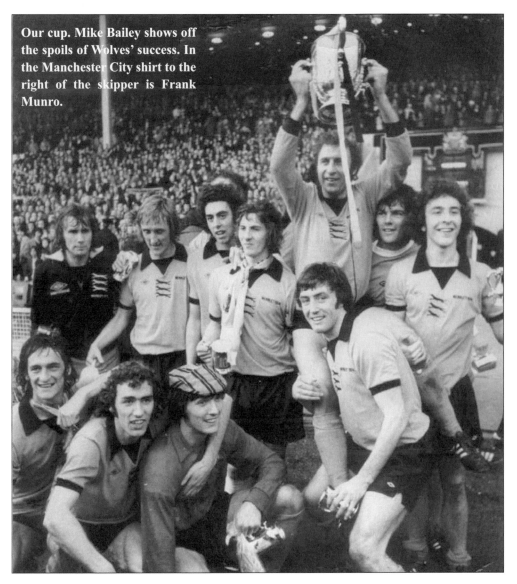

Our cup. Mike Bailey shows off the spoils of Wolves' success. In the Manchester City shirt to the right of the skipper is Frank Munro.

it was going out for a throw-in until it hit John Greig's heel and went in. He was good value in Wolves' team, Dougan was. Mind you, he was playing with a centre-forward as brave as a lion in Richards, a winger who could put the ball on a sixpence in Waggy and had Mike with the long throw. He was a bit of a character. You could say he wasn't shy. He was chairman of the PFA in those days and he'd always speak his mind. He had a bit of a temper on him, with his Irish streak. He didn't often come out second best in dressing-room discussions, put it that way."

The League Cup final presented Dougan with his first trophy win but Munro does not rate that game as the best of his own career, reflecting instead on a 1-1 UEFA Cup quarter-final draw in Turin two years earlier. "We won a trophy in 1974 but the match against Juventus was the best we played as a team, defensively and in attacking terms. By fluke, Mike was injured and I stood in as captain." Wolves had slalomed through the first three rounds, scoring 18 goals in six games, before defeating Juve 3-2 on aggregate. Danny Hegan and Dougan scored in the second leg in front of 40,421 on March 22. Munro himself scored in both legs of the semi-final as Ferencvaros were defeated 4-3 on aggregate, before Wolves met Tottenham Hotspur in the final.

"We lost it at home," Munro says. "What was incredible about that run was that we never lost an away game, not even in the final. We'd been all over Europe, picking up results every time, so it was an anti-climax to then meet an English side." It was the first time since a first-round stroll past Academica Coimbra that Wolves had had to play the first leg at Molineux. Spurs won 2-1 and, Munro recalls, Hegan almost scored the goal of that or many another season.

"I tried to find Wagstaffe with a long ball and Pat Jennings came out and sliced the ball to the corner flag," the acting captain recalls. "He went to retrieve it and cleared to the half-way line, where Hegan controlled on his thigh and volleyed, all in one movement, goalwards. Jennings was running frantically back and just managed to flip it over. One foot to the right and it would have been a tremendous goal. Martin Chivers scored from about 40 yards instead. Waggy scored with a cracker in the return leg to equalise Alan Mullery's goal and it was end to end but we lost 3-2 overall."

Five years later, Hegan became the central name in the most controversial match of Munro's career. The Irish midfielder alleged in a *Sunday People* article that Billy Bremner had attempted to bribe Wolves to 'lie down' and let Leeds United win their final game of the season so they could add the title to the FA Cup they had just won. Derby County, top of the table and already on holiday in Majorca, had finished their campaign by the night of Monday, May 8, when the title was to be decided. Liverpool, away to Arsenal, could nick it by winning if Leeds, needing a draw at Molineux the same night to finish first, were beaten.

"It was a real grandstand finish," Munro recalls. "Leeds had just played the FA Cup final and it was very unfair on them to have this game 48 hours later; a Wembley occasion takes so much out of you. Our game with them should have been on the Wednesday. Leeds stayed at the Mount Hotel and I saw them going there with the Cup. On the Sunday morning, they were training on Tettenhall Green, having a kick-about. Mick Jones had broken his collarbone so he couldn't play and others had to play with injuries. I was up against Billy Bremner, who was moved up front with Allan Clarke."

Bremner, who died in 1997, was a true great of that outstanding but oft-reviled Don Revie team. He was one of several Leeds players Munro knew from international football. Peter Lorimer, alongside whom the Wolves defender had played for Scotland juniors, was another. It is worth taking in the Leeds perspective on this game in the light of the High Court trial that was only concluded a decade later, after Bremner sued Odhams Newspapers, owners of the *Sunday People*, and Hegan for defamation of character. Bremner won and was awarded £100,000, with his accusers ordered to pay £60,000 legal costs.

In *Don Revie - Portrait of a Footballing Enigma*, by Andrew Maurant, Lorimer recalls: "There used to be the odd joke if we were playing a team in the last game of the season and we needed the points and they were mid-table. If you had some of your Scottish pals playing, you'd say: 'I hope you're going to take it easy.' But if you're talking about us going up to one of them with £200 to say: 'You're not going to have a go today,' I've never seen that. I remember saying [on match night] to big Frannie Munro, who was a pal of mine: 'I hope you're not going to kick us around.' That was a bit of banter. If you were going to put a story together, people could say you were trying to say something. But I was a pal of Frannie's; I said that as a joke. Wolves played out of their skin that night, perhaps because of a bit of hatred of Leeds. They wouldn't have played like that normally but I'd not know whether an approach was made that night, I'll be 100 per cent honest. If you got to one or two players, the other nine could still carry the match and you'd certainly have to go for the goalkeeper."

Lorimer is more candid in his autobiography, *Leeds and Scotland Hero: Lash*. He records: "The allegation was fuelled by an article by Gary Sprake (the Leeds keeper, who did not play that night at Molineux) in which it was said that Revie, with some involvement from Bremner, had tried through contacts to offer inducements to Wolves players to take it easy." The Scot says there were difficult decisions, including an apparent hand-ball in Wolves' area in the first half, but subscribes to the view that the referee (W. J. Gow from Swansea) had a huge task officiating a game that was surrounded by so much rumour.

Geoffrey Green, football correspondent of *The Times*, wrote in his match report: "When it was all over, the Yorkshiremen could justifiably point to two penalty kicks denied them, one in each half." Lorimer went on: "Wolves played like a team who had been given £100,000 to win. All the speculation had put them in a funny position. If they had been beaten 3-0, the headlines would have suggested that they had 'taken a dive.' They went at us tooth and nail and took a 2-0 lead through Munro and Dougan. They played brilliantly, steaming into tackles, and their goalkeeper, Phil Parkes, had the game of his life." Bremner himself reduced the deficit at the three-quarter stage but Wolves held on to win. Leeds were runners-up for the fifth time in eight seasons.

"One of the accusations after the match," Lorimer adds, "was that, with five minutes to go, Bremner had offered one of their players a good sum of money to hack him down in the penalty area." That player, of course, was Munro. But it was more than a last-gasp plea of desperation that the Wolves man says he received. He maintains to this day that attempts to fix the result were pre-meditated.

Hegan's allegation, that he had been offered a 'grand' for a penalty, took the case to the highest legal stage in the land and, there, Munro's central role became clear. In *The Daily Telegraph* of January 29, 1982, it is reported: "Frank Munro, 34, a former skipper of Wolves football club, claimed in the High Court yesterday that he was offered a £5,000 bribe to give away a penalty during a vital match against Leeds in 1972. The offer, made just after half-time, was repeated near the end of the game, by Leeds' captain, Billy Bremner. 'I was amazed,' said Munro." The *Daily Mirror* that day added: "Play was at the other end of the field when Bremner said to him: 'Big man, I will give you five grand if you give away a penalty.' No other player was near enough to hear Bremner's request - made twice - Munro told a High Court jury. On each occasion, he replied: 'You're not on, Billy.'"

The *People* paid £4,000 in air fares for Munro and his family to fly from Australia for the hearing. As he sits in his flat, more than two decades on, it is feasible to imagine he wishes he had never returned. He is conscious of the reverence due to Bremner, both as a great player and as a former colleague and compatriot who has passed away. Yet the case against Leeds becomes more complex as we talk.

"When I was in Australia, a fellow from the *People* called at my door four times. I was thinking about bringing my wife and two kids back for a holiday, so when he came back the last time, I thought I might as well have the paper pay for it and I could come back and tell the truth in court. That's what I did. Four of us were approached." Munro pauses, then names names: "Phil Parkes, Bernard Shaw, myself and Waggy."

There is not a 100 per cent concensus in the reports from Wolves players of the time and it is obvious how such a muddy flow of events failed to produce a water-tight case against Bremner, especially when Munro, the central Wolves player, suggests that Leeds' captain was only a middle man, acting on instructions.

No4 Billy Bremner is powerless as Frank Munro opens the scoring on the famous night Leeds were beaten at Molineux in 1972 - a game that cost them the double.

"Although Bremner was involved, it's not really come from Bremner," he tells me. "It's come from a higher source." Revie? Munro unequivocally nods in assent and adds: "It had been going on for many, many years. Even in this case, Gary Sprake, a Leeds player, had helped spark it off through his article. I walked into the High Court and Bobby Moore and Geoff Hurst were sitting there. I think they wanted to see what was going on. Bremner tried to get the case stopped before it started. All he wanted was an apology but the story was too much like good news for the papers to let it lie. So Billy was more or less forced into it and he ended up with a hundred grand.

"I was offered five grand to give away a penalty." Like you said in court, Frank, out on the pitch? "Aye, and before the game as well. It was tempting, I tell you. Five grand in 1972 would have just about bought you a house. Bernard Shaw went straight in and told Bill McGarry he'd been approached - and Bill called us together on the morning of the match and said: 'If I hear about any of you even *thinking* about taking a bribe, you'll never kick a ball again as long as I'm manager.'"

Munro, his white whiskers poking through an unshaven chin, stretches his legs up on to a foot stool and lights another cigarette. Physically, the years have not been kind to him. Mentally, however, he is as sharp as ever. He ponders for a few moments, then goes on. "I got a call as well, on the Sunday," he says, "from the Mount Hotel." He pauses but the question has to be asked: who was on the other end of the phone? "Bremner," he says. Again, he shuts off for a moment, weighing up his words. "That was when he first made the offer. He said I am to give away a penalty and I get five grand. I said: 'No, I'm not interested.' But I did think it was unfair on Leeds playing on the Monday, I did honestly. They had just played a Cup final."

The fact Parkes was among those allegedly approached brings back Lorimer's words that "you'd certainly have to go for the keeper." Yet there is another facet to it all. "Leeds should have won that league, you know," Munro added. "It was a massive game. There were more than 53,000 inside Molineux and about 20,000 outside. The gates were locked. I next spoke to Billy on the pitch." Munro will never forget these words either, for they came after he had made a telling contribution directly to the detriment of the Leeds cause. Green wrote in *The Times*: "[With Leeds] having been denied their penalty in the 24th minute and then seen Parkes make two great diving saves to Bremner and Lorimer, it was Wolves who scrambled the crucial opening goal four minutes from the interval. It came from a short corner on the right by Wagstaffe. Shaw's low diagonal cross was diverted into the goalmouth by Giles and, in the ensuing melee, there was Reaney just failing to stop Munro's quick stab going in." Parkes, Wagstaffe, Shaw, Munro...four fired-up Wolves players, it would appear.

"I remember, as I turned after scoring, Bremner calling me a Scottish bastard," Munro says, our laughing alleviating the tension hanging thick in the room. "He was more Scottish than I'll ever be. We went 2-0 up and Richards scored a goal that was disallowed that was never offside. It should have been 3-0. Billy was on at me again after a quarter of an hour. I was shocked. He was a tremendous player, Bremner, and I would imagine that, after the allegations came out in the press, this did affect him. Once you've been stained like that...

"From what I understand, I believe it had gone on for years. It is my understanding that when he was England manager, Don Revie told West Ham that, if he capped this young striker of theirs, did they realise his potential fee would go higher?" Munro raises his eyebrows. "Don Readies, they used to call him. I'm sure that's why he finished up so unpopular in the game."

Hegan never hit any great heights with Wolves, although Munro believes the Irishman could have helped complete the trophy-winning jigsaw if only he had not been obsessed with taking Bailey's shirt. Numbers were more than a means to selling shirts in those days. No4 usually denoted the holding midfielder, often the experienced anchorman. "Mike Bailey was a tremendous player," his vice-captain says. "I don't think he was fully appreciated here. I hate it when people say he was a tremendous captain; he was much more than that.

"That Wolves team should have won more. I think we lacked on the left side of midfield and, if Danny Hegan had screwed the nut, our middle three would have been Hegan, Bailey and Hibbitt. But Danny wanted Mike's shirt. I remember one day at Arsenal, when Mike was injured, Bill McGarry took the armband off me and said: 'I'm giving the captaincy to Danny Hegan, I'm having one more go with him.' Before the game, Danny had an imaginary coin in the dressing room and he tossed it and called heads. 'I've won,' he said. 'We'll play across.' When we played Juventus, he was up against Helmut Haller, and Danny kept him so quiet that he lifted the waistband of his shorts, looked in and said: 'Helmut, you okay in there?'

"Another time at Castlecroft, we were doing a skipping exercise as part of the warm-up. Every step, he'd chant: 'Mike Bailey's dead, Mike Bailey's dead.' Yet Mike was as good a No4 as there was in the country. He was on a par with Bremner at a time Terry Venables and Alan Mullery were at their best. We could have done better than we did."

Wolves went within one game of Wembley in 1973 when they renewed their great rivalry with Leeds in the FA Cup semi-final at Maine Road, 11 months on from the infamous title decider. Again, Bailey was struggling with his fitness. Both he and Munro were doubtful with

Mike Bailey - "a tremendous player."

Frank Munro: "For two years after the semi-final, the manager blamed me."

hamstring injuries. "We were about 80 per cent fit and Bill McGarry was going to play both of us. This is in the days of one substitute, remember. So after breakfast, in the team hotel, he asked us to go and see him in his room. I said: 'It's a hell of a gamble you're taking here. If you lose both of us, you'll be a man down against the best team in the country: you'll never get the ball back.' He was adamant he was going to play the two of us.

"He said to go back and see him after lunch. Then, I said: 'If I was you, I'd have one of us play and the other at sub.' So he made me captain and put Mike on the bench. Eventually, Mike came on for Ken Hibbitt and we both lasted. We were so unlucky. Richards hit the inside of the post and the ball rolled along the line. For their goal, I told Kenny to leave a cross but, not hearing, he tried a bicycle kick, the ball went straight up in the air and fell to Bremner, of all people, who scored. For two years, the manager blamed me. He was furious. He said: 'If I'd played the two of you, we would have won and got to the final.'" Instead, Leeds went on to their notorious Wembley defeat at the hands of Sunderland, from the old Second Division.

It was when Wolves were in Division Two that Munro's career at Molineux came towards its conclusion at the end of 1976-77. Again, as when they had helped Derby win the title by beating Leeds in 1972, they gave Brian Clough a crucial leg up in what turned out to be Munro's final game in a gold shirt. It was on May 14, 1977, when Bolton Wanderers needed to beat Wolves to be promoted along with them and Chelsea, the club Munro had played for as a schoolboy. Wolves and Chelsea had drawn at

Molineux the previous week to confirm their status as champions and runners-up respectively. If Bolton slipped up, Nottingham Forest, Clough's team, would claim the third automatic promotion place in the days well before the play-offs were introduced.

"We did Cloughie a few favours," recalls Munro, who had taken up smoking by this time. "We went up to Bolton for a bit of a stroll because we were already champions. Then Sam Allardyce started kicking Richards a bit so we decided it was time to start playing. They were still on top but, from a clever free-kick, Ken Hibbitt scored and we won 1-0 to leave them in fourth place. Forest snuck in, the following year they won the title and then the European Cup in the seasons after that. So you could argue Wolves won Forest the European Cup."

Munro, then approaching 30, is convinced he had two more years in him. But he fell out with Sammy Chung, who had succeeded McGarry as manager the previous summer, and was soon on his way back to Scotland. "McGarry knew the game and Sammy Chung was very good alongside him, on the coaching side," said Munro, who lived on the same estate as the new manager. "It's amazing how people change when they take over. Sammy, although a lovely man, had been a 'yes man' to Bill (they had worked together at Ipswich before Wolves) and to Harry Marshall, the chairman. I, as captain, stood up at a team meeting and told him as much in front of the other players. I knew then I had to go. The week after [October, 1977], I went to Celtic on loan."

On £300 a week at Wolves, plus £22 per point, Munro was paid £85 at Parkhead, where he was shocked that Jock Stein, the legendary manager, did not expect players to report until half an hour before kick-off. "I remember my first game," says Munro, a boyhood fan of Dundee - the club against whom he scored on his senior debut, as a 15-year-old, for Dundee United, so earning a slap around the face from his late United-supporting brother, Jimmy. "I drove five hours from here to Glasgow on the Friday, agreed to join on loan and stayed for the game against St Mirren on the Saturday.

"At 2.20, the other players arrived and, although they knew me, I hadn't been introduced. I knew Peter Latchford, the keeper, from his time at West Brom, but that was it. At five to three, Jock Stein threw me the ball and said: 'You're captain.' We lost 2-1 and I was credited with an own goal. I think Celtic were second bottom but we pulled up and were runners-up. I was due a testimonial from Wolves. They wouldn't give me a free transfer, so I went on loan for one month, then another, then another." He finally signed for Celtic for £20,000 on December 30 - six days short of a decade. "As my final incentive to go, Sammy said: 'You'll get a testimonial.' I never did. The deal was verbal. I got a note from Marshall, the chairman, but lost it over the years."

The season after playing against Rangers in the 1978 Scottish League Cup final at Hampden, Munro went on holiday to Australia for seven weeks - and stayed for 12 years. He played for South Melbourne Hellas under Dave MacLaren, a former Wolves keeper, and with two other ex-Molineux team-mates, Alun Evans and Bertie Lutton. A knee injury prompted him to retire at 32 but he settled in Melbourne and worked for several years as a traffic officer at the airport. As his marriage to Margaret came to an end, he returned to England. "When I came back, I contacted the club through Gordon Taylor at the PFA and reminded them I'd been promised a testimonial," he said. "But I was told it was all to do with a previous company, as Wolves had reformed after being through receivership. For me, though, Wolves will always be Wolves."

If there is a sadness about Munro's situation, he does not indulge it. He played his role in the finest Wolves team since the 1950s. He is conscious that, having performed 371 times for them, he is part of a great club. When he was in hospital for 19 weeks recovering from his stroke in 1993 - New Cross, then West Park - he received 45 cards. "The most special two were from Mike Bailey, and another beautiful one from Billy Wright, a few months before he died."

Wolves were his favourite English club as he grew up. "What I think is unfair is that the team in the 1970s were always compared with the 1950s side," he says. "Now, they have to put up with comparisons with the 1970s team. I've only ever seen him on video but Peter Broadbent was my favourite Wolves player. He was a great. Peter Knowles would have run him close if he hadn't packed it in to become a Jehovah's Witness. He was Jack the Lad in the late 1960s in his white sports car with his name on the side. But, if he had two halves of lager, he was drunk.

"I remember he started bringing a bible on the coach and reading it on the way to games. He didn't really talk to the other lads about it but we could see his outlook was changing. Then he told the manager he was going to pack it all in in six weeks. I can remember the very last game. We were 3-0 up at half-time against Nottingham Forest and they came back to draw 3-3. At the end, he just ran off the pitch - no fanfare or anything - and that was it.

"I believe the manager sent him a contract seven years in a row. He returned them all unsigned. I thought it was a gimmick and he'd be back inside three months. I was wrong. We keep in touch and he comes round to see me every now and then. He's still a Jehovah's Witness. He tells me that when he sees vidoes of the old games, he can't believe that hooligan running around is him. He was a strange lad. He scored in one game, picked the ball up and booted it out of the ground. Another time, with ten

porting Star

WOLVERHAMPTON, SATURDAY, OCTOBER 19, 1963

WEBBERLEY
for **COAL & CO**
Telephone   W'HAMPTON
            WILLENHALL
            WALSALL

A first goal - in only his second game - for young Peter Knowles. It came in a draw with Bolton 41 years ago.

One of those golden memories for a man bereft of material keepsakes...the Frank Munro goal that helped Wolves to a UEFA Cup semi-final draw in Ferencvaros in 1972.

minutes to go and Wolves winning, he ran the ball to the corner flag and sat on it. You didn't do that in those days. He liked to showboat but that person out there was not the one he wanted to be. Yet he'd have been as close to Broadbent as anyone."

Munro was a proud spectator at the Millennium Stadium, a month before we meet, as Wolves clinched their return to the top flight in such tremendous style. The club's former players' association took Munro, Bailey, Parkes, Gerry Taylor, John Holsgrove and many others to lunch at the Angel Hotel, near the ground in Cardiff, before the exhilarating play-off final against Sheffield United that Dave Jones' team won 3-0.

"The atmosphere was better than at Wembley in 1974," Munro says. "It was a fantastic day, from start to finish. I thought for weeks beforehand that it would be 3-1. The man of the match was Colin Cameron, up against their best player, Michael Brown. I was so impressed. I thought that was the best he had played for Wolves. The other Scot, Kenny Miller, did well too. I just hope he can do it in the Premier. He's certainly got great touch. These are exciting times. I can't wait to see the fixtures.

"Dave Jones has proved everyone wrong, hasn't he? He's done what several others couldn't manage. He raised the bar. Everyone's so pleased for Sir Jack Hayward. He's waited so long, spent millions trying to get the club into the

Premiership. I told Peter Creed, who runs the ex-players' association, he should book us a coach to Cardiff for 2004 as well - for the FA Cup final. If we could win the Cup, that'd be excellent for Sir Jack.

"Of this team, I can see Matt Murray and Joleon Lescott playing for England. At Cardiff, Murray was brilliant. He's got to keep coming for crosses like that, it gives the centre-halves such confidence. I think Lescott's a fantastic defender. Now he's got to work on his distribution. When Lee Naylor came on the scene, I thought then he was top quality. He hit a wall but, to be fair to him, he has come again. He might even be better in the Premier League."

As I pull out from the flats at the bottom of the Holloway, where I used to deliver newspapers at the time Munro was in his hey-day with Wolves, I can't bring myself to drive up the hill to where we lived. Nor the half mile to where I used to play with Stuart and Grant Munro, Scott and Gary Wagstaffe, Tim Chung, Mike Cox, Tony Amis, Simon Taylor, Jon Brayshaw, Tony Collis. There was a big gang of us who used to congregate to play football, ackey-ackey-one-two-three, cricket, bikes, to swap football picture cards. They won't remember me but I was almost in awe of the sons of these Wolves characters.

I had told Frank of the time I broke into his house because Stuart, whose enthusiasm for nocturnal adventures was less guaranteed than mine, had left the back door open for me to go and wake him if he did not make our midnight rendezvous. I bottled it once I got into the Munros' kitchen and went off alone in search of Enid Blyton endings. At the start of my meeting with Frank, I showed him the 1973 Soccer Stars album that my eldest brother, Dave, had acquired from Stuart in some childhood bartering. Stuart's name and address are crossed out, supplanted by my brother's. Dave and I filled the album meticulously and, 30 years on, we still have it. Stuart, out in Australia with his two children, has his father's League Cup winner's tankard.

Frank Munro, in the face of his disabilities, still has his dignity to go alongside the friendships and memories but it seems incongruous that we have more, materially, to show from his career than he does.

Frank Munro

Born:	October 25, 1947, in Broughty Ferry, near Dundee
Signed:	January, 1968
Wolves appearances:	371
Goals:	19
Left:	December, 1977
International recognition:	9 senior Scotland caps

Kenny Miller

TURMOIL, TRIUMPH AND TANTRUMS

July 14, 2003: RAF Cosford training camp, near Wolverhampton

If Cardiff, May 26, 2003 provided an unimagined degree of catharsis for Wolves supporters nursing 19 years of pain, then it was the also the day that healed some fairly deep wounds for Kenny Miller. Wolves' top scorer in the so-long-dreamed-of promotion season had a brilliant five months.

In the period he discovered he was to become a father, Miller finally established himself in Dave Jones' team and equalled a post-war club record of scoring in seven successive games. His exploits culminated in the games of his life: first the clincher just before half-time on that surreal May Bank Holiday afternoon in the Nationwide League First Division play-off final; then, as his season blossomed into June and he wore Scotland's No9 shirt at Hampden Park, he netted the point-saver against Germany, the World Cup finalists, in a European Championship qualifying match.

As he looked forward to life in the Barclaycard Premiership after justifying the club's £3million record transfer outlay, life could barely have been sweeter, even as he recuperated from a double hernia operation in the close season of 2003. And the heights he had just hit were all the more rarified for the depths he had plumbed in the year prior to his purple patch.

If Wolves fans remain grateful for Miller's contribution to the club reaching the Premiership, their appreciation is intensified when they realise he could have been long gone before that glorious run-in. Things became so bad in 2001-02, what with breaking his collarbone, wallowing in rented accommodation and falling out with Jones, that he wanted to leave. Even in the promotion season, Miller could have preceded Wolves into the Premiership - with another club. Thankfully, that did not happen and his 26 goals for club and country established his as a name to be reckoned with. Breathe in and reap.

The temperature in mid-July, 2003, reached 34 degrees by Lee Naylor's open-top Boxster outside the Nuffield Pavilion at RAF Cosford sports ground. George Ndah, with an amiable hello, is being worked by Barry Holmes, the Wolves physio, as he steps up his rehabilitation. Inside the tiny stadium, as he intensifies his, Miller laps the track. Punctual and tidily kitted out even after a morning's running, the team's current pin-up soon calls me in from my diminishing spot of midday shade, as the sound of military helicopters vies with building work at this modest training base.

In the players' lounge, Miller is affable and relaxed. We work out that the season - the Premiership season, that is, not the other one Wolves fans usually have to rush back for - is four weeks and five days away. He rates his chances of being fit for its kick-off at 70-30. It has been a miniscule close season for the former Hibernian and Rangers forward and the memories, the fantastic memories, are still fresh. Miller was watching the video of the game against Sheffield United - for at least the fourth time, he admits - the day before our interview. Now that's what I call homework.

I tell him that, for Wolves fans of my generation, Cardiff is one of the best three days of our footballing lives. My mate Chris told his wife it was one of his best four days ever, in there with his wedding and the births of their two children. Then he came out and admitted that he was lying. It was just the best.

"It's up there," Miller muses. "With what was at stake, and what was achieved for a big club that's been away so long, it was probably the best day of my career. Scoring was great but walking out in front of 70,000 fans was incredible as well. To score just before half-time… every fan, every player, everyone connected with the club, must've thought to himself: 'We're there.' 3-0. That was such a massive advantage for us, it was probably the first time we had relaxed at all because there wouldn't be many teams who would come back against us from three down. So, for the supporters - their relief, their joy - that goal was a big moment. If Sheffield United got a goal back at 2-0, it's game on, but 3-0 felt like a bridge too far."

Take your time, Kenny, take your time. Tell me everything about it: the goal, the match, the build-up, the dressing-room. This is a special time we're talking about. Don't peak too soon. Wolves fans have waited a long time for something like Cardiff. We'll be happy to relive this in 20 years time when Sheffield Mergers are playing in the Unibond League and Wolves are pushing for the Inter Stellar Cup.

"I just tried to get anything on it," he says. "It was one of those horrible ones. From a spectator's point of view, it's a great cross from Shaun Newton - between the defenders and the keeper - but, from a forward's perspective, when it's bouncing in front of you like that, it's so hard to judge. You don't know whether it will stick or fly, so, for all the excellence of the cross, it was one of the worst balls you can deal with." Did Miller mean to let Newton's centre run across him and take it with his left, to skew the ball up and past the keeper into the far corner? "It was just reaction," he admits. "I knew I hadn't caught it properly but I looked up and saw it go in. I was delighted."

Dreamland. Kenny Miller races away in celebration of his killer goal in the 2002-03 play-off final.

The goal allowed Wolves the breathing space to enjoy a half-time of unprecedented glee; sheer unbridled elation. As you queued for your drinks in the bar, supporters who would ordinarily have stayed strangers traded proclamations of utter rapture and admiration for the performance. It must have been very difficult for the players not to do the same. Miller admits that, privately, he thought the game, even at the half-way stage, was won.

The triumph was borne of the most single-minded play-off campaign. Both wins over Reading had been greeted by a resounding absence of triumphalism from the Wolves players as they undertook a vow of public silence. This, in part, sprouted from the agonies of the previous year when every utterance of confidence ended up in the newspapers as bravado, while West Bromwich Albion peaked with perfect timing. This was no-one's fault. Jones and his players, although fading at the end of 2001-02, did not want to let their conviction slip and genuinely believed they would still go up. The media men needed their stories. If Paul Butler said Wolves were determined to go to Norwich and gain a three-goal lead from the play-off semi-final first leg, then surely it is fair game that the reporters take this to the top of their story?

Paul Ince, Butler's successor as captain, was thought to be the ringleader in the media silence during the 2003 play-offs, aping the us-against-the-world mentality that had served Manchester United so well. Miller, however, maintains it was down to the local paper's critical attitude, as well as the manager's bid to shut out distractions. "We didn't speak to the press, left that to the manager and the coaches. The manager kept saying: 'Play the game, not the occasion.' He said this before the semi-final as well.

"We knew it was going to be a massive day and it turned out to be a great occasion but the build-up was as normal as could be. I think the only interview you see from us is when the gaffer said it was okay for me to do a quick one pitch-side before kick-off. Sky had their cameras at the Sheffield United golf day, interviewed about five or six of their lads. They went down that route, we went down ours. Maybe it helped us on the day, I don't know.

"The previous year, we were getting crucified in the local paper and a lot of the lads were nae happy that the reporter was caning us personally. I wasn't playing so I wasn't getting that. So it wasn't that we took against the press as a whole, more a local thing, and that played a part in our silence. Incey made the point that if we blanked one paper, we had to blank them all. It was a group decision and it showed the togetherness of the team that we stuck to it. No matter which way you approached the Cardiff final, it was always going to be one of the biggest games you're ever going to play in. Our lads were just up for it, as were theirs, but we blew them away with that opening."

Wolves stayed at the Vale of Glamorgan Hotel, as did all the winners of the 2003 play-off finals, and Miller roomed with Colin Cameron. The night before, he ate soup, pasta, chicken and salad, and finished with yoghurt and banana. He slept so well he did not awake until 10am, when he had a flick-read of *The Sun* and the *Daily Record*. After a walk in the hotel grounds, while the early-risers had moved back on to the chicken for their pre-match meal, he ate cornflakes, banana and yoghurt.

After a 15-minute coach ride, when the atmosphere in the squad remained jovial, and a warm-up on the pitch when Miller conserved his energy by focusing on his touch and getting the feel of the turf, he found the occasion getting to him. "It was the most nervous I've ever been before a game," he says. "We were in the dressing-room, lining up ready to go out, and I experienced a feeling of anticipation like never before."

Miller's only superstition is to have a shot into the net before kick-off. Little could he have hoped that his team would be doing the same so soon after it, when the forward - having had the first touch of the match, and the first shot - played a key role in setting up Mark Kennedy for a wonderful opening goal. "I've watched it many times on Sky and thought I played a big part in that goal without getting much credit.

"Two of the goals came after long kicks from Matty (Murray). From the first, I've managed to get a couple of touches in, hold the defender off and lay it in there into the path of Sparky. As soon as I've passed it, I've thought: 'Sod it, I've not hit that hard enough.' Not for his left foot anyway, because I know he's hardly going to swing with his right leg. Then he's absolutely pinged it, right in the bottom corner. What a start!

"The second goal was also down to good play. It was in the 22nd minute. Mickey (Cameron, so called because of his similarities to Disney's Mouse) has run through the middle, not a team-mate near him, and managed a wee jink, a shot and done great to hit the target and win the corner. A good ball from Sparky kept it away from the keeper, Incey's done well to get a run on (John) Curtis to head it on and Blakey's come off and flicked it, just got enough on it to get past the keeper. I was right behind him, thinking: 'Miss that and I'm there' but he's done it, 2-0. I'm thinking we're not going to lose a 2-0 lead if we can get to half-time.

"We're nearly there when I went up for a challenge. While I didn't win the ball, I maybe did enough to put the defender off. It's knocked right into the centre circle, where wee Mickey has passed to Blake, who's stretched and managed to knock it wide over Rob Kozluk to wee Newts on the right. I've got off the floor, run in and there's nobody near me. So I've pointed to Newts where I want it. He took a touch, stalled a bit so I had to check my run and, by that time, Phil Jagielka had actually got back. I thought: 'This is going to have to be one hell of a ball' and then, just as Newts has gone to hit it, Jagielka's moved out and left me in the space. Newts has whipped in a great ball and it's bounced right in front of me but I've managed to get enough on it to knock it in. You can't really explain how that feels.

"From watching the video, in that first half, I thought our attacking play was incredible. Everyone from middle to front, we absolutely tore them apart. To get three goals in a game of that magnitude is incredible. But the thing that struck me was that every time Sheffield United got to within 20 yards of our goal, there were three or four bodies on them: Incey, Mickey, Sparky, Newts, Butts, Jo, Nayls, Denis. They couldn't get near so everything's come from deep and, for big Matty, that's bread and butter. He had a great game and was a worthy man of the match."

Murray made a remarkable save to Ince's back-header with the score at 2-0 but the jam came when he saved Michael Brown's penalty three minutes into the second half. "We'd been working on penalties all week in case it went to a shoot-out," Miller

Paddy Kenny is grounded and Sheffield United are down and out, too, in the splendour of the Millennium Stadium. Kenny Miller has just scored to make it 3-0 to Wolves.

reveals. Wolves' first-choice takers would have been the Scot himself, substitute Dean Sturridge, Blake, Kennedy and Cameron. "Matty had been working on his penalties. If you watch, he doesn't stand in the middle for Brown's penalty. He stands to the left as Brown looks, and invited the shot to go in the other corner, where Brown has hit a few. It's gone that way and he's got there. He was there waiting for it! He was up quickly for the rebound as well, so he has done well."

At half-time, when Neil Warnock was losing his head, Wolves were keeping theirs. "I was thinking: 'We don't have to play well now, we've produced our stuff, scored our goals, now we can just scrap it out, do whatever it takes to get there.'" Miller came off with about 15 minutes left. "When the final whistle goes, that's when it kicks in," he says of the adrenaline of victory, the sweet taste of success. The players' celebrations, as they bounced up and down on the podium as Butler and Ince lifted the play-off trophy, revealed a group as united as could be. "I've never played at a club where the team's been as tight as this," he says. "It's like we're family. You could see that in that game, the way people were throwing themselves in the way of shots, going that extra yard to get on the end of things. We took a hell of a lot of stick the previous year and we came back stronger and better."

Miller missed out on the joyous celebrations in Wolverhampton 48 hours later, as did several of his team-mates. "It looks an unbelievable night," he says, with regret. "It was sprung on us pretty late, the day before the game I think, that, win or lose, we were going back to Molineux on the Wednesday night. Looking at the pictures, all the streets are rammed, Molineux's rammed, and I'm pretty disappointed I could nae be there. I'd already got things booked up. It wasn't the best organisation on the club's part."

Consolation wasn't too far away. After a week in Scotland with his girlfriend,

Something worth celebrating: goalscorers Kenny Miller and Mark Kennedy in the party mood at Cardiff.

Lorna, he and Cameron teamed up again - for the goal that announced Miller's arrival on the international scene. Trailing 1-0 to Germany, Scotland won a free-kick, from which the duo showed the quick-thinking that typified their end-of-season form. "Christian Worns had been penalised for handball and I started to make my way forward. I've seen the space and said 'Play it' without actually saying anything." It was all in the body language. "Me and Mickey just made eye contact and he put it in the space. I managed to get on the end of it and put it away. It was a special one, obviously, against the World Cup finalists. It was a great day, when we did ourselves justice, and it rounded off a great season for me."

Miller's rapport with Cameron had helped him bed in at Molineux. They played against each other in Edinburgh derbies and, after Miller's Wolves debut on loan from Rangers, away to Preston North End in September, 2001, went out with friends in Manchester for a few drinks, an initiation that was continued a week later. After Miller had gone on as a substitute to set up Blake for an equaliser against Stockport County, the Wolves players went out in the city to welcome their new team-mates.

It was an auspicious start for Miller, but deceptively so. After earning a starting berth alongside Blake to score in successive games against Gillingham and Walsall, as Wolves won five in a row to go top of the table, he broke a collarbone in a horrendous fall late in the home victory against Nottingham Forest. He went back to Glasgow for surgery on October 22 and, as his loan was for three months, was back at Wolves training in three weeks. But his career was between a rock and a hard place, and the next year proved the worst of his young life.

His two clubs started negotiations over a transfer but it was a slow process. "Rangers were nae happy to extend the loan and the manager wanted to make a permanent deal. I'd had a great start and was really interested as long as all parties could agree," Miller says. Eventually, in December, the forward became Wolves' joint record buy at £3m, along with Ade Akinbiyi, who arrived from Bristol City two years earlier. "I was training back with Rangers when I got a call saying the deal was on. During the loan, I'd been in a hotel and, what with being injured, it was horrendous. Even when I signed, I was in a rented gaffe and it was crap. I didn't have the games to focus on and I just hated it, to be honest. It was the worst six months of my career. Lorna finished work and came down and looked after me but it wasn't a nice place."

Although at ease with his new team-mates - "straightaway, you were part of the lads," he says - there was no honeymoon period. Wolves' wonderful form early in 2002 meant he couldn't find a way back in as Sturridge, signed as a stop-gap, scored goals for fun and promotion looked a formality. "You can handle living in a house you don't like if things are going well on the pitch," he recalls, "but I felt in turmoil. I was on to my agent [then Gordon Smith, the former Brighton & Hove Albion forward] saying: 'What have I done? I'm in the same situation I was at Rangers, not playing.' There, at least I was up the road from family and friends. Here, I had nothing. You can't rely on the lads 24-7. It was a frustrating time. I'd moved here to play football and it wasn't happening. What with living in hotels and rented places, it was a killer."

Did he knock Dave Jones' door? "Every week," he says wryly. "I was a pest. He'd say 'Play your way in' and, at the time, I'd understand it. When I wasn't playing, it wasn't the best relationship in the world between us. When I signed, then when I was injured, I was told: 'You're going to be one of the main players to get us up.' And it wasn't happening."

This was also the period when Wolves' hopes of promotion blew up in their faces, when Albion made up an 11-point deficit to claim second place behind Manchester City. "I'm not saying I'm a better player but I felt that if I'd been playing, I could have done something," he says. "We lost that massive lead. It was an absolute disgrace. People pointed the finger and it was a collective criticism but what could I do? I was playing ten minutes here and there, starting the odd game.

"I was sitting watching us lose leads against Forest and Birmingham and could see it slipping away. The boys never considered we weren't going up. I understood that because, when I signed, the position we were in and quality of the players we had, I thought there was no way we'd miss out. It was nothing to do with complacency. Just because we're Wolves and sitting top, we never decided to let up. Stories that the boys were discussing before games where to go on holiday were nonsense. Because of Sir Jack's links in the Bahamas, it had been said for years that if the team went up, they'd all go. But the bonuses were agreed before the season and they stayed the same."

As Miller was given only two starts when Wolves' wobble set in, he remained in a permanent grump. Unable to gain full match fitness, he could not reproduce his form of the autumn, so he could not stay in the team. It was a vicious circle, a helter-skelter spiralling inexorably downwards. "I must have been an absolute nightmare to manage. I was losing my rag in training, arguing with TC [Terry Connor], John Ward and the gaffer. I was at the lowest point of my career. Straightaway, I thought about leaving. It was the same at the start of 2002-03. Studge had had a really good season, scoring 20-odd goals, Blakey's the sort of powerful player you'd have in your team every week then George Ndah was playing before me and young Adam [Proudlock] was even coming off the bench before me, so I thought: 'Sod this, I'm off.'"

Premiership clubs were alerted and interest was there. Miller had cost Rangers £2m from Hibs and, already a Scotland international, had potential that was widely acknowledged. "My agent was working to get me away. Last summer, I was hearing the team plans and I wasn't figuring. I couldn't believe what I was hearing. I was absolutely enraged. I changed agents [to Dave Baldwin and Chris Bromage, who also worked for Carl Robinson] and told them: 'If I'm not playing, I want to get away. I can't have another year like the last one or I'll end up chucking it.'"

Bromage met Jones to hear his verdict and was encouraged. "Chris told me I was to keep working hard, not give the gaffer any excuses and I'd be playing," the striker recalls. Sure enough, albeit with Sturridge injured, Miller played the first three games. Although he did not score, Wolves clocked up six goals and seven points. Miller was promptly dropped. When he came off the bench to score in a 4-1 win at Derby County that put Wolves top, he thought he'd be recalled. The following match, a 2-2 draw at home to Sheffield Wednesday, he spent almost the entire second half warming up, to get two minutes at the end. "That was the one game I spat the dummy out," he says. "My body language just said I did nae want to be there. It was wrong and I haven't behaved like that again.

"I was straight on the phone. Chris went in, asking what's happening and was told: 'I'm the manager, I pick the team.' The usual nonsense. A permanent transfer was ruled out because of the fee paid for me. Imagine if I went on the cheap and started banging in goals in the Premiership. How would Wolves look then? A loan deal to a First Division rival would hardly have helped the club, either. It was difficult, so the first target was to get back in this team."

This Miller managed, but Wolves still didn't find top gear despite going ten games unbeaten. A home defeat by Coventry City, followed by an international call-up, could have sounded the death knell of Miller's Molineux career. "I was due to go with the Scotland Future squad to Germany and said to the manager: 'If you want me to go, I'll go. If you don't, just say. I don't want to jeopardise my place in the team.' He told me straight: 'Don't worry about your place, get yourself away with Scotland and get back on track there.' I was dropped for the next game. I was fuming. Chris went in and said: 'You've told him one thing, done another, what's happening?' I was out only for three games but it still hurt.

"It was a horrendous time. The manager's a similar person to me in that we don't hold grudges but I think he was coming to terms with a bad six months when I was practically unmanageable. I was out of order on a lot of stuff and some of the knocks on his door probably weren't justifiable. But, from my point of view, coming here from Rangers, a big club, I've been told so much to convince me - not that I needed much convincing, but it was still said - that the frustration was difficult to take. I have got a short fuse - I'd be in the top two or three at the club. But I feel I'm good enough to be playing and that I should be playing. If I'm not, it kills me."

The turning point came on New Year's Day as Wolves slid to tenth in the table. Sir Jack Hayward let rip in an interview in the *Express and Star*, warning that such underachievement would not be tolerated. Derby escaped with a 1-1 draw but Miller, Butler, Naylor and Cameron all returned to the team, so Jones' strongest mix was coming together. "I didn't read the article but you hear about these things," Miller recalls. "It was a time of frustration for the fans, for the board, for Sir Jack, and there was a general determination to put things right. Maybe subconsciously, Sir Jack's words had a timely impact but, personally, I never felt Dave Jones' job was hanging on a shaky nail. You never know how to take things reported in the media, how serious the threat is, because, obviously, a line gets magnified to make a story. For all the previous season's collapse, we'd finished third and were still in contention now."

The following game brought Newcastle United to Molineux for an appetising FA Cup third-round tie that turned into one of the matches of the season. It also offered Miller and his team-mates a glimpse of the fun - and opportunities - to be had playing against opponents from a higher class. "People said we had no chance, up against the third-placed team in the Premier League. But we were confident. Teams had been coming to Molineux and sitting in, eager to kill the game and get a point. It is easier to be destructive than take you on. But Newcastle were always going to come and play us and that did give us more space."

Ince and Kennedy scored in a game televised live on a Sunday evening. "It was two going on five," Miller says, "and it was daylight robbery that Newcastle came in 2-2 at half-time. But George scored early in the second half, we deserved to win and that gave us a taste of playing against the big lads. It brought us confidence and we really kicked on from there." Miller would like to have swapped shirts with Alan Shearer, a hero since childhood, but, for once, was not quick enough off the mark. "The gaffer had got in there first," he says with a grin.

Wolves lost only three times in the rest of the season - at Southampton in the Cup quarter-finals and at Brighton and Portsmouth. It was after Miller had scored for the fifth consecutive game that he discovered he was to become a father. "It was great news and we were absolutely delighted," he recalls. "I found out after the Rochdale game (a fifth-round FA Cup tie live on TV). I wouldn't say my scoring run was down to it, but there was definitely a feel-good factor that, subconsciously, can only help."

Miller missed out on the feat of scoring for an eighth consecutive game (he still equalled Micky Holmes's 16-year club record) as Watford held on for a 0-0 Molineux draw at the end of February. In the next match, however, the forward clinched his first Wolves hat-trick when Sturridge urged him to take a late penalty in a 4-0 drubbing of Crystal Palace. All told, Miller scored 20 times after Christmas in 26 games, the hernia problems only affecting him minimally. It was the best run of his career and helped lift Wolves into the Premiership and Scotland into contention for Euro 2004.

With a new house being built in Bridgnorth and his first child on the way, Miller has plenty of domestic reasons to be cheerful. Professionally, he cannot wait to get on the same pitch as Ruud Van Nistelrooy and Thierry Henry. He is having caps and shirts from the Sheffield United and Germany games and pictures of goal celebrations framed ready for mounting on the walls.

As he prepares to go back to Molineux, where Barry Holmes is waiting to put him through another session of rehab, Ince comes in to snaffle his beans on toast and sign his new contract. "You doing interviews already, Kenny?" the captain banters. "What have you ever done for this club then?" Miller lets out the laugh of a man whose answer has already been given.

Goal hero once more: a happy Kenny Miller is acclaimed by Mark Kennedy following his famous winner against reigning champions Man United during his momentous few days in the early weeks of 2004.

May 11, 2004: Wolves' training ground, Newbridge, Tettenhall

That is the drawback, of course, of chronicling a year in the life of a football club. We are hostages to the passing of time. Don't assume a snapshot taken in a player's life will represent the whole album. Miller is now a proud father to Coby and can add a couple of glorious moments to his video collection, having scored the winner against Manchester United and, four nights later, a cracking last-minute equaliser against Liverpool. I never expected anything less but it is evident I have rather a higher opinion of the player than Dave Jones does.

Those were Miller's only Premiership goals in 2003-04, although they did follow a brace in an FA Cup replay with Kidderminster Harriers. Last I spoke to him, he said he hoped still to be at Wolves in 2004-05 but, after a campaign in which he was injured at the start, scored just five goals, often played wide right and seemed to be hauled off like a naughty schoolboy every time Wolves were losing, who can tell? He is not training this morning and is not even a substitute in the final games of the season.

I put it to Jones that Miller did at least produce his best for a couple of weeks in January. "No, he scored for a couple of weeks. There's a big difference," the manager says. "Kenny's probably been disappointing this year but he's a young player who is still learning his trade. He needs to work harder if he wants to fulfil the potential he has. Sometimes young players don't realise this. If they're in the team and had the kind of season Kenny had [in the promotion year], it seems everything is swimming along nicely. But you have to remember to work twice as hard to keep that standard up. If you want to stay at the top for many years, you have to put all the work in. Good players work harder than average players; great players work harder than good players."

Surely, Miller suffered from missing his pre-season? "Perhaps so but if a player's not having a good time, it's always the manager's fault. Sometimes, what players need to do is look at themselves and say: 'Am I doing enough?' It's easy to place the blame at someone else's door. Take Vio Ganea. He's an unbelievable pro, just gets his head down, works hard and knows that if he gets an opportunity, it doesn't matter for how long, you go and perform."

Henri Camara ends up winning the player of the year award. His dazzling boots, close control and scintillating pace earned him a place even when his finishing was so wide of the mark that the corner flags were frightened. When the goals started flying in, Jones' perseverance was rewarded. Carl Cort, needing several weeks to shake off the rust, was similarly afforded patience and a regular place before looking the part.

"If, unfortunately for you, people have got the shirt and are playing better," Jones continues, "you have to bide your time. The only way to deal with that is by working harder and taking your opportunity, whether it's for five minutes or 50." But, other than that, Kenny Miller's the bees-knees, right? I reckon, if he can stay on track mentally, he will prove a decent Premiership striker. With which club, sadly, I'm not so sure.

Kenny Miller

Born:	December 23, 1979, in Edinburgh
Signed:	September, 2001 (on loan) and December, 2001 (permanently)
Wolves appearances:	105
Goals:	31
International recognition:	11 senior Scotland caps

Steve Daley

BURDENING A GOOD PLAYER WITH GREAT EXPECTATIONS

July 24, 2003: The Codsall Station pub, near Wolverhampton

A lcohol threatens to ruin our meeting. We are due to convene at his local for 11.45am but Steve Daley, a salesman for Highgate Brewery, has got caught up in a rush, ferrying kegs of ale for a barbeque to be hosted by Dave Jones. Eventually, Daley pulls into the car park, rather flushed, apologises for my wait and makes a bee-line for the bar.

The waitress brings our coffees over. The table is adorned by a recent copy of *The Times,* turned to the page on which Real Madrid's new No23 is depicted, fresh from his sponsored medical and resplendent with double pony tail and ballerina-style shorts, greeting supporters. A £1.5million transfer may seem like small beer these days, perhaps tantamount to David Beckham's signing-on fee, but, 25 years ago, when Manchester City paid Wolves that amount to land Daley on a ten-year contract, it was enough to make him the most expensive player in the country.

"People ask me who the first million-pound footballer was and the general answer is Trevor Francis," Daley says, alluding to the forward Nottingham Forest bought from Birmingham City in 1978 who scored the winning goal in the European Cup final the following year. "Trevor cost something like £975,000, which only went above the million-pound mark when you added all the bits and pieces. The actual fee paid for me was £1.15m, which, with all the stuff on top, ended up as £1.45m."

There was not half the fuss over that transfer as there was surrounding Beckham's departure from Old Trafford but the scorn poured over the Barnsley-born midfield player when his move did not pan out would be enough to rattle the mettle of an England captain. "Malcolm Allison (the cigar-toting City manager who bought him) would say any publicity, whether it's positive or negative, is good publicity," Daley says. "Moving to Man City has given me the stories to tell on the 'after dinner' circuit that makes me more money than I ever made as a player."

Daley earned £8 a week from his first professional contract at Molineux after inadvertently becoming Bill McGarry's first signing in March, 1969. "Mark Crook called me for a trial with Wath Wanderers, Wolves' nursery side in Yorkshire, and, after playing games against Chesterfield and Doncaster Rovers at Saltergate, I was asked down to Molineux for a month's trial," he recalls. "That turned into three months and I didn't go home for the first five weeks."

When he did, the homesick 16-year-old, son of Arthur, whose own substantial career included around 60 games for Coventry City, and brother of Pat, briefly a professional with Sheffield Wednesday, nearly stayed put. "I said to my parents: 'I'm not going back.' They were all right about it. Mum phoned Bill McGarry and said: 'We've got a slight problem with Steve.' He replied: 'Take as long as Stephen wants to get himself sorted out but, between you and me, I want him back at this football club.' I went back five days later, not a problem.

"It was a nice side of him that people didn't know much about. He had this reputation as a disciplinarian, which was justified, but he also cared about his players and he was good with the youngsters. Wolves had a talented youth team then and I remember he used to take me, Alan Sunderland and Peter Eastoe down to Newbridge and play us at squash. He'd give us a seven-point lead, then beat us, one by one, 9-7, 9-7, 9-7. I don't know why, whether it was to boost his ego or to let us know where we stood."

McGarry's man-management evidently worked and Daley, an England youth international who was initially considered the heir apparent to Dave Wagstaffe, had a memorable 1971-72 debut season. He found out only on the afternoon of his first senior appearance that he was starting against Southampton - playing on the right wing in the No8 shirt - but October 9, 1971 is a day Daley will never forget. "I'm 18, making my debut in the First Division for a club who, with their history, are one of the biggest in

Steve Daley in his days as an eager Wolf cub.

Europe," he says, declining the offer of a lunchtime beverage. "It was fantastic. And then to score as well..."

The goal features on one of my Wolves videos, *Molineux Magic,* largely culled from ATV's *Star Soccer* archives. Daley goes ape after tapping in Wolves' final goal in a 4-2 victory, jumping vertically upwards, from a two-footed take-off, punching both hands above his head. "To be fair, you couldn't plan that celebration," he says after a beer-mat re-enactment of how he pulled off his defender to convert Danny Hegan's pull-back. "I was so embarrassed when I watched it on *Star Soccer* on the Sunday, Hugh Johns commentating. But it was great to get off to that sort of start."

Further goals followed that season, including a winner away to Huddersfield Town that helped relegate McGarry's former club on April 22, and, three nights earlier, in Daley's European debut, at home to Ferencvaros in the second leg of the UEFA Cup semi-final. Wolves had drawn 2-2 in Hungary but Wagstaffe was injured for the return game. "I scored after 22 seconds," Daley recalls proudly. "We kicked off, the ball went back, up the line to Sunderland, he crossed it and I smacked it in the bottom corner. That was it: European debut, first minute, 1-0 up, scored. To be fair, it could have gone anywhere."

In full flow...Steve Daley in his Wolves prime.

Daley's Wolves career continued on a rather hit-and-miss basis for the next four years as he struggled to force his way into the regular starting line-up. He might have thought he had cracked it just before the League Cup final of 1974 when, with Mike Bailey injured, he played the two games leading up to Wembley. "We were at Man United the week before, drew 0-0, and I had a great game," he says, recalling an afternoon when Alex Stepney, the United goalkeeper, took a penalty that Gary Pierce, another of Wolves' young Yorkshiremen bidding for a place in the final, saved. "I reckoned if Mick was fit, he would play in the final anyway but I remember Alex Higgins coming up to me in their players' lounge afterwards and saying: 'You were head and shoulders above everybody today.' Knowing what

Alex was like in later life, he was probably pissed anyway," Daley laughs, ordering another two coffees.

"Bill McGarry loved Mick Bailey, because he was a great captain, a great player and a great leader. If Mick was having a bad time himself, it wouldn't prevent him from encouraging everyone else. He was brilliant. Years on, I wondered if Bill simply rested Mick, who was getting on a bit, to make sure he didn't get injured before Wembley. He might have had a toe injury but maybe Bill was thinking: 'I'll hold him back and let him prepare for the final.'

"The manager called me in early in the week leading up to the game and said: 'You know I've got to bring Mike Bailey back in, don't you? I know you'll be disappointed but Mick's years in the game are numbered, you're only a young lad and you'll have plenty of opportunities to come back here.'"

All justifiable enough but Daley never did make it back to play at the stadium, leaving Wolves just before they returned there six years later. "I played at the Empire Pool at Wembley, though," he grimaces, "when we won the *Daily Express* five-a-sides. I got a winners' tankard as a squad member in the 1974 final. It was a mixed experience for me. There was the disappointment of not playing but then the

Steve Daley (in distance) leaps in celebration as Steve Kindon briefly raises Wolves' hopes with this early goal against Liverpool on the fateful last night of the 1975-76 season.

elation for the team winning, for the manager, for Sammy Chung, for my team-mates and for the fans.

"Unfortunately, Parkesey [Phil Parkes] was injured but Gary Pierce was absolutely phenomenal. I remember that save he made from Rodney Marsh. If that'd been Parkesey, knowing his luck, the ball would have hit the post and gone in off the back of his head. To be involved in winning something felt good and, when you looked at the players we had at the club, with the young talent coming through, the future looked very rosy."

Within two years, however, Wolves were relegated. With Wagstaffe in his final season and Bailey, when fit, filling a more defensive role, Daley played more than half the games in 1975-76, including a theatrical last evening against Liverpool. A crowd of 48,918 packed into Molineux and, as if to further underline the significance of the occasion, a commemorative poster went on sale.

"If we had won, we would have stayed up and Queens Park Rangers would have taken the title," Daley recalls. "But we lost and went down while Liverpool finished as champions. Bill McGarry, in what turned out to be his last game in charge, gave me a man-marking job on Kevin Keegan and we took the lead through Kindo [Steve Kindon] after about ten minutes. It looked good at that stage. The closest I got to Keegan was in the players' lounge afterwards, to be fair. He scored from a flick-on from John Toshack. He drifted away from me and got goal-side and finished us off. It was pure inexperience on my part, getting caught ball-watching.

"In our dressing-room afterwards, no-one said a thing. That's as bad as it gets. You just sit there, your mind drifting back to games you could have won, games you could have saved." Relegation marked the end of the old guard. Daley, at 23, played every game of the next season, taking over Bailey's No4 shirt, although adopting a more advanced position than the former captain, and producing some scintillating displays that started gaining him recognition farther afield as Wolves returned swiftly to the top flight. He played on the left of a midfield three and averaged ten goals a season over the next three years, mainly under the management of Chung.

"That was the best midfield I ever played in," he says, "with Kenny Hibbitt on the right, Willie Carr sitting in and me. The season we won the Second Division title, we contributed 34 goals from the middle of the park. The consistency of selection helped us: Pierce, [Geoff] Palmer, Squeak [Derek Parkin] and I were ever-present, with Alan Sunderland, Frank Munro, John McAlle and, once he was fit, John Richards barely missing a game. Me, Kenny and Willie had this understanding, this willingness to work for each other, that gave the team a real momentum. It was built out of respect, I suppose. Sammy was all right as a manager but his coaching was phenomenal and he stayed 'hands on' even when he became the No1. He was probably more relaxed in his approach than McGarry."

Daley's free-scoring midfield contribution earned him many admirers, among them Ron Greenwood, the England manager. He toured the Far East with the England B team, whose manager, Bobby Robson, gave him a glowing end-of-term report. "Ron Greenwood met us at the airport to welcome us back," he recalls. "He pulled me to one side and said: 'I believe you've had a good tour.' I said: 'Yes, I've enjoyed it, thanks.' He said: 'Keep doing what you're doing and I'll bring you through to the full squad next season.' Then I signed for Man City in that next year and never got the call."

Malcom Allison's opening gambit was that his record signing would jump into the England team but Daley's high-profile transfer turned into a personal nightmare as City tried to rebuild their team with him as the fulcrum. As he says, though, declining the bar meals on the menu, signing for City provided him with some amusing material, especially now middle age allows him to look back without anger.

He did not figure in the first four games of Wolves' 1979-80 season, with John Barnwell now at the helm, having succeeded Chung the previous winter in time to lead the team away from relegation. Barnwell had clearly lined up Andy Gray to join from Aston Villa with the proceeds of the sale of his star midfield player. But for three days, at least, Daley was the most expensive footballer in Britain. What's more, the transfer, from Daley's perspective, happened overnight. Quite literally.

34 *The Daily Telegraph, Thursday, September 6, 1979*

DALEY SETS RECORD FEE: GRAY WILL BREAK IT TODAY

By DENIS LOWE

THE latest British transfer record, set up yesterday as Steve Daley at last left Wolves for Manchester City in a £1,450,277 deal will be shattered again this morning when Wolves pay £1½ million for Andy Gray, Aston Villa's much admired Scottish international striker.

While Daley, 26, the England B midfield player, was completing the transfer forms at Maine Road before lunch, Gray, 23, was on his way to Molineux for talks with the Wolves' manager, John Barnwell, and the signing should go through without hitch today.

John Barnwell, the Wolverhampton manager, yesterday said: "We had a long discussion over lunch. The talks have been favourable and I'm optimistic that we'll finalise the situation tomorrow."

Steve Daley, flanked by the Manchester City management team (left) Tony Book and Malcolm Allison signs on at Maine Road.

least, Daley was the most expensive footballer in Britain. What's more, the transfer, from Daley's perspective, happened overnight. Quite literally.

"It's 2 o'clock in the morning and the phone rings," he says. "I reach over to the other side of the bed, lift it up and a voice says: 'Is that Steve Daley?' I said: 'If it's not, I've just made love to his wife.' Not really - I've added that bit for my after-dinner routine. It's Tony Book, Malcolm Allison's assistant, and he says: 'We've just agreed a fee with Wolves. John Barnwell will call you into the office in the morning. We've done the deal, but you're to act surprised.'

"We're laid in bed and Lyn says: 'Who the hell was that? It's 2am.' So I tell her I'm talking to Manchester City in the morning about a £1.5m transfer. She says: 'Phew! I thought it was something serious,' turns over and goes back to sleep. I say to her back: 'Fair play, love, thanks for the support.'" Richie Barker, Barnwell's assistant, duly summoned Daley into the manager's office the following morning and the player was officially informed of the clubs' agreement. As Daley went into the car park behind the old North Bank - a rubble-ridden, pot-holed area in stark contrast to that which looks up at the Stan Cullis Stand nowadays - he bumped into Peter Daniel, a team-mate, and told him about the transfer and the fee. "Rather you than me," Daniel replied.

The burden had started falling on Daley's shoulders even before he had driven off to meet Book at Knutsford. City's assistant drove Daley and his wife to a hotel to meet Allison and, from there, the player travelled to Maine Road, underwent a medical and was offered terms that he accepted by the next morning. Done and dusted. Compare and contrast that transfer with the circus that followed Beckham around for the six months preceding his sale. The Spanish and English press wrote entire features speculating on which part of Madrid David, Victoria, Brooklyn and Romeo may live in. Daley had 14 houses in 12 years; no wonder he is now so contented that he and Lyn live in Codsall, with their three children - Ryan, Kerry and Gemma - and four grandchildren settled in the same village.

Daley harbours no envy of Beckham or the players who become millionaires even before their first big transfer. "Good luck to them," he says. "A lot of players don't make it at all and fall by the wayside early in their careers. I was lucky enough to earn a living in a job I loved. Better players than me haven't made it. I played for 18 years and now all my family live near us in Codsall. That to me is worth more than anything football's riches could bring you."

Daley knows at first hand of the caring, paternal side to the Beckham personality. Whether England's captain is a victim or a protagonist in the fame game that envelops him is up for debate. "When we played, we were very uniformed," Daley says. "You wore a shirt and a tie when you went to a game. Now, he goes in with his hair-band, pony-tail, his kimono; he's a style icon, and he's married to a celebrity. People want to follow that.

"After I had been manager at Telford United, I fixed up with Jim Ryan, a coach at Old Trafford, to take my old centre-forward, Tim Langford, and his son Adam, who was suffering from leukaemia, to United's training headquarters at The Cliff. We met several of the United players and got autographs but Adam was just starting to think he wouldn't get to meet Beckham. Then this long pair of legs comes down the stairs and it's David Beckham. He has photos taken with Adam and everything, goes back to Old Trafford with him, shows him the trophies. He was absolutely brilliant. When people talk about David Beckham, I say: 'Do you know David Beckham?' He probably invites a lot of the attention that surrounds him but a great deal of it also follows him whether he wants it or not. Good luck to him, that's what I say. You get all this publicity and money but you have to live in a goldfish bowl. It will be even more intense at Real Madrid because their players are treated like film stars."

Daley's goldfish bowl was more your domestic circular variety that fits next to the microwave than the spanking great room-size receptacle in which Beckham swims. But, as Allison's hastily-assembled team struggled and Daley became the prize scapegoat, it was no more accommodating a place in which to flounder. It was said that he was made for life, what with a £64,000 signing-on fee, although Daley refutes that. "They made my wife rich, to be fair," he laughs. "I just tagged along.

"I went for a lot of money and every man and his dog had an opinion," Daley reflects. "You're never going to please all the people all of the time. Some players say: 'Daley? He worked hard, could knock a ball.' I do the after-dinner circuit in Manchester and people say: 'You were a bloody great player at Wolves. What happened?' Well, I know they sold Mick Channon, Peter Barnes and Gary Owen on the day I joined, and Asa Hartford had not long gone. Instead, in came the likes of the late Tommy Caton, who was 15, Steve Mackenzie, Ray Ranson, Nicky Reid, Steve Robinson. Malcolm was buying a whole new team. He told me I'd be playing for England in no time and I saw no reason to disbelieve him. After all, Ron Greenwood

had told me he was keeping tabs on me.

"It was a transitional period but the team never came together. When Malcolm went, John Bond came in and bought experience, which you can understand. I'm a proud fella and I wanted to do well. The team were broken up very quickly and that puts the onus on two or three players to keep it all together. With results poor and the inexperienced survivors struggling, you needed a Mike Bailey figure to see the team through. That wasn't me. I was an attacking midfielder, not an anchor-man, and I wanted to get my own game in order.

"People seem to think I had a nightmare every time I pulled on a boot for City. Yes, it was a bad

Steve Daley in new surroundings at Manchester City - and immediately under big pressure.

53

experience but it wasn't that black. I had my good games, my bad games, my indifferent games, like everyone else. But when you've cost a million pounds, you're not expected to be like everyone else.

"It did affect me. You get so fed up with being ridiculed that you end up staying in. Then one Sunday, John Bond went public and slaughtered me, slagged me off on TV something rotten. He wanted me out - he needed to finance his new signings and wanted someone to take the rap. I was sure it all went back a couple of years to a game at Molineux when he was manager of Norwich. Kevin Bond, his son, tripped me off the ball, so I grabbed him by the windpipe and pushed him into the dug-out, where his Dad was. Kevin got booked, which triggered a suspension, and John Bond said: 'I'll have you for that.' After the match, he chased me up the tunnel but Richie Barker caught him and held him for me. I could've smashed him in the face.

"When he took over at City, the first thing he said to me was: 'I don't bear grudges but if I'd met you a couple of years ago, I'd have killed you.' Anyway, as it went from bad to worse for me at City, he went on television and told the world I wasn't fit to be a father, had no respect for my fellow professionals and was causing unrest in the dressing-room. I went into the ground the next morning and the first team-mate I saw was Joe Corrigan. I said: 'Joe, is that true?' He said: 'No, you're sound.' So I went in and saw him, the manager. I said: 'That's it. I'm not playing for you, I'll go.' Even then, he put a story in the *Manchester Evening News* that ran with the headline: 'Bond offers Daley olive branch.' It simply wasn't true."

Denis Tueart returned to the club after a short spell in the United States to find Daley struggling. "I went to New York Cosmos, a 28-year-old England international, for £235,000," the City director recalls. "Within a year, they'd bought Steve, uncapped and relatively unproven, for £1.5m. I couldn't believe it. When I came back for my second spell at Maine Road and he was here, I felt sorry for him. He was a good lad but it was such a massive fee, I don't think he could cope with it. The expectations were just too great."

Daley was put up for sale at £450,000. Chelsea nibbled but eventually the outcast negotiated his own move to Seattle Sounders, with a transfer fee of £300,000. The club were soon on the verge of collapse when Daley and Bond were reunited. Briefly. "John came out to watch his son Kevin play and we beat Tampa Bay Rowdies 4-2. I scored two and made the other two. We had a beer after the game and agreed that a lot of water had passed under the bridge. Then he told me he had just taken over at Burnley and would I consider signing for him?

"He signed Kevin Reeves, Tommy Hutchison, Dennis Tueart, Bobby McDonald, Gerry Gow and me, then he turned on us all again. I saw it coming. The chairman told me: 'We want you to go, you're costing too much to play in the reserves. Can we sort something out?' I said: 'No problem.' He was surprised. 'You sure?' he said. 'Don't worry, it's fine.' So we came to a settlement. Then I said: 'By the way, I'm off to San

Diego next week on a three-year contract.' The fingers of the clock always meet. If I could have paid £1,000 never to see John Bond again, it would have been money well spent. In the States, I loved it. Nobody knew me, so they couldn't slag me off."

Daley's playing career ended at Walsall, Rhyl and, in 1986-87, Kettering Town, where he played under Alan Buckley. Perhaps surprisingly, he considers Buckley, who signed him for Walsall, to be the best manager he worked with. Daley has had various modest jobs since, mainly in sales - of washing machines, of beer and of sportswear in Beatties department store, Wolverhampton. But then, his Dad was christened Arthur...

There is a humility about Daley, an acceptance of his lot, and his bonhomie and banter remain this side of arrogance throughout our meeting. As a player, he had a swagger about him that could veer towards petulance when things were not going so well. But I remember him as a decent player who could occasionally produce the extraordinary; that's not such a crime, is it? I remember him sliding into a tackle next to the touchline yet managing to scoop out the ball to retain possession rather than concede a throw-in.

Most passers-by in the hostelry recognise him. One is my mother and, while I would not want to give the impression that my bond to Wolves is in any way umbilical, it does seem entirely natural that she should order a coffee and baked potato and join us at the table. Daley is undeterred by her attendance and treats her questions seriously and politely. For all his ups and downs, his feet remain on the ground, his self-deprecating sense of humour always hovering. "My Dad was a miner when he wasn't playing football," he says, "and my Mum a nurse. I was brought up in Barnsley in a two-up, two-down, with an outside toilet. In fact, there were that many houses boarded up in our street, the window cleaner was a sander."

The showman declines the offer of another drink before bidding farewell to return to his day job, selling fine local ale. We speak by phone the following week and he recounts that Sky Sports have been doing a piece about Maine Road being sold that weekend. "They went into the boardroom and said: 'This is the place where some momentous business decisions were made. Do I hear £1m for Steve Daley?' They still remember me," he says, ruefully, "still for all the wrong reasons."

Steve Daley

Born:	April 15, 1953, in Barnsley
Signed:	July, 1971
Wolves appearances:	244
Goals:	43
Left:	September, 1979
International recognition:	England youth and B caps

Matt Murray

A GIANT IN THE MAKING

August 13, 2003: The players' lounge, Molineux

It was three days before the start of the 2003-04 Barclaycard Premiership season that Matt Murray acknowledged he and Wolverhampton Wanderers were to be personally involved. As he sat down to discuss his remarkable rise to prominence over the previous 12 months, the goalkeeper who had been associated with the club since he was at primary school finally accepted the unlikely truth he had helped establish.

"It just takes ages," he says, despite having pulled off the penalty save that helped clinch victory in the Nationwide League First Division play-off final against Sheffield United and having watched the game on video ten times since. "Only now, with all the publicity, the fact that we've got Blackburn Rovers away on Saturday, then Manchester United just after that, Arsenal and Liverpool over Christmas, is it sinking in with me."

The source of Murray's incredulity partly derives from his lengthy association with the club and his ready understanding of Wolves supporters' desperation to reach the Premiership, but also from the injury-wrecked teenage years that left him doubting whether he could establish himself as a professional footballer. Getting in (to the team) and getting up (to the Premiership) had taken less than a season.

Raised in Lichfield after being adopted at ten weeks of age, this well-mannered and modest character has been grateful for the love and support of a large overlapping family throughout the times when a succession of knee operations left him tearfully pondering alternative careers. It was only when he finally made his breakthrough into the Wolves team, early in the promotion season of 2002-03, that he dared believe he could make it as a top-level goalkeeper.

Dave Jones, his manager at Molineux, had challenged him to prove he could stay fit enough for long enough to show that his potential could come to fruition. It might have sounded cruel at the time but Murray responded with form that was sufficiently eye-catching and consistent as to make him the England under-21 keeper.

When injury struck again, he took the summer to recuperate from a double hernia operation he underwent two days after the play-off final. The plan was to give himself the best possible opportunity of being fit for the start of the new campaign. Mission apparently accomplished, the pre-season press day is just coming to its conclusion when Murray, having munched his way through copious amounts of Doritos snacks as Paul Ince and Dave Jones were inundated with interview requests, happily re-parks his car and agrees to come back inside for a chat.

"I thought no-one wanted to talk to me," he says, as he looks around for a bin on spotting my dictaphone. "Excuse me, but I'm just going to lose the chewing gum. It doesn't sound too good champing away. I didn't know which was better after I'd been battering the Doritos, to come back in with cheesy breath or keep chewing." When he hears of the plans for this book, he asks who else is being lined up. "You doing Bully? What about Robbie Keane? Ring Simon at SFX - his agent - and I'm sure he'll get Robbie to ring you. He's a mate of mine, Robbie."

Murray still almost sounds like a fan. When he hears he is one of only two keepers in this book, he demurs. "I've been in the team less than a season," he argues, without wishing to appear unwilling to help. I counter by suggesting that the mantle of hero often falls upon a character that plays his part at a critical juncture in a team's history, regardless of longevity of service.

"It's fair to say that 12 months ago the majority of Wolves fans would have said: 'Matt who?'" he says. "Nobody had really heard of me. I was just trying to establish myself as No2 goalkeeper at the club when Oakesey (Michael Oakes) got injured. That was the only way I was going to get a game, really."

He made his first senior appearance in a 3-2 defeat away to Wimbledon, in "a surreal atmosphere," with Wolves fans outnumbering the home following. "I count my debut proper as the game at home to Reading," he says. "Disappointingly, we lost 1-0 but the atmosphere was fabulous and I was fortunate enough to get man of the match. It was a great day and gave me the taste for it. I've never really looked back.

"Having got in the Wolves team, I was then picked for England under-21s after five games. You have to pinch yourself. Looking back at that season, with international recognition, promotion, the FA Cup run, beating the likes of Newcastle United, I experienced in one year so many of the kind of games Wolves fans will remember for a long, long time."

Murray should know as he counts himself among them. Originally, he liked Everton, following the example of his step father, Steve, and admired Neville Southall and Mike Stowell. "At the end of the day, I've been at Wolves since I was nine," he says, "so it's deep in my heart. Stowelly's my hero and we're still good friends now.

Matt Murray pictured at his second home three days before his Barclaycard Premiership debut - just before his season was decimated by yet more injury misfortune.

He's goalkeeping coach at Bristol City. We speak often and he'll always give me advice.

"Stowelly was just joining Wolves as I arrived and he was there for me as I moved through the age groups. For me, he's the man. We used to get free tickets for Molineux as schoolboys and I remember big nights like the FA Cup game against Sheffield Wednesday, when Paul Jones saved from Chris Waddle in the penalty shoot-out, and the play-off semi-final against Crystal Palace. We were knocked out despite winning on the night but the buzz made me desperate to play in this team.

"I've seen how close we've come over the years. I've wanted it so much for the fans. They've been great to me. You come in - big club, big stage - but it's like they know you're going to make the odd mistake. They understand that. So you make sure you give 100 per cent, and that's a burden off your shoulders."

Murray appreciates the guidance he received from Rob Kelly, Chris Evans, Martin Thomas, Stowell and Bobby Mimms. "The facilities, the coaching," he says, "it's been a Premiership set-up ever since I came here."

Support was essential in keeping Murray on track, psychologically, as he suffered during his teens from a bone-growing disorder known as Osgood-Schlatter disease. "I wasn't that tall as a kid," he explains. "I was a late developer and, at 15, I was still under 6ft. Then I just shot up. That's what gave me the growing pains. I missed a big part of my development through injuries. In three years, I probably only played for about six months. Bobby Mimms really helped me with confidence because I used to get really nervous, then beat myself up if I made a mistake. I think that's why it took me until I was given my debut and a five-year contract before I thought I might do something in the game. Before that, in my heart of hearts, although people could see an ability, I wasn't convinced. Bobby kept saying: 'You can do this, you can.'"

"Matt Murray was lucky still to be here," Dave Jones recalls. "He got into the mode where he loved the treatment room too much. It's not so much the players' fault but they reach the point where every niggle becomes a major injury, because they want to be absolutely right before coming back. That cycle needed to be broken with Matt.

"I remember [the players] getting measured for club suits and Matt complaining about the material. So he got both barrels from me. He was pasted all over the wall. Here was a player who had hardly kicked a ball for this football club, complaining about his suit. He had a few home truths blasted at him. Players can moan for England, nothing's ever right for them, and Matt needed a few realities drummed into him.

"I threatened to kick him out the club. He was hanging around with players at other clubs who were at the height of their careers and, every time I spoke with people in the game, they'd say: 'Oh I've seen that big fella from your club out and about.' Nobody knew his name. He was just 'the big fella.' They know his name now: he knuckled down and earned his place and had a fantastic promotion season."

Yet it was not an easy cycle for the young player to break. One injury would beget another. Murray, rapidly growing into the 6ft 4in man-mountain you encounter now, underwent six operations on one knee or the other. "Injuries mess with your head more than anything," he recalls. "You just get back from one and then, bang, you're back to square one. Surgery, strengthening, the whole process - you rehab yourself, you know what to do so well.

"It's so disappointing because you just want to go out and play football. It makes you appreciate it all the more when you can play. I was never jealous of the other lads but they're out there, making progress and I'm sat in the treatment room, getting left behind. You're happy for them going on in their careers but you're thinking: 'If I was fit, what could I be doing?'"

Stowell had a high regard for his young protégé; still does. The youngster's vast eating capacity has been a topic of fascination round Molineux for years but the one part of his appetite he could not satisfy for so long was the desire to play games. "It seemed to sum Matt up when we were training one match-day on a pre-season tour of Sweden a few years ago," Stowell said. "Away from the other players, I was testing him with some shots just before we finished for lunch. Suddenly, he dived to his left and caught his head with a sickening blow on the post of the aluminium goal we were in. Blood poured from the cut and I pressed my hand on it to stop the flow, so much so that I remember my glove almost stuck to his head. It was no more than a minor injury but it typified the misfortune he suffered at that time. There seemed to be no end to it."

The lowest point came when Murray was loaned out to two non-league teams and, rather than reap the benefit of playing games, came back with his most debilitating injury yet. "I'd just got back from one year out with my right knee," he recalls, the recalled frustration redolent in his expression as he stares up at Molineux walls adorned by previous players' international shirts. "I went to Slough Town and that was a nightmare, a disaster.

"It makes you realise, with no disrespect to Slough, that you just don't want to be there. Then, at 19, I went to Kingstonian, who were playing in the Conference, and I was enjoying it when, 20 minutes into my debut, I went to kick the ball, as innocuous as anything, and I did my 'cruciates.' I played on. I was struggling so much that I kept falling over, just couldn't stand up, but I didn't realise the extent of it. I saw a specialist and was told I'd injured my cartilage, which would take between one and three months to recover from. I thought: 'I can deal with that.' When I woke to hear I had damaged my interior cruciate ligament and would probably be out for another year, I cried.

"I thought: 'I can't take this any more.' At best, you get labelled injury-prone. But you know people who haven't come back from that. I was even considering other careers and started looking into teaching and the property business. I thought: 'I can do without this.' You're a kid and the game's hurting you, football's hurting you. That's when you need your family and friends."

Just as well, then, that Murray had a family tree like an oak to lean upon. It takes some explaining but, after much calculation, it becomes apparent that Matthew William Murray has seven siblings, plus Charlotte, the daughter of Jan and Pete Morris, with whom he lodged in Penn for six years after leaving school.

"It's been a really good stable base for me," he says. "Everyone talks about adoption but it's the best thing that's happened to me. They say you can't choose your parents but I really would've chosen mine. They've stood by me all the way, been there if I've made a mistake, never put pressure on me and just offered support. My biological parents aren't allowed to contact me. I was adopted almost from birth. My blood father's Nigerian, I know. My biological mother, I don't know. They might have an inkling of who I am but they're not allowed to approach me.

"It has not hurt me at all and I would not class them as my parents anyway because they have had no input into the person I've grown up to be. I never felt awkward when I was growing up. The only times I was asked about it was when I came to Wolves as a youngster and people said: 'How come you are black and both your parents are white?' But I wasn't embarrassed or ashamed about my upbringing, I was proud of it."

Murray's adoptive parents, Ian and Linda, had already adopted Ben, whom Matt considers his brother. They divorced amicably before both were remarried; Linda to Steve, who had two daughters from a previous marriage. They are Matt's step-sisters. Ian's second wife, who gave birth to Matt's half-brother and half-sister, died and his third wife, Alison, already had two boys, so they are Matt's step-brothers. Got that? Simple really.

"We're all close and support each other. Because I'm from such a large family, if ever any of us have problems, we can go to each other. Obviously I've had a lot of problems with my knees and everyone's had their own situations. My step-Dad and my brother come everywhere with me, my step-sister comes to some games, but the whole lot of them are proud of me, I think." Murray now lives in Lichfield with Chloe, his fiancée from Leeds, and their kittens, Bootsy and Blossom. "Chloe chose the names," he laughs. "They're wrecking the gaff."

Other key sources of support through his injuries were his closest team-mates at Wolves. "Robbie [Keane] was a big help," he says. "He was the kind who would ring you and keep you going. When you were down, he'd come round and see you or give you that phone call to make you laugh. He'd point out the players who had come back from such injuries, like Paul Gascoigne and Alan Shearer."

"Friends are friends," Keane himself says, when I catch up with him a few months later. "Just because I leave Wolves for another club doesn't end a friendship. When I went to Coventry and Matt was injured, he was struggling, had some really hard times and thought of packing the game in. I kept on his case, kept telling him he'd be back in no time. Although it was hard for him, I wanted to be a mate, to be there for him."

"Robbie's the type not to let things bother him unduly," Murray continues. "We only played one game together in the youth team because he was straight into the first team at 17 but we clicked from day one. I'd be in the squad sometimes when we were travelling away and they'd take a few young lads for experience, and he'd look after me. We'd sit together on the bus plus we'd go out together because we were both single and had more free time whereas a lot of the other lads were married and had kids.

"Mark Jones was the young striker everyone was raving about at first but Keaney just came from nowhere. I was with the schoolboys still when he came into the youth team. I remember him in training, doing nutmegs, trying everything and anything. Ever since I've known him, he's been one of the main characters in the dressing-room. He's never arrogant, just has a good sense of humour, enjoys good banter. The proper Irish craick.

"I was on holiday in Portugal last summer when he was playing in the World Cup finals. I was watching him take these crucial penalties on television and I was probably more nervous than he was. We'd speak on the phone in between the games and, obviously, he did himself justice. Our game with Tottenham Hotspur was the first I looked for when the Premiership fixtures came out."

Another of the talented young internationals to progress from Wolves' youth academy has been Joleon Lescott. "I roomed with Joleon when I was called up for England under-21s and, as he'd been there before, that helped," Murray says. "I've played with him right through from youth-team level at Molineux. He's improved every year and he's a great lad as well, down-to-earth and willing to learn.

"I'm only young but if you listen to people in the game, they say he's got what it takes to go right to the top. He's strong, quick and improving all the time. He's only 21 this Saturday and he's already played around 150 matches for Wolves. I can see him playing for England. You look at him in training with the other under-21 lads and he's awesome."

Lescott chooses not to do many interviews. "He prefers to let his feet do the talking," Murray reveals. "If he doesn't know someone, he's quite reserved but he's

Wimbledon F.C.

NATIONWIDE LEAGUE DIVISION ONE
Wimbledon – V – Wolverhampton Wanderers
Saturday 31st August 2002 – Kick-off – 3.00.pm.

WIMBLEDON		WOLVES	
1	Kelvin DAVIS	13	Matthew MURRAY
3	Peter HAWKINS	3	Lee NAYLOR
5	Mark WILLIAMS	4	Alex RAE
7	Jobi McANUFF	5	Joleon LESCOTT
8	Damien FRANCIS	6	Paul BUTLER (C)
9	Neil SHIPPERLEY (C)	7	Shaun NEWTON
12	Trond ANDERSEN	8	Denis IRWIN
18	Wayne GRAY	9	Nathan BLAKE
22	Rob GIER	15	Kevin COOPER
23	Alex TAPP	21	Ivar INGIMARSSON
24	Jermaine DARLINGTON	29	Dean STURRIDGE

SUBS		SUBS	
2	Gareth AINSWORTH	12	Adam PROUDLOCK
4	Chris WILLMOTT	14	Ludovic POLLET
13	Paul HEALD	16	Kenny MILLER
17	Adam NOWLAND	24	Marc EDWORTHY
20	Mikele LEIGERTWOOD	36	Lewis SOLLY

Referee : Brian CURSON (LEICESTERSHIRE)

A new name appears at the top of Wolves' line-up.

not arrogant. Once he's comfortable with you, he's a very funny guy. He'll back you on and off the pitch. We've grown up together so we speak on the phone, we go out together. Because we're a similar age, we have similar lifestyles. We get noticed around Wolverhampton a bit now, perhaps in Birmingham as well, but, outside the area, not at all. Perhaps with my height, I stand out a little more but everything I've had has been positive. I can't complain."

At this point, Pete Colley, a Sky Sports reporter from Lichfield, walks through and indulges in a spot of light banter with Murray. "I'll see you in the Three Tuns later," he laughs. Murray adds: "He used to go to the same school as me. He interviewed me once but I'd lost my voice, so I was struggling." Then Nick Potts, staff photgrapher with the Press Association, wanders in and asks to take a couple of pictures of Matt out on the hallowed turf. "No problem," Matt says. "Pottsy..." he adds, after the snapper leaves us, "...now there's a legend round here."

Nothing appears too much trouble for Murray. Perhaps it is this congeniality that represents the flip-side of the diffidence that held him back earlier in his career. He needs pushing to pick out his biggest personal contributions to Wolves' promotion season, as if he has been taught to speak up for himself.

Favourite game from the regulation season? "Preston at home," he recalls. "It was a great team performance but even though we won 4-0, I also made a few important saves. It was my first clean sheet, my first win and a night match with a brilliant atmosphere. We'd been under a bit of pressure after a bad run. And for atmosphere, the Newcastle game was just a classic Cup-tie." Does he have the video? "Yeah, don't worry about that," he laughs. "I've watched that and the Cardiff game a few times."

It must have been nerve-wracking playing in such a massive game, with a place in the Premiership at stake. "I was nervous in the build-up but, once I got into my warm-up, I adapted to my surroundings and felt good," he recalls. "The early goal settled us and it all grew from there. But I was never as nervous for that game as I was for the semi-final games with Reading. I have to admit, in the away game, the whole atmosphere got to me. It was taking over me and I stiffened up and just couldn't relax, whereas, at Cardiff, I just embraced it all.

"I don't know what the difference was. Maybe making the final was better than we'd done before as a club. I remember Nayls [Lee Naylor] cleared one early on [when Reading nearly scored in the second leg] but I got more into it and made one or two good saves. It certainly intensified the relief when we were through. That felt fantastic but nothing compares with beating Sheffield United at Cardiff. You know you're there then. It doesn't really sink in but it was memorable all the same. The most important thing I did in the final? The save after the ball cannoned off Paul Ince, when we were 2-0 up just before half-time."

Matt Murray, complete with novelty head-gear, savours the moment as Wolves players go on their lap of honour at the Millennium Stadium, where he was named man of the match. It would appear the Sheffield United end is in the background.

That preceded Kenny Miller giving Wolves a 3-0 lead before United were awarded a penalty early in the second period. "I'd done loads on penalties in the week before," Murray confirms, "getting my technique together, deciding which way I'd go. Michael Brown had scored in our league game at their place a few weeks beforehand, so I gave him a little extra to go his favoured side. Things like that come from preparation. The defence pride themselves on a clean sheet and it was nice, with the penalty save, to get a bit of the spotlight. But it's a team game."

It is the unity in the camp that gives Murray faith in Wolves' top-flight prospects. "People are writing us off but we've got a lot of pride," he says. "We're not just going into the season to make the numbers up, but to give a good account of ourselves. I think realistically a good season would be Premiership survival but we've worked hard for this, we feel ready and it'll be nice having the shoe on the other foot. We're not one of the big guns now, where teams come here and set up with ten behind the ball.

"The pressure's on other teams more now. We feel we've a lot to prove because we've got our pride. We've got this squad with a lot of spirit generated from all that's gone on in the last couple of years. The XI selected against Blackburn will be making history, playing in Wolves' first game in the Premiership, so there'll be that extra stab of excitement. We understand it's going to be difficult and there'll be long periods when the likes of United, in the third game, the defending Premiership champions, with a star-studded line-up, will have the ball. We'll have to do our jobs, not let up for a moment, and be patient. This is what we've worked for and it's brilliant to be here."

Almost exactly 72 hours later, Murray is signing autographs outside Ewood Park. He grabs his bag out of the team coach and comes to shake hands but there is no smile. Wolves have lost 5-1, their spirit doused too easily and, if it had not been for his excellence, the baptism of fire could have been even hotter. "I realised this was going to be a step-up, a whole jump in class. Everything Blackburn did was so sharp," he says. "But we've got to give it more than that." After all Wolves have been through and after all Murray has been through in his young life, the pride will surely resurface.

Matt Murray

Born:	May 2, 1981, in Solihull
Signed:	August, 1997
Wolves appearances:	50
Goals:	0
International recognition:	England under-21 caps

Little did we know after the Blackburn debacle that Murray's Premiership season was over. Added to the absence of Joleon Lescott, his enforced withdrawal from the fray proved to be truly significant over the subsequent months. The lack of a central defender of genuine pace, and of a goalkeeper of physical presence who can come for crosses, has cost Wolves dear. The pain of another thrashing, at home to Charlton Athletic (0-4), is alleviated by the pride of a great performance at Old Trafford, where Wolves are unfortunate to lose 1-0. Imagine if Henri Camara had a radar. A goalless draw at home to Portsmouth brings a first Premiership point.

THE GAMES BARCLAYC.

WOLVES SUFFER STAGE FRIGHT

August 2003

BLACKBURN ROVERS (2) 5
Amoruso 22, Thompson 29, Emerton 53, Cole 79, 87

WOLVERHAMPTON WANDERERS (0) 1
Iversen 72

Referee: J Winter 6. Attendance 26,270.

★★★★

Scintillating Blackburn highlight the gulf in class

THE NEW BLACKBURN ROVERS sponsors were giving out "stress-relieving rabbits" at half-time on Saturday. On their entry into the Barclaycard Premiership, however, it was Wolverhampton Wanderers who froze in the headlights. Clenching the foamy rubber animal helps to assuage anxiety. Wolves, on this evidence, should place a bulk order of the executive toy for their club shop. Angst will be furrowing many a Black Country brow this winter.

Blackburn were scintillating, their performance testimony to the job Graeme Souness has done and a template for the progress that can be made within two years of promotion. They were helped, however, by Wolves coming down with first-night stage fright. Dave Jones's team started on the back foot and regressed. All the positivity of their promotion evaporated as they stood off in awe of the home side until they were two goals down. By then it was game over and Blackburn finished in mickey-taking mode.

Wolves have been so obsessed with reaching the Premiership that, on Saturday, they neglected to call upon the attributes that had got them there. The very least to be expected of a newly-promoted side is to play with maximum commitment. The sooner Jones is able to have fit his "big hitters" — Nathan Blake, Mark Kennedy, Joleon Lescott and Kenny Miller — and accept that a commanding defensive midfield player does not come cheap, the better.

"The club and the city have been wrapped up in us getting into the Premiership," the Wolves manager said. "Now we have not only got a kick in the teeth but a bash on the head as well. But it shouldn't be all doom and gloom. We're here; now we have to earn the right to stay here. I'm angry, I'm frustrated but I'm realistic as well. Sometimes you need to hit rock bottom before you can bounce back."

Jones cited the example of Sunderland, four years ago, who were similarly outclassed in a 4-0 defeat by Chelsea and went on to finish seventh. Only three of the Blackburn players who started on their return to the Premiership were playing on Saturday and Garry Flitcroft admitted: "It's always hard when you come up. You've got to spend big now to stay up and if you can scrape through in your first season,

then you've done well. I'm sure Dave Jones will get things right. It is early days."

Lorenzo Amoruso and Brett Emerton, both making their debuts, powered home with head and foot respectively either side of David Thompson's looping volley. Steffen Iversen slashed home a rebound after heading against a post as Wolves did at least make five clear chances. However, Andrew Cole, whom Blackburn can afford to name as a substitute, emphasised the gulf in class with superb movement to score twice from passes from the inspirational Tugay. Scottish sources suggest Barry Ferguson could still follow Amoruso to Ewood Park if Rangers miss out on the Champions League while Markus Babbel is set to join on a free transfer from Liverpool.

"I'm eager to spend money," Souness said. "It's burning a hole in my pocket."

PETER LANSLEY

Blackburn Rovers (4-4-2): B Friedel 5 — L Neill 5, M Taylor 6, L Amoruso 7, V Gresko 6 — D Thompson 7 (sub: C Grabbi, 79min), Tugay 9, G Flitcroft 7, B Emerton 8 — M Jansen 8 (sub: A Cole, 74 8), D Yorke 6. Substitutes not used: N Johansson, A Todd, A Kelly. Booked: Thompson. NEXT: Bolton Wanderers (a).
Wolverhampton Wanderers (4-4-2): M Murray 7 — D Irwin 4, P Butler 5, J Craddock 5, L Naylor 5 — S Newton 6 (sub: H Camara, 85), P Ince 4, C Cameron 5, Shaa 1 (sub: N Blake, 60 6) — S Iversen 3, D Sturridge 4 (sub: O Leahy, 71 4). Substitutes not used: A Rae, M Oakes. Booked: Blake. NEXT: Charlton Athletic (h).
Shots on target: (h) 18 (a) 6. Fouls: (h) 8 (a) 14. Offsides: (h) 6 (a) 1

Steve Bull

HE PLAYS FOR WOLVERHAMPTON AND HE IS A LOVELY CHAP

September 4, 2003: The Bull residence, Newport, Shropshire

It felt as if there had been a bereavement in the family when Steve Bull retired from playing for Wolverhampton Wanderers in 1999. Yet, for me, the end of his England career at the start of the decade had proved the greater burden. So, when we meet at his resplendent rural retreat in Shropshire, I want to discover whether I did actually put the kibosh on his international prospects.

Back then, just before pasta and mineral water supplanted lager, fish and chips as the average footballer's staple diet, I interviewed Bully for the Wolves programme. One of the set questions appertained to a player's favourite meal. When I subsequently placed a piece with a national magazine, it seemed rather quaint to mention that Bull loved to scoff a double Big Mac and fries, with chocolate shake, after training.

Working at the same time at the *Bucks Free Press*, I covered England on the somewhat tenuous grounds that they trained in our county and were therefore one of our local teams. When *90 Minutes*, a shiny, laddish mag spawned from the fanzine age, came out, I proudly posted a copy to Steve Bull, Molineux, Waterloo Road, etc, with the note: 'Thanks for the interview, Steve. Look forward to seeing you at Bisham Abbey for the next England camp.' The scenario, sadly, never materialised. Bull, having played in Italia '90 and in Graham Taylor's first two games as manager, never appeared for his country again.

In no time, it became strictly off limits for top-level players to sample anything more exotic than chicken and broccoli. I was convinced the health people within the increasingly enlightened England set-up had read *90 Minutes*, realised Bully was a walking culinary dustbin and banished him to international exile with no more ado.

I have interviewed Steve on several occasions since, and pinned hopes of Wolves reaching the Premiership on his broad shoulders for a decade. Yet writing this book brings the more relaxed opportunity to delve into critical junctures of his career. "Doh worry abou't, mate, it weren' yow," Bully says, when I relate the burger botch-up. "You want your coffee stronger than this?" Clearly, he holds no grudges. Phew!

For a man who came as close as any contemporary player to being bigger than his team, Wolves meant remarkably little to Steve Bull the boy. Perhaps the freshness with which he zapped into an eventual total of 306 goals for the club was borne of a lack of expectancy. We may have wanted him to score the 50 goals a year with which he had led us from the Fourth Division to the Second, in order to haul Wolves to the top flight, but, as a teenager, he never anticipated playing professional football. Everything was a bonus. Becoming the club's latter-day legend, their record scorer, thrashing home a debut goal for England against Scotland, going to a World Cup. His whole story defied its opening chapter.

Bully was a Liverpool fan whose knee operation at 17 prompted a specialist to tell him the Sunday park would be his field of dreams. "I had a foreign body taken out and the surgeon said afterwards: 'You know you won't play pro football, don't you?' I said: 'As long as I can play Sunday mornings, I ain't bothered.' So I defied the laws of gravity by playing for the next 17 years. The knee he told me was no good (the right one) has stood up ever since." Playing on a Saturday afternoon for Tipton Town in the Black Country epicentre where he was born, after turning out for West Bromwich Albion youth team in the morning, Bull would take on a third game of the weekend the following morning. No wonder his knees have given him such gyp.

In such a hectic schedule, watching football came a poor second. "The only game I remember going to was when Chris Taylor, a neighbour, had two tickets for West Brom v Chelsea. Not only was I playing at weekends, there wasn't much money around. Getting to The Hawthorns, though, I thought: 'I like this, I wouldn't mind some of this.' But I was so busy playing, always first out the school gates and over to Jubilee Park, getting home for a clip round the ear-hole for having muddy trousers and all my homework still to do."

So which soccer sticker did *he* most covet? Which team did he beg to stay up to watch on *Match of the Day*? "I'd just get other people's swaps," he says, "but Ian Rush was my hero, and Heighway, Callaghan, Neal, Keegan and Toshack before that. Once I was old enough to get a paper round, I did fill one of those Panini albums, eventually. It took me ages. I was Liverpool mad but it was football in general. Hugh Johns used to commentate on ATV on the Midlands games on Sunday afternoons but if Wolves came on *Star Soccer* or *Match of the Day*, I felt nothing at all. They were just another team. I didn't think: 'I wonder if I'll play for them one day.'"

After his knee operation, Bull trained below his age group two evenings a week at Albion. He was earning £27 a week in a bed factory before Nobby Stiles, the club's youth-team coach, finally persuaded Johnny Giles, his brother-in-law, to give him a 12-month contract, on £120 a week. In April, 1986, Ron Saunders, Giles' successor, gave Bull his one and only taste of top-flight football, a 24-minute run-out as sub in a 1-0 defeat away to Queens Park Rangers that confirmed Albion's relegation. Three first-team goals in the lower grade in the early weeks of the following season failed to convince Saunders that Bull had the necessary touch for the top divisions and, at the age of 21, he was offered a somewhat disheartening alternative.

"I've never seen Ron Saunders," Bull says, "since the day he said: 'Someone's come in for you.' Me and Thommo (Andy Thompson) went across to Molineux and, within eight minutes, we'd signed. Albion were a great club, only just out of the First Division, and they'd got all tiles on the floor and everything. Beautiful! We went to Wolves and they had absolutely nothing. We thought: 'What have we done?' But we didn't say that to each other until after the nightmare against Chorley."

That was the FA Cup first-round second replay for which the newcomers were ineligible, 48 hours after they had made their debuts in a 3-0 home defeat by Wrexham, Bull wearing the No8 shirt. It remains the nadir of the club's history, that so-called giant-killing by the Multipart League part-timers. Five days later, away to Lincoln City, Andy Mutch was dropped and Bull claimed the No9 jersey he was to wear with such distinction for the best part of 13 years.

"I retired the year they brought names in on the back of shirts," Bull says. "They were going to have one season when they were going to have the shirt, with Bull and the nine on it, in

Wolverhampton Wanderers F.C. (1986) Limited

Molineux Grounds
Waterloo Road
Wolverhampton
WV1 4QR
Telephone (0902) 712181

IT IS HEREBY AGREED that in consideration of the transfer of the transfer of registration of STEPHEN GEORGE BULL from West Bromwich Albion Football Club Ltd to Wolverhampton Wanderers Football Club (1986) Ltd a transfer fee of £54,000 plus VAT of £8100 will be paid by Wolverhampton Wanderers Football Club (1986) Ltd as follows:-

1. £39,000 plus £8100 VAT forthwith.

2. £15,000 on the 13th May, 1987.

3. A further sum of £5000 plus VAT after the player has played in twenty first team league matches,.

4. A further sum of £5000 plus VAT after the player has played in forty first team league matches.

5. It is further agreed that Wolverhampton Wanderers F.C. (1986) Ltd will pay to West Bromwich Albion Football Club Ltd 33½% of any transfer monies obtained on the player being transferred by Wolverhampton Wanderers to another club over and above the amounts already paid above.

6. It is further agreed that in accordance with the Football League Regulations Wolverhampton Wanderers Football Club will be responsible for the payment of the 5% transfer levy to the said Football League.

7. The foregoing is subject to the player passing a medical examination to the satisfaction of Wolverhampton Wanderers Football Club (1986) Ltd.

....
Wolverhampton Wanderers F.C. (1986) Ltd.

26/11/86
Date

....
West Bromwich Albion F.C. Ltd.

26/11/86
Date.

A highly cherished document from Molineux's archives - the signed paperwork for Steve Bull's move to Wolves.

the club shop and not have anyone play in it. It never bothered me at the time what number I wore but I suppose the nine was my shirt."

This is not the book for statistics but the 19 goals Bully knocked up for Wolves in the following six months, as he and Mutch formed the ideal lower-division partnership and players such as Micky Holmes and Phil Robinson found their feet, took Graham Turner's team into the Fourth Division play-offs. On the last day of the regulation season, May 9, Bully scored his first Wolves hat-trick, against Hartlepool United, but only after the players had had to run off because of a pitch invasion, with four minutes to go, following his second goal. We wondered whether the referee would bother restarting the game but he did and, in honour of the 15th birthday of my brother Simon (obviously), our new hero completed his treble.

It was a heady old time, the delirious joy of winning so many games and cheering so many goals providing an exhilarating contrast to the depressing five years Wolves had endured prior to Bull's arrival. The numbers are awesome, of course, as this lean and hungry young striker with such a primeval lust for goals racked up 100 in the following two years, hence the fanzine's name, *A Load of Bull*.

Just as important as the legend Bull created are the surviving images. Hereford United away, when he turned the last defender 30 yards out and whacked the ball into the roof of the net without further fuss. At Peterborough United, when we stamped our feet on the wooden terraces all match and sang the song of that time: 'Everywhere we go, people want to know, where the hell are *you* from, we're from Wolverhampton, lovely Wolverhampton, sunny Wolverhampton.' And, of course, as every chapter then seemed to have a happy ending, scoring the late winner on his first return to The Hawthorns after Wolves had climbed back to the old Second Division. 'Thank you very much for Stevie Bu-ull, thank you very much, thank you very very very much.'

Part of the enjoyment of following Wolves then was the earthiness epitomised by Bull. Muck-and-nettles, roll your sleeves up, get at 'em. There was little sophistication about Turner's team, with Mutch as the attacking pivot off whom Bull fed, with Keith Downing snapping his way round the field and Ally Robertson and Floyd Streete forming an uncompromising defensive partnership. Robbie Dennison added class - yet another steal off Albion - and the likes of Thompson, Nigel Vaughan, Mick Gooding and Mark Kendall were crucial players in the barnstorming success.

It was a working-class triumph, Turner putting together a team on a pittance. But everyone pulled for one another, even if Bully was the star. After the drain of the preceding years, the two dicings with death when the club went into receivership, Wolves were still impoverished, but this only added to the glee with which they won the Fourth Division, Sherpa Van Trophy and Third Division. Bull going to the World Cup, only a year out of Division Three, capped it all.

"My best day? Probably the one when I signed for them," Bully reflects. "They gave me a tremendous 14 years I didn't think were going to happen. Every day was classic, I loved every single day. We had this fantastic team spirit and I wouldn't have changed anything at the club back then, because we had the same goals, the same drinks, even the same bath water. After games, it was two in a bath. It was a wonder we didn't catch anything. We used to fight to get in first, while the water was still clean, and, if there was anyone dodgy, you'd scramble to team with someone else.

"Once a couple of goals went in, me and the Wolves fans just clicked. They started trying to get a song together. You'd be coming in for a game and they'd say: 'Alright, Bully, you'll score today, no problem, we'll be fine,' with this beaming smile on their faces. So I thought: 'I've got to score for this lot, that's my job.'"

One of the best songs was: 'Oh, Stevie Bull's a tatter, he wears an England cap, he plays for Wolverhampton, and he is a lovely chap. He scores goals with his left foot, he scores 'em with his right, and when he plays the Albion, he'll score all fuggin' night.' I had no idea what a tatter was but still joined in with gusto.

Fans and hero celebrating together - yet again.

"A tatter's a rag and bone merchant," Bull explains now. "They'd come round the streets and, if you had an old jumper you could chuck them, they'd give you a toy, like one of those helicopters where the propellers whizzed round when you pulled the string. I knew what the fans were on about. Coming from Tipton, it was like: 'He knows where his roots are, he's willing to work hard,' like a tatter. I never felt it was disrespectful. It was a compliment because I always felt I worked hard."

The crowning glory of the club's ragged-edged renaissance does not, ironically, rank among Bull's favourites. Nigh on 50,000 Wolves supporters descended on Wembley for the Sherpa Van final with Burnley on May 29, 1988, and, so swept up were we all, that even Jacqui, then my fiancée and a football-free zone for most of her life (despite driving me to Exeter City the previous Easter and Aldershot for the play-off final) went along. Bull crossed for Mutch to head in and Dennison swerved home a free-kick. Wolves 2 Burnley 0.

"We had a dinner that night," Bull recalls, "but I'd got one on me because I didn't score. There was a disco and a few drinks in a Wembley hotel and all the wives and girlfriends came. I was disappointed but I got out of it after a couple of pints. In those days, if I didn't score, I thought I hadn't done my job right."

Two 50-goal seasons earned Bull local-celebrity status and brought him international recognition. After maintaining his goal-scoring form for England at B and, as an over-age player, under-21 level, he got the call to join the seniors at Hampden Park. The back-street international, they called him, the working-class hero. It was as though our Bully was acting out the archetypal rags-to-riches drama. The Tipton Terrier was Wolves' very own Roy of the Rovers.

When John Fashanu was injured in the first half and Bull, jumping up and down on the touchline in the No16, prepared to go on, he entered the national consciousness for real. This was England v Scotland. "I had 55 minutes," he says, "and it was a great experience. I loved it but I have to admit I was crapping myself to start with, with all those Scotland fans. But, up in one corner, I could see about 500 Wolves fans, with their banners saying: 'Let the Bull loose' and 'Raging Bull.' In the middle of all the white shirts, there was this band of gold and I thought: 'This is class, this.'"

One humdinger of a shot, early in the second half, rebounded from the advertising hoardings just as Jim Leighton, the Scotland goalkeeper, made his dive. The shivers ran down my spine as I watched on Grandad's old telly in my front room in Foxhill Road, down-town Reading, where Jacqui and I had moved in together. He's up for it, I thought, he's going to come out with credit. And how. With about ten minutes left, Bully challenged Dave McPherson for a high cross, the ball bounced off his shoulder and, as he came down, he was facing the right way to hammer his shot low into the corner. I smashed my head on a shelf as I leapt around maniacally.

Bully himself admits he hardly knew how to react. "I thought: 'I've scored, I'm off.' But where can you go, in a ground full of 80,000 Scots? So I just fell to my knees. I could have cried. I could've died then. There's Robson, Gascoigne, Waddle giving it some. When I'm running back for the restart, I have to stop and take a breath because the excitement just goes right through you. It was unbelievable, mate, unbelievable."

Such a storybook debut meant Bull had to stay in Robson's squad and, by the time he scored twice in a friendly with Czechoslovakia in the run-up to the World Cup, he and Paul Gascoigne had booked their places to Italy. As a Wolves supporter unaccustomed to having local heroes on the international stage, I found the whole competition lifted on to a new plane. Our man went on a couple of times and started against Egypt, although unable to make much head-way against a deep-lying, five-man defence. "It all went that quick," he says. "We were together for six weeks and there's not a lot I could've done different. Everything was really well organised and it was just great to be involved, with the whole nation watching you doing something for your country. I was rooming with Platty (David Platt), a nice bloke, and that World Cup made him a superstar. That great goal he scored against Belgium, in the last minute, I was right behind him. You wouldn't have caught me if I'd scored."

Watching with Andy Michael and Jamie Biggins, my mates from Uni, I thought it *was* Bull who scored. I was convinced there were no limits to the heroic heights he was to reach. "I nearly scored just before, with a 30-yard shot that skimmed the post. If that had gone in, maybe I would've become the multi-millionaire," he suggests. Instead, he has a fourth-place medal "somewhere in the loft" and shows me all his caps, framed neatly on the staircase wall. There's no envy of Platt but Bull will always wonder, in his dotage, what would have happened if he had left Wolves for a top-level club. He certainly had the opportunities.

"In the warm-up to the World Cup, in Sardinia, I remember swimming with Gazza and Lineker to the Tranmere chairman's boat. Doug Ellis (the Villa chairman) was on board and said to me: 'After the World Cup, I'm coming in for you.' I never saw or heard from him again until recently, at a dinner, when he was on the top table. I said to Kirsty: 'I'm going to ask why he never followed that up. I was nervous, don't know why. When I asked him, he just said: 'I don't know.' You'd have thought he'd have had an excuse, like the money wasn't right, or Wolves said no. I was always intrigued."

Ironically, it was Graham Taylor who left Villa to become Robson's successor after Italia '90. He evidently had faith in Bull. "If people think I don't rate Steve, they must be crackers," said Taylor when managing the forward at Wolves. "They seem to forget that, as manager of England, I picked him for my first two games." Taylor nevertheless tried to sell Bull in 1995 and rebuild a game-plan that remained reliant on a man who continued to score goals at the new, sub-Premiership, Division One level.

"I never had a rift with him," Bull states. "I respect him. I was in his England squads a few times but gradually dropped out, maybe as other players regained their form. He said to me after he took over at Wolves that he had been planning to come and buy me at Villa before he took the England job."

There were at least four other clubs who, Bull is aware, tried to sign him. Don't misunderstand; it isn't that he wishes he had left. He kept believing he could play at the highest level with Wolves. Since he can now look back and accept that he didn't play in the Premiership, though, it is only natural he should reflect on paths not taken. "Graham Turner told me a couple of years later that, in the World Cup, Torino had a bid rejected. Then, Andy Cole was only Newcastle's second choice. I had a phone call from an agent up north and he came to the house. I wasn't tempted at all but, if I knew now how things were to pan out, I should have gone. Newcastle are a massive club.

"There was a four-year deal on the table from Coventry City and, with Wolves' permission, I met Ron Atkinson (then the Coventry manager) four times. Eventually, I told Big Ron: 'I'm happy where I am.' He accepted it. I thought to myself: 'What have I got to prove to myself here? Next season, hopefully, Wolves will get promoted.'

"The last one was Celtic. I remember stretching out on the training ground. Graham Taylor came up and said: 'I know you've turned Coventry down but Celtic have come in for you.' I just said: 'It's too wet up there.' He laughed and said: 'That's a shame.' End of conversation. He was getting stick from the fans by this stage and, if he'd pursued the transfer when I wasn't interested, he might have got slaughtered. He needed some money to keep rebuilding the team, so I understood where he was coming from. But he was a good manager; if he'd stopped another year, I'm sure he'd have got us up."

The perennial pursuit of

"Our Dad says you used to score lots of goals and play for England." Author's sons Tom (left) and Joe Lansley, aged eight and five, meet a legend they never saw play. Picture courtesy of Shaun Fellows/newsteam.co.uk.

promotion became Bully's burden. He remained prolific, averaging exactly 20 goals in eight seasons before the last couple were beset by injury. While he remained convinced Wolves could provide him with the top stage, he accepts on reflection that something got left behind when finances allowed Turner to start rebuilding his squad.

It's ironic Wolves' best-paid player should cite the increasing wage bill as a factor in their momentum stalling. By 1990, Bull was earning £2,500 a week from the club, before boot deals kicked in. "After my first year, my money kept going up and up," he says. "The other players knew that but I wasn't one to go round the dressing room with my collar up and a mobile phone on my ear. The club chose to reward me and I don't think it bothered the other lads until some big-money players came in.

"The likes of Geoff Thomas, Neil Masters, Tony Daley and Steve Froggatt arrived and, while the original lads didn't mind having one, me, as long as I was scoring all them goals, when four of five others came in on big money, people asked questions. They'd say: 'I'm doing the same job as him. Why aren't I earning the same?' Players talk, so they know what others are earning. My pay went up from £2,500 after I got back from the World Cup but then other so-called bigger clubs were supposed to be willing to pay me more and Wolves wanted to keep me."

Turner, later to give Bull a coaching role at Hereford, certainly did. "He was the focal point of the club's resurgence," says the manager who signed him. "But because of his manner, there was never any resentment whatsoever from the other players."

Bull became the face of Wolves, a marketable local icon. He had his hair shaved off in his first season at Molineux - "grade three on top, two on the sides" - but, after establishing his commercial pulling power, noticed others cashing in. "There was an advert in the local paper for a hairdressers, saying: 'Come and get a Bully cut' with a picture of me alongside. I thought: 'Can they do this?' Nowadays, your agent would be in getting the best cutters to buy the right to use your mug.

"I was just happy to have my picture in the papers. I loved scoring for Wolves and loved the whole job." Was the celebrity status not a pain in the backside sometimes? Would he have got the 12-month driving ban, for drinking three halves, if he hadn't been recognised as Steve Bull? "You live and learn," he says. "But, generally, I never abused my position, so it wasn't a problem. I never did anything for the papers to have a go at me and say: 'Look, he's a bad boy, look at the scandal he's causing.'"

Bull did stop talking to all newspapers for a couple of years when he felt the media intrusion into his personal life went too far. "It was when my parents weren't coming to the wedding with Julie," he recalls. "I thought: 'Sod it, the press need me more than I need them,' so I cut them off. I just felt it needed doing. If they'd let me get on with my life, that would have been okay, but no-one likes having their own life pried into, then put in the papers in a negative way."

The *Express & Star* took his uninvited Mum and Dad to the church with a present they had given them as a prop for a picture. "That started it off," he adds. "Then, when we finished, and broke up four or five years ago, the papers started again. I thought: 'They haven't got the facts right, not that I want to talk about it anyway, so let's leave it.' It does your head in."

At least Bull's relationship with Kirsty has helped heal the wounds with parents he now sees regularly. "Ah, they'll be over later," he says. "I'll have a drink with my Dad. I lost them for a bit but now we're back together and that means a lot to me. Sorted. They're your family, aren't they?" So are Jack (12) and Joe (8), his sons, who live with their mother. "The older one is getting bigger, getting stronger, wants to score all the goals, selfish, like his old man.

"It was after I retired that I met my parents again and my Dad tells me he'd been going to watch me all the while. They've been all over and I didn't know. They even went on a pre-season trip to Ireland. Everybody has regrets but I haven't got any bad

The first published photo of Kirsty and Steve's wedding in Malta in June, 2004. Pictured top left is George Bull.

regrets. You do good things in your life, you do bad; the good things in my life outweigh the bad."

Bull enjoyed one of the happiest days of his life nine months after this interview. On perusing an early draft of this chapter, Kirsty and Steve let me know the book would be out of date before publication - unless I could keep a secret. This I managed so well that Mum rang me the other day to inform me Bully had wed and would it be too late to include in the book? Kirsty became Mrs Bull as the pair married in Malta, the Mediterranean providing the cool backdrop to a ceremony attended by 50 family and friends. They kept their plans under wraps and went abroad to ensure some privacy but Bull was still identified by some Wolves fans on the island, who added their own congratulations.

"Kirsty looked stunning and we are still on cloud nine," Bull said on their return home in mid-June. The groom even had supplies of *John Smith's* rushed over for the reception, to keep his father happy, and chip butties were served with brown sauce in the evening. Appropriately enough, Andy Thompson was best man and did not let the side down with a prank right out of the wedding-night manual. When the couple retired for the evening, they discovered Thommo had led a raid to steal their bed, leaving the sheet laid out on the floor.

The birth of Joe Bull, in February 1996, provided one of those heart-warming tales that his indefatigable Dad delivered so regularly. Bull travelled with Mark McGhee's squad to East Anglia on the Friday, when news of the imminent arrival of his second child prompted him to return home by taxi. Having happily seen Joe clock in and had one hour's sleep, the proud father was driven back to Carrow Road, where he promptly scored twice in a 3-2 win over Norwich City.

Wolves finished in the play-offs in the seasons either side but, losing to Bolton Wanderers after Bull had given them the lead in the 1995 semi-final, and to Crystal Palace at the same stage two years later, meant the manager in each case was on borrowed time. Bull remains a firm admirer of Graham Taylor but rates McGhee less highly. The Scot found immediate favour when he succeeded Taylor in December, 1995, by placing himself firmly in the Steve Bull fan club, insisting the 30-year-old striker was good for another 100 goals. But his man-management, Bull suggests, was not as good as his predecessors'.

McGhee bought Iwan Roberts to partner Bull and this helped take some of the physical pressure off the senior man. When Roberts scored a hat-trick in a 4-2 win at Albion and Bull netted the other, I floated all the way back to Reading. *The Daily Telegraph*, for whom I was now a regular, even let me follow up my completely objective match report with a big piece the next day. Life felt pretty good. By the following March, with Bull in a purple patch of ten goals in as many games, I bumped into McGhee in Bailey's wine bar in Bridgnorth the morning after the main man had scored, almost straight from kick-off, in a win away to Birmingham City.

I was having coffee with Mum and Dad when the manager walked in. Like a sad groupie, I could not resist showing him my report in the *Telegraph*. To my surprise, he asked if he could take it away. He wasn't being tight. He simply wanted to devote the necessary attention to studying such a work of art. All 315 words of it.

He came back to say that he agreed with my sentiments except that, within a couple of weeks, it would come to pass that there would be no fears over Wolves not going up. If we all simply remained relaxed - fans, players, press - then the team would be promoted without any hassle. I was staggered at his nonchalance. It did not strike Mum, Dad or me as arrogance, more as an educated assessment of a situation from someone who knew best. The fact is we relaxed so much in the run-in - and Bull was sent off away to Oldham Athletic at the start of a three-game losing run - that Barnsley nicked the second automatic promotion place out of our grasp.

The following year, we reached the semi-finals of the FA Cup, when McGhee, buying strikers like they were going out of fashion, named Bull and Robbie Keane, a startling and unpredictable teenage talent, as substitutes. Bull, after knee surgery, was still club captain and I remember tears pricking my eyes as he got all the players in a line, during the warm-up at Villa Park, to run over right in front of the Wolves fans and applaud us. I felt that this was Bully's twilight, his last chance of winning something big for the club, *his* club. Paul Simpson, out on the left wing, wore No9 that day. The other strikers - Steve Claridge and Don Goodman, I think - did not dare. We lost 1-0 to the first magnificent Arsenal side of the modern era, and McGhee's number was up. He left the following November.

"He started losing the players' respect," says Bull, who had no problem with him personally. "Once one player falls out with a manager, it's like a bad apple in a basket. He talks to another, who talks to another. Before you know it, it's spread right through the squad. He probably did rate me, as a goalscorer. You might lose a bit of respect the way they act on the training field, the way they coach; not me so much, more other players. He falls out with them and you're fighting a losing battle. If one link in a chain goes, you've had it. That's why it's so hard for a manager to keep every player happy. It's man-management, basically. Graham Turner knew when to give the pat on the back, when to give the kick up the backside, whereas McGhee might say something behind your back and then it would spread."

Bull remains on good terms with all his managers and would relish the chance to have a crack at the job himself. As he curls up on the sofa in his kitchen, one eye on the racing on the muted television, it is difficult to escape the notion the opportunity has passed. His life has become comfortable in its new ways. And why change? He trades in Spanish properties, does after-dinner speaking, appearances at weddings and birthdays, has a *306* clothing range. He goes to the gym four mornings a week, does his ten hours a week PR work at Molineux, plays golf with Andy Thompson, Mike Stowell, David Kelly and Don Goodman. Why trade such a pleasant lifestyle?

Kirsty comes in, asking for the car keys so she can move Steve's BMW and go and practise on her new hands-free car phone. She starts to ask: "Steve, can you…" but

A precious array of keepsakes for Wolverhampton Wanderers' all-time record goalscorer to have close at hand following his retirement as a player.

he replies, sharply but fondly: "I can't empty this and I can't do that. We'm busy." Once Kirsty is out of earshot, he admits he is appreciative of the woman who is also his business partner. "She's great," he admits. "She helps with the properties abroad, does all the arranging, keeps on top of everything. She gets paid loads, though.

"I'd love to have a go at management, preferably non-league to set my stall out and see if I can do it. I did a year coaching with Hereford, with Graham. He said I can go down any time I want to join in. I enjoyed my year there but I had the divorce to deal with so I knocked it on the head. Do I want all that? The grey hair and everything? I've done my UEFA B coaching badge and I'm half-way through my A licence but the longer I leave it, the less I'm fussed. I don't want to coach, I want to manage."

He'd want Keith Downing with him - "I'll eat my hat if he doesn't go further" - and would love to have more involvement at Molineux. "I love watching Wolves and like doing my hospitality stuff at matches but sometimes I'd like to just go and be among the fans," he says. "Have a pie and a pint at half-time rather than sit in a collar and tie. I'm not bitter about not getting a coaching role there but I thought they'd give me something more for all the years I'd been there. But a new manager comes in with his own staff, so it's probably better for me to go somewhere else, then come back."

He applied for the Walsall job before Colin Lee, his last manager at Wolves, was appointed and was on the short-list for the vacancy at Telford United in the summer of 2003. "I said to Kirsty I'd drop everything tomorrow to be a manager. The drive would be there immediately. I'd love to manage Wolves one day, love to be in that dug-out. That'd be an absolute dream but if it don't come off, I had a great time there, the best days of my life, and I'm enjoying my life now."

The facial scars, gained shifting slabs at school and repeatedly reopened during battles with defenders over the years, have healed now. The hair has regrown. The MBE from Buckingham Palace resides in a drawer upstairs and, in the garage, behind the enormous orange stone football in the garden, is his Suzuki Bandit 600, the bike he can ride incognito. On the dining room mantelpiece sits a photo of his sons. Twenty miles away, where 35 years ago the old clock was housed in the gold gables, where 25 years ago a £2million redevelopment became known as the John Ireland Stand, where nowadays the away supporters often sit, one side of Molineux is now called the Steve Bull Stand.

"They said I'd earned it, like Stan Cullis and Billy Wright," Bull says, "for all my efforts on the field for the club. What an honour; I can live with that. I just hope they don't take it off me. It's a nice thing to have and I long for the next Black Country derby. Then I can go out on the pitch with the microphone and say: 'All you Albion fans, you listening? You're sitting in my stand.' I could give them loads. I'd clap them all and say: 'Thanks for coming and filling my stand.'"

And we would sing in the time-honoured fashion: "Thank you very much for Stevie Bu-ull."

Steve Bull

Born:	March 28, 1965, in Tipton
Signed:	November, 1986
Wolves appearances:	569
Goals:	306
International recognition:	13 senior England caps
Left:	July, 1999

September 2003

At this rate, Wolves will finish the campaign with nine points and nine goals; that is, one of each for each month of the season. When defeat at Southampton (0-2) is followed by a total roasting from Chelsea (0-5), it appears Wolves are wholly out of their depth. Our Joe had prepared himself for the first Premiership game of his life by committing himself equally to both Chelsea and Wolves, as insurance, so he is less devastated than me. Still, beating Darlington (2-0) in the Carling Cup is appreciated and Alex Rae speeds to the top of our scoring charts by adding to that midweek goal with an absolute screamer away to Bolton Wanderers, who, cruelly, equalise in the dying minutes.

Campbell Chapman

A BIT OF TALENT AND VISION AMID SO MUCH DROSS

October 10, 2003: A long transatlantic call from Derbyshire

The story of Campbell Chapman reads like a backpackers' guide to trying to make it as a professional footballer. From bikes and hot dogs in Finland to the coldest room in a house shared with David Platt at Crewe Alexandra; from a dressing-room brawl at Molineux to meeting Alan Sunderland over breakfast in Qatar. From buying an engagement ring for England's captain to being handed shampoo from the terraces when playing for West Bromwich Albion reserves.

"People will say this guy's done so much to achieve so little," he laughs. "I went to watch Birmingham City play Tottenham Hotspur recently and there was Platty to my left, Brian Kerr, the Ireland manager, and Mark Hughes to my right. Anyone looking on would say: 'That guy in the middle, he should be someone. But he's not.' It was like a Who's Who, only it was more of a Who's He?"

It is useful that Chapman has such a self-deprecating sense of humour. At 40, he has found contentment as a successful coach in Atlanta, where he runs the Gwinette Soccer Association - a non-profit-making organisation for 1,500 children. But he must have acquired a thick skin back in his playing days with Wolves. The son of Sammy Chapman (manager at Molineux in 1985-86), a skilful if lightweight midfield player became the scapegoat for die-hard supporters who were witnessing their team's tumble through the divisions.

He was an easy target. Not just because of the inevitable charges of nepotism. He was a flair player who would try a trick when what Wolves required primarily were ten human bricks to block up Tim Flowers' goal. Ten and a half stone 'wet through' and 5ft 8in tall, he was not built for relegation battles. Even when the youngster had left the club on his wide and varied travels, they used to sing from the terraces: "If you still hate Chapman, clap your hands."

Personally, I saw a player with a bit of talent and vision trying to stick to his principles amid so much dross. I even filed a piece to the Wolves fanzine, *A Load of Bull*, in 1989, standing up for him. It was entitled 'The Campbell Chapman Fan Club' and signed off 'by Pete Lansley, sole member.' Yet Chapman, whose younger brother, Cavan, was an apprentice at Molineux where their father was initially the chief scout, turned Wolves down at the first time of asking. Having graduated through the ranks at Peterborough United as schoolboy, apprentice and first-year pro, he had returned from an uplifting summer abroad to star for Bilston Town and earn a trial with Shrewsbury Town. When Tony Painter, a Wolves scout, moved in, Chapman said: "Thanks but no thanks. People would say I'm only getting in because my Dad's there."

The confidence that would later be terminally undermined by Wolves' terrace critics was at a high in 1984 following the first of several Scandinavian summers. After being released by Peterborough, he was playing non-league for Stamford Town and signing on the dole when the Professional Footballers' Association gave him a list of foreign telephone numbers. "I rang the first one with a name by it," Chapman recalls. "I told him I was an English player who wanted to play in Finland. He said someone from Bolton hadn't turned up, so it was good timing. And could I score goals? Of course, I said. He asked: 'Great, how many?' When he told me they played about 35 games, I said I'd get him 20 goals. We had a deal." Chapman became KAIK's only full-time player. "They were on the coast of Finland, below a big town called Vaasa, and I was to play up front - clearly not because of my size and strength. I was on £50 a week, which would go up to £75 if I reached ten goals, and £100 if I got to 15. I got there, as well. They also said I'd have an apartment, transport and two meals a day.

"I found I was sharing with a US college kid. When I asked about transport, they said: 'No problem, we'll bring it tomorrow for you both.' Brilliant, we thought. The manager turned up with two bikes. One meal each day was at a restaurant, fine. For the other, we ate as many hot dogs from the stall outside the ground as we could. The folks were so hospitable and I was so happy to be playing professionally. I was a big fish in a small pool. They asked me to go back the next summer - they play from April to October - but I said I'd go back to England first and try again to make it."

Unbeknown to Chapman, Tommy Docherty, Wolves' manager, went to watch him play for Shrewsbury Reserves against Stoke City. "Afterwards, Tony Painter said there was someone who wanted to see me. It was the Doc. He said: 'The first thing is, your Dad doesn't know I'm here. I've seen enough to think you've got what it takes.' He asked me if I'd like to sign non-contract terms with Wolves. I checked with Chic Bates, the Shrewsbury manager, and he had no problems.

"I even scored for Wolves Reserves against Port Vale behind Dad's back. Then I asked him about it and he said: "You won't even see me. If you fancy it, just go and

THE CAMPBELL CH

Wolves plummetted to some staggering depths in the eighties, as regular readers of ALOB might have gathered, and many cite the Chorley disaster as the nadir. For me, the era was epitomised when my favourite player of the time, having been booed into a truly awful performance against mighty Wigan in late 1985, ran off the pitch almost unnoticed as soon as he saw Paul Dougherty get his kit off. When the number 11 placard was raised and the linesman had checked that Peewee had tied his laces up properly, Campbell Chapman was already in the players' tunnel, and in vain, everyone looked around to tell him to get off the pitch.

I still claim Campbell Chapman was a good player. Sure, not very effective in those dark and dismal days, but then, there were several players of talent who passed through the club's line-ups without stopping the

our hero - sorry, my hero - continued this rich vein of form, scoring with a near post header the following Tuesday against Bury in a 1-1 draw, thus helping set up an impressive unbeaten run of four games. He was never to score for Wolves again as this burst of Liverpool-like form failed to prevent us from slipping into the Fourth Division, and Campbell into obscurity somewhere in Scandinavia.

So why did everyone else hate him? He couldn't help it that his Dad was manager, and it was actually when Tommy Docherty was in charge that he finally forced his way into the first team, after failing to persuade previous managers to take him on at Molineux. I remember this flimsy waif of a youth coming on as substitute, and brilliantly beating the Carlisle full back down the line with same trick that Johann tyff

do what you can do.' I asked my brother, and he said he was treated well, so I signed and lived with my parents.

"Wolves didn't have a lot of players, so I got my chance relatively quickly. I'll always thank Tommy Docherty for that. He saw something in me and I did have some attributes: decent engine, tried to pass it, quick feet, honest. But there were better players than me who couldn't reproduce their best in that side. We were struggling so much. If I'd scored the goals I was capable of, it might have turned out better for me."

Chapman made his league debut for Wolves as substitute away to Manchester City on December 29, 1984, after Docherty, half an hour before kick-off, was alerted to the fact that his team-sheet had been handed in with only 11 names listed. The new boy, only along for the experience, got his chance, and went on early in the second half for Danny Crainie. He promptly collided with Mick McCarthy - not the wisest move considering their relative physiques.

"I went up and protected myself with an elbow," Chapman, never the best in the air, adds. "We ended up flat on the floor and Mick, a foot taller than me, said: 'Do that again and I'll break your legs.'" That was it; Chapman had landed as a pro footballer.

APMAN FAN CLUB

It was stylish, it was arrogant. For Johann, followed two World Cup finalist's medals and immortality from the most repeated slow motion piece of skill on "Saint and Greavsie". For Campbell, a place in the Wolves relegation side of that particular year, and soon a goal, in a 2-2 draw away at Sheffield United.

Style

Three of my hero's four goals in his entire Wolves career have now been covered, and no reason for the hate campaign yet occurs to me. Even after the lad had departed, the South Bank's cries of "If you still hate Chapman, clap your hands", were greeted with ironic raptures from the majority. Was it his slight build and unwillingness to let his hair get dirty then, that caused such rancour? He might have been a bit of a poseur, possibly. But is the same not true. Maybe? I supp

Campbell's defence. Pleas from the Doc for more aggression in an end of season victory against Huddersfield brought the tiger out in young Chapman, as he went up to a Town player after the ball had been released and simply kicked him. The ensuing booking may have received double the censure away at Gillingham 12 months later on, when, anguished by the injustice of a red card to David Barnes, Chapman made a satanic studded lunge into the back of David Mehmet look like just another mis-timed header.

Not that Campbell Chapman ever meant to head the ball. He believed in playing the ball on the turf, like all the game's conoisseurs, caressing it here, cajoling it there. Anyway, it might have spoiled his hair.

By Pete Lansley, sole member

Within a month, he volleyed his first senior goal, past John Burridge in a 2-2 draw at Sheffield United. Playing wide on the right, he was a regular in midfield alongside Alan Ainscow but so badly were Wolves faring that, when Chapman netted against Oxford United on April 13, it was the first time the team had scored at Molineux in five months.

"Even though we lost, I was on a high for about 20 minutes," he says. The inevitable relegation soon followed, however, and Sammy Chapman was promoted from chief scout to manager by the start of his son's first and last full season in English professional football.

"Campbell wanted to be a player but I hadn't really wanted him at Wolves," his father says. "I think he was a good footballer. He had two good feet and good control but lacked upper-body strength. He could never play against a Vieira - not that many can - but he had terrific stamina. It would have been nice if he'd had another yard of pace. Handling him at the club wasn't easy. It doesn't generally work with a father and son - but he's a very honest lad who loved his football and did his darnedest."

Campbell started 1985-86 in the No6 shirt, in the heart of midfield alongside the former Everton player, Andy King. Not even the injection of several exciting young players such as Jon Purdie and Neil Edwards, though, could arrest the fall. "They were tough times," recalls the player, who trained with Northern Ireland's under-23s that summer. "We had to take our own training kit home to wash every day. Purds was too lazy so he'd leave it in the corner and it would be there waiting for him, smouldering away, the next morning, from Monday to Thursday. No-one wanted to touch it. Eventually, the gear would get up and move off itself in protest.

"Jon had a lot of talent. He was an Arsenal youth-team player and played at the level he wanted to. He could have played at the top level; he had speed, skill, strength." Purdie started at centre-forward, scoring in a sunlit Milk Cup tie at Walsall one August evening before moving to the wings and, at one stage that season, back as the midfield anchor-man. "I think his favourite position was wherever he had the least running to do," Chapman jokes. "Only Jon Purdie stopped Jon Purdie."

With King scoring ten goals by the end of November, Chapman started the season in reasonable form and, for his own good, perhaps that was the time he should have moved on. After a thrilling 4-2 defeat at the Baseball Ground, in which this young fan was just elated that Purdie and Edwards scored and Chapman looked good, he had the opportunity. "The one thing I regret about my time at Wolves," he volunteers, "is that I turned down the chance to go to Derby. Following that Bank Holiday game, Roy McFarland (Arthur Cox's assistant) wanted to talk to me next morning. Wolves asked for £10,000 but, realising Derby were keen, the price escalated and the move collapsed."

Chapman dropped out the Wolves side. "Derby came back in a fortnight later and I met McFarland for a chat. But he couldn't assure me of a first-team place so I said no. Big mistake. I should have gone and forced my way in. It would've been great for

How Wolves' programme captured Chapman scoring his first goal for the club - in a 2-2 draw away to Sheffield United on January 26, 1985.

my Dad as well for me to move on and be backed by someone else's judgement."
Instead, as Wolves plummeted and King departed, Chapman became a whipping boy
for the dwindling crowd. In the *ALOB* article, I recorded how even before the player
was substituted in one game, he was off the field and down the tunnel. "There's always
a scapegoat and, because I was the manager's son, I was an obvious target," he says.
"You're playing for £100 a week, so you're playing because you want to. Sometimes
the player in the thick of it is making the mistakes because he's not hiding. But there
were games when you felt like you wanted to get the hell out of there."

In mid-March, my Dad and I were among the 2,367 sad souls who saw Plymouth
Argyle win 3-0 in the pouring rain. We stood on Molineux's decaying South Bank and,
for supporters, it could barely get any worse. Chapman confirms that it felt pretty bad
as a player too. "We were struggling to stay up and a lot of the players were frustrated.
There was a lot of hurt pride and, although everyone was trying his hardest, the club
was in a mess," he says. "Peter Zelem came in after that game and stood up in the
middle of the changing-room and said: 'We've got some cheats in here.' I looked up
and he was pointing at me. I couldn't believe it.

"He'd played me a ball from sweeper and, as I tried to turn with it, I got tackled.
They broke and scored. Everyone felt this was the lowest point. But one thing I felt at
Wolves was that I always gave it the best I could. It might not have been the best
people wanted, but it was the best I had. So, when he said that, I went for him and we
both swung at each other and had it out.

"By the time we reached the players' bar, both of us with a good old shiner, we
had all agreed to keep it quiet. In the next day's *Express & Star*, however, there was
this 'dressing-room brawl' story all over the back page. It was over by the next
morning, though. The following week, my Dad asked if I wanted to be left out. I said:
'The best way to get over this is to get out there and play.' As fate would have it, away
to Doncaster Rovers, we won 1-0 and I got to score the winner."

"They did have a bit of a ding-dong," says Sammy Chapman, the genial Irishman,
laughing. "It didn't do too much harm. I've been prone to taking the odd swing myself
and dressing-room bust-ups have always gone on. Campbell's time at Wolves was
character-building and probably gave him resilience. You could understand the fans'
feelings towards him. They want to vent their frustration at the team not doing well and
the manager's son is an easy target." Campbell's 18-month contract expired that
summer as Wolves were relegated for the third consecutive year. Despite the
concession of 98 league goals, the arrival of Dean Edwards and, significantly, Andy
Mutch helped them sign off with a flurry of goals themselves. Better times were
around the corner for Wolves - if not for Campbell Chapman. He went to watch his old
team-mates for a while and refutes the notion that they did not care for the club.

"The Wolves lads had a tradition of being boys about town," he admits, "but
you've got to remember that, when I was playing, we weren't celebrities. With crowds

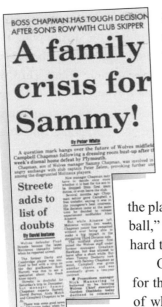

BOSS CHAPMAN HAS TOUGH DECISION AFTER SON'S ROW WITH CLUB SKIPPER

A family crisis for Sammy!

By Peter White

A question mark hangs over the future of Wolves midfield Campbell Chapman following a dressing room bust-up after the week's dismal home defeat by Plymouth.

Chapman, son of Wolves manager Sammy Chapman, was involved in an angry exchange with club captain Peter Zelem, provoking further unrest among the disgruntled Molineux players.

Streete adds to list of doubts

By David Instone

of 3,000, people in the pubs wouldn't recognise us like they would Steve Daley or John Richards. The Rock was the place for Danny Crainie: he had the playboy image, with the leather trousers and long hair, but I'd have been under the table on four halves of lager. It couldn't have been me you saw in The Mermaid two hours before a game. We weren't big time. How could we be, on £100 a week, watched by such small crowds?"

Brian Little, taken to Molineux as a coach by Sammy Chapman, took over as acting manager after the player had been released. "Campbell could really hit a good ball," the former Aston Villa manager recalls, "but they were hard times."

On leaving Wolves, Chapman signed for IFK Ostersund for the first of two summer seasons in Sweden, in the second of which the club won the third division title and a cup. In between, he trawled round the lower reaches of English football, injuring his knee when on the verge of joining Brian Horton's Hull City, driving from Walsall with Bob Hazell to train with Port Vale and befriending Platt when joining Crewe in November, 1986.

"Several of us shared a club house - Platty, me, John Pemberton; Geoff Thomas had just moved out - and the last ones in had the top floor. It felt like it was open to the elements," Chapman recalls with a smile. "There was only heating on the bottom two floors. It was so cold in the room I shared with Platty that you'd wear your next day's training gear to bed. Two ladies came in to cook for us but no matter what you had, it tasted exactly the same. If you had roast duck with exotic vegetables, it seemed identical to yesterday's shepherds' pie.

"Platty had this unbelievable desire to improve, this enthusiasm and confidence and energy, in games and training. You knew that if someone had the confidence to take him, he'd go all the way. My Dad was chief scout at Leicester by this time and was busy recommending him but the club's attitude seemed to be that they wouldn't pay £200,000 for a player from Crewe."

"Platty was a big thorn in my side," recalls Sammy Chapman, who signed Russell Hoult on YTS at Leicester, kick-started Scott Barrett's "nice little career" and also took Purdie, Micky Holmes and Mutch - three men who played their part in the club's revival - to Molineux. "We should have bought him. I wanted to buy him for Wolves but we couldn't find £20,000. He'd just moved from Manchester United Reserves and got into the side at Crewe playing wide on the right. I got to know him over the years because I always wanted him as a player. When he went into management, I ended up working for him, at Nottingham Forest and then scouting for England."

Chapman junior made one appearance for Crewe - as a substitute in a 5-0 home defeat by Northampton Town when Dario Gradi blamed him for the final two goals - but he has kept in touch with his old room-mate. "I went through David Platt's rise with him," he says. "I'd go and watch him at Aston Villa and saw all of his England games at Wembley. I also went out to Bari when he moved to Italy and he and Rachel were doing the long-distance relationship thing. We were having dinner one night when he told me they were getting married. Brilliant. Then he said: 'I want you to buy the rubies for me, because I don't want the press jumping on my back making a fuss. We'll go to the bank and get cash' - this is, like, millions of lira, about £8,000 'and, because I speak Italian, we'll pretend it's you getting married. I'll ask for the rubies.' But because it's David Platt, when we got into shops, everyone came out hugging him - then hugging me because they wanted my custom. It was a right circus."

The pair opened a wine bar, Amici Mai (Among Friends), in a fashionable complex near Wolverhampton railway station in the early 1990s. "There was this disused cinema, a total shell," Chapman went on. "I fancied converting but the council weren't interested in selling. But, when David Platt rang and said he'd put his name to it, they acted quickly enough. Rachel was the general manager, I ran the bar and another mate of Platty's ran the restaurant."

Chapman, by this time, was player-manager of Willenhall Town and had a transatlantic relationship, so eventually he gave up his commitments in the Black Country and moved to America. He had fallen in love with the States on one of his forays abroad, coaching there in the summer of 1988. This was after his latest tour of English outposts had been interspersed with an interesting spell in Qatar, early in 1987.

He refused to accept that he was not destined to make the grade. "When you've just been released from non-contract terms at Crewe, the only way is up," he says. "An agent from London rang, knew I was available and said I could fly out on January 1 to Doha for a three-month deal. 'The only thing I would advise,' he said, 'is that there's no alcohol allowed over there, so get it out your system at Christmas.' I flew out there on New Year's Day with the biggest hangover of my life.

"Players were always coming and going out there. One morning, Alan Sunderland walked in at breakfast, said he'd just got in. 'Come on over,' I said, 'have a seat.' We had a chat - I knew he'd been a good player at Wolves in the 1970s, then at Arsenal and Ipswich - and I said: 'I thought your knee was crocked.' He said: 'It is.' He got a grand signing-on fee just for showing up." Chapman earned his best money from football playing in Doha - £400 a week tax-free - but still hankered for the opportunity to prove himself in England. He flew out, the night he returned from America, to Malta, where a chance meeting with another former Ipswich player brought him a trial with West Brom. Is this what failed Wolves players have to do as penance? Travel the world on short-term contracts, trials here, there and everywhere, only to end up playing at The Hawthorns for the Baggies Reserves? It seems harsh.

David Platt and Campbell Chapman pictured in the unlikely setting of Willenhall Town Football Club in the early 1990s. It wasn't their only tie-up in the West Midlands.

"When I landed at the airport in Malta, this chap was waiting to meet me, with my name on a card. He said: 'I'll take you to the club right now.' I said: 'But it's 11 o'clock at night.' He replied: 'Don't worry, it's always open.' We're driving along and he told me they played at the national stadium. I thought it sounded great but, when we got there, it was all dark and I couldn't see any floodlights. So we knocked on a door, walked in down these steps to a smoky bar. Then it dawns on me what kind of club he was referring to. Down some more stairs, everyone was drinking liqueur and gambling away. I stayed a while to play there for Birkakara and, in one game, recognised Paul Mariner. Afterwards, he said to me: 'You're too good for this' and asked if I wanted him to arrange a trial at Albion, where Brian Talbot had just become manager. So I got my release from the club and came back to England."

Trials went well and Chapman signed for Albion until the end of 1988-89, around the time Steve Bull was becoming a legend at Molineux after failing to make it at The Hawthorns. "I was playing regularly for the reserves and doing okay, even if I didn't look the part. I'd grown my hair really long and hadn't had it cut for about a year. After one match, a kid ran on to the pitch and said: 'My Dad says you need to get your hair cut.' I was on £100 a week and joked: 'I can't afford to wash my hair, let alone get it cut.' After the next game, the same kid ran on and handed me a sachet of shampoo."

Chapman's playing days at league level were rounded off, neatly enough, with another spell in Finland in the summer of 1989 before he joined Willenhall. His sheer bloody-minded stubbornness could take him no further. He could barely have tried any harder, yet his professional career was ended prematurely in his mid-20s.

Campbell's Dad, who had played alongside Bobby Charlton and Duncan Edwards in Manchester United's youth team, had the privilege of seeing his sons play once in the same Wolves team, away to Cardiff City on February 23, 1985, before successive broken legs ended Cavan's career when at Bilston Town.

"I'm sure the most enjoyable part of my Dad's career was his time at Wolves," Campbell says. "Although it was a skeleton of a club under a huge banner, for anyone to be manager of the Wolves, even with only two sides of the ground open, still stood for something. I'm sure he feels people don't appreciate the effort he put in and that's true of a lot of the characters who were there, such as Greg Fellows, a big, fat friendly guy who helped run the youth team; always upbeat, having a laugh and a joke.

"This was a time when first-team players were having to play for the reserves in midweek to make up the numbers. Reserve regulars also had to play for the youth team and I'd call up lads from Bilston Town if the reserves were short. I'd only seen Wolves on TV before I joined them but I knew what a big club they were. But no club, whatever their history, has a divine right to play in the top grade. Any club can slide right back down like we did. You look at Ipswich, Derby and Sheffield Wednesday, and see that mismanagement, especially right at the top, can hit anyone.

"Losing is a horrible habit. We were going into games hoping to win rather than expecting to. Then again, if the fans are booing you, that affects confidence and a rot can set in. Die-hard fans were entitled to their opinions but if some of those 20,000 others that were there in the 1970s and came back in the 1990s had turned up instead of staying away, they might have made a difference."

Chapman accepts with good humour his role as the unwitting villain in the pantomime that was Wolves in the 1980s. "When I was over last year, I played for Old Wolves with Robbie Dennison, Mel Eves, Stuart Watkiss, Andy De Bont and my brother," he says. "I even got booed by some of my own players. We didn't tell the Wolves fans where we were playing in case they came and booed us."

John Richards has his Wembley match-winner to remember; Tim Flowers a Midlands player of the year award. Steve Bull might pick his famous winner at The Hawthorns in 1989 or his first cap when going on to score against Scotland at Hampden Park. Kenny Miller hit the killer goal in a play-off final that clinched a Premiership place; Steve Daley can tell his grandkids he became the country's costliest player by dint of his deeds at Molineux. What about Campbell Chapman? "There's no one thing," he says after deliberation, before adding with a chuckle, "mainly because they couldn't afford to let us keep anything." He pauses for another moment, then concludes: "I've got my memories framed. It may only have been for two years but I played professionally for Wolves."

Campbell Chapman

Born:	June 28, 1963, in Sutton-in-Ashfield
Signed:	December, 1984
Wolves appearances:	58
Goals:	4
Left:	June, 1986
International recognition:	None

October 2003

Where were you on October 25, 2003? I was at Andy Chelsea's wedding. His real name is Andy Michael but at Childs Hall, Reading University, circa 1983, he went by his team's name. As we came out of church at 3.45pm, I switched on my mobile, so my brother's texts beeped in quick succession. As I announced to my Dossers United mates that Wolves were 3-0 down, a Leicester City fan celebrated noisily. I didn't catch his eye at the reception later on. Tom and Joe had taken the season tickets, sitting with their Grandpa, and can forever say they witnessed one of the best comebacks in Premiership history. Marvellous. In a month when we also beat Manchester City (Mark, over from America for the weekend, and Dave, my elder brother, joined us for this one), Wolves were unbeaten in six matches, including the Carling Cup, and were 15th in the Premiership. I'll never forget Andy and Jo's wedding.

Derek Dougan

ANGEL OR DEVIL, A MOLINEUX ICON TWICE OVER

November 20, 2003: Doog's place in Tettenhall, Wolverhampton

Perhaps we should have known Derek Dougan would end up as the talisman of Molineux when the rebel without applause asked for a transfer from Blackburn Rovers on the very eve of the 1960 FA Cup final. For that was the occasion when Wolverhampton Wanderers framed their period of greatness with their last trophy for 14 years. By the time they next visited Wembley, the controversial Northern Ireland forward had etched himself into Wolves' folklore: a daring, colourful character, the daddy of a promising batch of cubs, the elder statesman who provided the perfect foil for the emerging England forward, John Richards.

The Doog was a television pundit renowned for speaking his mind and writing his books and it was clear long before he waved his first farewell to Molineux - as a substitute against Leeds United in the final league game of 1974-75 - that he cared deeply for this club. Richards scored in front of a 34,875 crowd as Dougan went on for Steve Kindon for a sentimental send-off.

A year later, Wolves went down, Dougan's retirement signalling the dismantling of Bill McGarry's under-achieving team; the old heads just too old, the youngsters just too young. When this decline, seemingly temporary at the time as Sammy Chung led them straight back into the top flight, proved ultimately unstoppable, it was Dougan who rode back in on his silver charger. When he became chairman of the club in 1982, he was a hero all over again. He was the saviour, the main man heading up a consortium that prevented Wolves going to the dogs, three minutes from the deadline set by the receivers for the club's liquidation.

Yet those two and a half years working with the Bhatti brothers, the supposed financial power behind the takeover, seemed to be the undoing of Dougan's good name at Molineux. For nearly 20 years, by dint of legal restrictions, the voluble Irishman had to keep his own counsel. As Wolves lurched through the divisions during the Bhatti era, as the ground fell to ruin, as 30,000 of those fans who had cheered him off in April, 1975, stopped going and another lapse towards liquidation approached, so the Doog had to keep his powder dry. Silenced and stigmatised, his angst was evident. So when we spoke, in the summer of 2002, and he told me that the legal binds that had followed his departure from the club in 1985 had been tied up, it was clear he had a story to tell.

Dougan had in some quarters started to resemble the devil who had pulled Wolves down into a footballing hell, the front man for the abhorred and anonymous Bhattis who bought our club on the cheap and almost razed the place to the ground. Was this a just image? As I was busy moving back to the Midlands, Dougan visited my parents in Bridgnorth, to swap some books for background reading over a cup of tea. The Doog has this charisma, this totemic quality. For some, it is a charm to be wary of. But it is there nevertheless and it underscored the entire playing career of a striker with a reputation for the explosive temperament that often accompanies genius.

Perhaps it was this mercurial character that had him moving from club to club every couple of years, that prompted him to test Blackburn's team spirit to the limit by asking for a transfer just as they were completing their preparations to play Wolves in that final. He shouldn't have played, he maintains now, having pulled a muscle against Birmingham City the week before but, after scoring twice in the semi-final win over Sheffield Wednesday, he considered it his call. "I'd earned the right to play," he says.

We meet for the first time, face to face, at his home, an immaculately kept bungalow in Tettenhall, one of the better-heeled areas of Wolverhampton, in the midst of a hectic schedule. He is preparing to spin off to a dinner at Port Vale that evening, race down to Reading the next morning, then off to Wales, meeting publishers about a prospective book before flying to Ireland. Yet he is a cordial and relaxed host.

The best-dressed man of 1972 - according to the Tailor and Cutter - Dougan is still a dapper figure at 65, in blue chinos and a red shirt buttoned to the neck, his silver hair combed forward, the moustache long since gone. He pours a coffee and we make our way through his lounge to a conservatory overlooking a large, tidy garden. Since the football life of Derek Dougan - Northern Ireland captain, prolific marksman for six clubs over 18 years, PFA chairman, political spokesman - far exceeds the boundaries of one chapter, we come to a gentleman's agreement. We will hold up a white flag if we stray off the subject of the Doog at the Wolves. Since he's the one character in this book to have played against Billy Wright and alongside John Richards, this should keep us going.

"My connection with Wolves could have started when I was 16 and playing at centre-half for Distillery," he tells me. "Their scouts came over and said I wasn't good enough to get in their third team. Little did they know I'd be scoring my first league goal in English football against them within a couple of years. I remember watching on television as Hungary beat England 6-3 at Wembley, in that legendary game 50 years ago, when Puskas performed that drag-back to hoodwink Billy Wright. I never thought Billy was that outstanding a player. Although he had an enormous reputation, I always thought Eddie Clamp was the best Wolves player of that half-back line, a phenomenal figure and a tough guy as well.

"It was Clamp who scored for Wolves down at Fratton Park [on November 9, 1957; crowd: 38,320] the day I got my first goal. They were to be the champions that season and the next, the climax of Stan Cullis' great period as manager. I got the equaliser; I always tended to do well against them for all my other clubs.

"Reputations can exceed realities and Wolves were probably just as famous for those floodlit European friendlies as for being a great team who won three titles. I used to find Ron Flowers extremely slow, for instance. Then again, Peter Broadbent was a beautiful inside forward, a majestic footballer. When I came to Wolves, it was to a club with a great reputation, a great history, a great standing. I used to get a thrill because I

Photographers' friend...the Doog obliges on the day of his signing by depicting his leap down from First Division Leicester to Second Division Wolves.

have this in-built projector where I could play footage of those great European nights in my head. Wolves had become pioneers in investing £25,000 in floodlights in the early '50s and it paid off for them."

Dougan finally joined Wolves at 29, for £50,000 in March 1967, scoring three on his home debut against Hull City and netting nine times in an impressive 11-game run-in that secured promotion back to the top flight. It seemed the act of a man intent on enjoying his Indian summer. Ronnie Allen was manager but John Ireland, the chairman - and later, when Dougan returned to the club in 1982, president - played a part.

"I developed a really good relationship with John Ireland and he subsequently

Wolves meet The Monkees in LA in 1967. Pictured with the quartet are Graham Hawkins, John Holsgrove, Fred Davies, Dave Wagstaffe, Les Wilson, Phil Parkes, Gerry Taylor, Dave Woodfield, Derek Dougan, Ronnie Allen, Peter Knowles, John Ireland. Front: Ernie Hunt, Terry Wharton, Dave Burnside, Alun Evans, Paddy Buckley, Bobby Thomson.

told me he had suggested they sign me long before they did," Dougan reveals. "Jim Marshall, a director for years and years and chairman for a time, father of Harry Marshall, told me when we were in the United States [in summer, 1967] that he'd suggested to Stan Cullis they brought me to Molineux. John Ireland knew his football. Oddly enough, he didn't interfere with managers' tactics, neither was he responsible for sacking Stan Cullis. That is a Molineux myth. It was a board decision. John Ireland tried to sign me when I was at Peterborough United [1963-65] and then told Ronnie Allen to sign me from Leicester City."

It was a decision few at Molineux regreted as Dougan proceeded to batter in 123 goals in 323 games over eight years. With his theatrical presence, long loping run and increasingly wild hair, he stopped being a wanderer once he settled in Wolverhampton. He was the Catweazle of the First Division, a wizardly figure whose ability to climb early and sustain his leap laid on innumerable goals for the likes of Richards, Bobby Gould and Hugh Curran. Yet his wanderlust, allied to his undoubted ability and an uneasy relationship with Bill McGarry, his manager at Molineux from November, 1968, meant he nearly left Wolves on several occasions. Only eight months after signing and with the goals continuing to flow, he almost joined Coventry City. "Noel

Cantwell told me he agreed to pay £80,000 and Ronnie Allen agreed," Dougan recalls. "John Ireland got Ronnie in his office and they summoned me from training. John confronted Ronnie and said: 'What's going on?' Ronnie was very good in the transfer market and felt that, having gained promotion, a £30,000 profit on a so-called ageing player was good business.

"Ronnie was stacking his treasure chest. He had just sold Ernie Hunt to Everton for £80,000 and had agreed to sell Alun Evans and Peter Knowles to Liverpool for £180,000. Evans went for £100,000 but Knowles got the huff because he was only rated at £80,000." So Dougan, with Ireland's intervention, stayed but McGarry's arrival did not settle him. The two sparked against each other from the off. Like David Beckham with Sir Alex Ferguson at Manchester United, Dougan believes he had become too big a character for the manager to control.

"I know McGarry stopped me going to Liverpool, Arsenal and Leeds United," he says. "Don Revie had been trying to get me when I was at Leicester, where he came round my house. Just after I joined Wolves, he came back for me. Then Gordon Clark, my old manager at Peterborough, became chief scout at Arsenal two years before they won the double. Bertie Mee and Don Howe were in charge and Gordon came to my house to talk through the move. McGarry asked for £80,000 but, when Arsenal agreed to pay, his backside went, thinking he was selling me to a better team. I went to see him and said: 'You'd happily sell me to Shrewsbury Town or Carlisle United but you haven't got the bottle to sell me to a rival in case I show you up.'

"In 1971, Manchester United came in for me, then there was Liverpool. I spoke to Bill Shankly a lot. I loved him, with that thick Scottish accent. 'The two players I regret not buying,' he told me in later years, 'were you and Gordon Banks.' Shankly had been McGarry's manager at Huddersfield in the 1950s and I know McGarry told him: 'You don't want Dougan. He's trouble. He can play a bit but he's too big for his boots.'" Dougan maintains it was McGarry's poor man-management that prevented Wolves progressing from a potent cup team to championship contenders. "McGarry was a bully. He never wanted me at the club in the first place. He wanted to control everything. He bullied Waggy [Dave Wagstaffe], Phil Parkes and younger players were frightened of him. But I was chairman of the PFA, remember. I didn't treat him with contempt but I never listened to him. I don't mind hard guys but I couldn't listen to his team talks. How could he tell me how to play centre-forward?

"In one week in September, 1971, I scored back-to-back hat-tricks, against Nottingham Forest and away to Academica in the UEFA Cup. That was the only time in eight years he said to me: 'Well done.' When I think about the goals I scored and made, the performances I gave... people like to hear compliments, it's human nature. I was a different personality to David Beckham but it was a similar situation. I was never off TV, I was writing for a national newspaper, I was captain of my country, I was running the players' union and I never had to ask his permission about anything. He hated it. If he sold me and I did well, he'd have never lived it down; plus he'd have had to convince John Ireland and the board it was right I should go.

"He didn't like me getting more attention than him. The TV people always wanted to interview me after a match ahead of him. Beckham's a fantastic professional - doesn't smoke, trains well - and why does Ferguson get rid of him? Because he doesn't like the celebrity baggage? What's that got to do with it?" Once Dougan was into his 30s, however, happily married to Jutta and with two sons, and with Wolves a settled side packed full of quality players, he laid down his roots. "It was only after I'd been here a few years that the gold of the strip I was wearing got into my blood," he recalls. "I was as proud to wear that shirt as Billy Wright was. Football's about players."

Yet Wolves enjoyed the best days of the past 40 years during McGarry's reign. Surely the manager did something right? "He inherited some good players, didn't he? You name me one player he bought who significantly added to what we had," Dougan challenges. "I rated Jim McCalliog and, to a degree, Hugh Curran. But a manager's role is to bring the best out of people and, tragically, he never did. With signing the right players, we should have won the title. I think we had nine elevenths of a championship side and, dirty as he was, we could have had Terry Paine, from Southampton, on the right wing."

Dougan maintains Gordon Banks, England's World Cup winning goalkeeper, would quite happily have followed him from Filbert Street to Molineux as Wolves were about to join Leicester in the First Division in 1967. "Phil Parkes had just broken into the team when I came and, at 19, 6ft 2in and with this big Black Country accent, I told Ronnie Allen it'd be ten years before he'd be a good keeper. It was the weekend I made my debut, at Plymouth, that I told Ronnie I'd spoken to Gordon and he would be available for £50,000 and willing to join Wolves if things were right. Leicester were grooming Peter Shilton and wanted to sell Banks before he hit the big three-o.

"Ronnie said: 'He won't last. He's 29, too old.' I said: 'He'll keep you in work for another ten years.' Ronnie barely lasted another 18 months. I saw him at Tranmere a few years later at the start of our successful League Cup run and he said: 'Remember that time you lined me up with Banksy? Do I regret not buying him!'"

To say Dougan has attitude is rather akin to suggesting the Pope likes to dabble in Catholicism. "Once at Wolves, we had about 16 players in dispute over contracts," he adds. "Who resolved them all? I did. McGarry was limited with his vocabulary. When John Richards was just starting and McGarry offered him new terms, John was happily getting up to leave when he said: 'That's fine, I just want to speak to Doog first.' McGarry went off at him. 'Why the fog do you want to speak to him?'

"Another time we beat Arsenal 5-1 at Molineux after trailing 1-0 at half-time. The interval used to last only ten minutes, so, by the time you came off, walked up the tunnel and the 60 yards to the left to the home dressing-room, the manager would have a maximum six minutes to speak. On this occasion, I delegated Kenny Hibbitt to count the number of times McGarry swore. I said: 'Kenny, don't listen to what he says, just count the swear-words. I went off to the toilet, had my cup of tea and could hear McGarry ranting away as normal in the background. The printable bits would have been about us being a load of cheats, people paying good money to watch this rubbish, then he'd start picking on someone. Never a constructive word.

"When we went out for the second half, Kenny came over and said: 'I'm sorry, Doog, but I stopped counting at 59.' We put five past Bob Wilson in the second half. I wish I'd been a fly on the wall when McGarry held court to the press in his little office afterwards, cigar in one hand, a scotch in the other, and they'd asked him what message he had conveyed to the team to inspire us in such a manner."

The following summer, McGarry bought Steve Kindon from Burnley with the intention of training him up to succeed Dougan. The striker known as The Tank almost accelerated the process unintentionally when, as a substitute, he was preparing on the pitch before the FA Cup quarter-final against Coventry City in March, 1973. "I'd warm up in the dressing-room, then go out on to the pitch and do my runs up and down, getting tuned in - they call it focused these days," Dougan says wryly. "Kindon, who could hit the ball so hard, would be practising bulging the net. Suddenly, I see this blur coming out of the blue and it's one of Kindon's shots going well wide. Next thing, I'm down. When I start coming round, I remember this water-sucking noise Kindon used to make through his teeth and he's nearly crying, saying: 'Doog, please make it, come on. I'm sorry.' McGarry's up in the directors box and bowls right over the top and comes running on the pitch. All the medical people are running over, Sammy Chung's got the smelling salts out and McGarry's effing and blinding at Kindon.

"The kick-off was delayed for ten minutes. I had double vision for a lot of the game but remember Frank Munro thundering this header all the way from his own half towards me. I'm thinking: 'Which ball should I go for?' Thankfully, I chose the right one and off went Richards like a hare to score." This anecdote arises when I ask Dougan his opinion of Richards' calibre. His appreciation of team-mates tends to be equivocal. He says: "I used to say to Bobby Gould - and this is where John Richards started to pick things up - 'Bobby, no-one can beat me in the air, so watch the way my body shapes up because I can only head it one of four ways: to the left, to the right, flick it on or nod it down to you. Start your run as I'm starting to climb, then get it down, under control and hit it early.'

"John was a substitute watching this for a whole season (1970-71). It was part of his apprenticeship. He was more powerful than Bobby Gould and I used to say to him: 'Don't think about it. From the knockdown, just hit it. You'll catch the defenders and the goalkeeper unaware. If you take extra touches, you'll miss out on the opportunity.'" It worked, clearly. For their three seasons in tandem, the Dougan-Richards alliance plundered 128 goals (the highest in England), culminating in the League Cup success of 1974. "It was a unique combination," Dougan says, "one that comes along only

Derek Dougan and Bobby Gould test defenders Mike England and Cyril Knowles to the full in Wolves' 0-0 draw at Tottenham in December, 1969.

every 20 years or so. The sad thing was, I suppose, that I was 15 years older than him.

"Waggy doesn't get the credit he deserves, mind. He could put the ball where he wanted. I'd say: 'Davey, put it on the near post, never mind where I am. I'll get there.' In training, he used to put the ball on the centre spot and ask who'd challenge him. Frank Munro would take, say, 50 shots to hit the bar; then Waggy would do it straightaway. Every time Jonny Wilkinson lines one up, I think of Davey Wagstaffe.

"I never really had an enjoyable relationship with Mike Bailey. We didn't mix as we should have done. He was McGarry's boy. I know McGarry pushed Bailey to Sir Alf Ramsey but never Dave Wagstaffe, which was a travesty. Waggy had the best left foot I've ever seen and he could pass and cross like no-one else, including Beckham. Alf Ramsey told me that every time he spoke to Bill McGarry about Waggy, he was told he smoked too many fags and drank too many pints."

Other team-mates Dougan rated very highly were Munro - "the best footballing centre-half I've seen at Wolves - and Ken Hibbitt. But, as the careers of Munro, Bailey, Wagstaffe and the Doog drew closer to a conclusion, so the end of an era beckoned. After the Wembley triumph in 1974, Doog barely played in his final season, managing one last UEFA Cup goal in a 3-1 victory over Porto and a farewell effort in the league

Personal File 'Doog'

FULL NAME: *Alexander Derek Dougan.*
BIRTHPLACE: *Belfast, N. Ireland.*
DATE OF BIRTH: *January 20.*
MARRIED: *Yes.*
WIFE'S NAME: *Jutta Maria.*
CHILDREN: *Alexander, Nicholas.*
CAR: *VW K. 70.*
FAVOURITE COLOUR: *Green.*
FAVOURITE FOOD: *Anything my wife Jutta cooks.*
FAVOURITE DRINK: *Dry Red Wine.*
FAVOURITE TV SHOW: *Morecambe & Wise.*
FAVOURITE SINGER: *Frank Sinatra.*
FAVOURITE PLAYER: *George Best.*
FAVOURITE OTHER TEAM: *Wolves Reserves.*
PET LIKE: *Driving.*
PET DISLIKE: *Leeds United.*
HOBBIES: *Training in afternoons.*
PERSONAL AMBITION: *To win League Cup at Wembley.*
PROFESSIONAL AMBITION: *To win League Cup at Wembley.*
PREVIOUS CLUBS: *Portsmouth, Blackburn, Aston Villa, Peterborough, Leicester.*
JOINED WOLVES: *March 15, 1967.*
DEBUT: *Manchester United October 1957.*
REPRESENTATIVE HONOURS: *Schoolboy, Youth, Under-23, 'B' and 47 full caps.*
BIGGEST DISAPPOINTMENT IN CAREER: *Not joining Wolves in 1956.*
MOST MEMORABLE MATCH: *Wolves debut at home scoring hat-trick against Hull 1967.*
BIGGEST DRAG IN SOCCER: *Brian Clough, Malcolm Allison.*
BIGGEST INFLUENCE ON CAREER: *Cliff Lloyd, Secretary P.F.A.*
BIGGEST THRILL IN SOCCER: *Becoming first Irishman to score 200 League goals.*
IF YOU WEREN'T A FOOTBALLER WHAT WOULD YOU HAVE BEEN: *Journalist.*
CUP MEMORY: *Getting to League Cup Final with Wolves.*

Left: A League Cup final brochure feature in 1974 on one of Wolves' main men.

at Middlesbrough in the space of three days in the October. "My goals have kept teams up for nearly 20 years," Dougan says without self-deprecation. He runs through his teams, recalling the subsequent relegations of each, although only half went down within two years of his leaving. Point taken, though. "I have always thought one man doesn't make a team," he says, "but one man can make a hell of a difference to a team."

We break off and the Doog offers fresh caffeine. Leeds United have been in the news, with a member of the Bahrain royal family said to be on the point of helping take over a club only two years out of the Champions League semi-finals. If they were to be relegated, their potential fall into the arms of the administrators would be almost as rapid as when Wolves, League Cup winners in 1980 and sixth in the top flight, slipped into receivership in 1982. Harry Marshall was the chairman who over-reached with the building of the £2million John Ireland Stand. Doug Ellis, against whom Aston Villa supporters are still rallying at the time Dougan and I are talking, had been in the chair at Molineux for six weeks when he called in the receivers. Wolves were up for sale for £2m.

"What I do smile about," Dougan says, his frustration tinged with bewilderment, "is that history gives us hardly any credit. Yet Wolves were within 24 hours of going out of business." After time was called on Marshall's regime, the two other consortia interested in picking up the baton were led by Ellis, assisted by Malcolm Finlayson, the former Wolves goalkeeper, and Ken Wheldon. "Up until the 11th hour, Doug Ellis was saying: 'My group will get £2m together' as he went up and down the country passing round a begging bowl. Ken Wheldon's lot couldn't get the money together either."

Dougan recalls he was told by John Bird, leader of Wolverhampton Council, at a meeting at South Staffs Golf Club, that his consortium were the most credible. No-one at that stage had cause to doubt the substance of Allied Properties or the Bhattis. "John Starkey, a Manchester architect, and Mike Rowland, the very articulate MD of Allied Properties, came in. When you see Mahmoud Al-Hassan Bhatti drive up in a Rolls Royce, at his own aviation company, and know of his luxurious offices in London, you can't help but feel impressed," Dougan says. "When Peat Marwick and Co, the accountants dealing with the receivership, show you a bank draft for £2,000,050, you have reason to think the club can be saved and built up again."

Having met the Bhatti brothers at Grosvenor Aviation's offices in Manchester on the Sunday night, Dougan was celebrating with Starkey, Rowland, Roger Hipkiss and Doug Hope, his fellow board members, by the following Thursday. The paperwork was signed and sealed by 4.57pm the following day, July 30, 1982, three minutes before the end of business, even when the Football League insisted on an extra payment of £50,000 to guarantee Wolves would fulfil their fixtures. "Our backers were outraged and not inclined to provide the extra but we managed to find it," Dougan later told the *Sunday Express*. "We had come so far, achieved so much, in such a short time, that we couldn't walk away. Had we done, Wolves would have disappeared. The other two groups we thought were competing with us just didn't have the money.

"It was a desperate situation. The League were so doubtful about our future that we weren't even on the pools lists. And remember, as a precaution, Peterborough had been promoted to the Third Division and Lincoln moved to the Second to replace us. I'm not an emotional person but, when I walk down the corridor at Molineux and think of all the great figures who have trod the same path, men such as Stan Cullis, Billy Wright and Major Frank Buckley, for instance, I would have wept with thousands of others in the town had the bulldozers gone in."

It is appropriate to recall the jubilation, not to mention relief, at that time. I was at the *Express & Star*, on work experience from Regis Comprehensive sixth form, and was on the news desk when David Harrison, now a widely-respected sports reporter on the *News of the World*, started writing the story that Wolves had been saved.

Although Wolves made a fine start under Graham Hawkins and went nine games unbeaten, including an opening-day victory over Blackburn that Dougan watched from the North Bank terraces, the honeymoon period did not last long. "Within three to four weeks, we were told we would have to have an overdraft for £1.5m for a month, which the Bhattis got off Lloyds Bank," he recalls. "It remained for 15 months. I had no money to spend on players and the tragedy for me was that we all knew Graham was a fine manager and a fine bloke. It was my role to produce the resources for him to strengthen the squad.

"Rowland had told the press I had £1m to spend. I [*sic*] got promotion that season on £141,000, with which John Burridge, Alan Dodd and Billy Kellock were bought. That's something Sir Jack Hayward has never been able to do. We had a better than average side - [Mel] Eves was still young and, although Richards was finished, [Andy] Gray was a wonderful fellow, John Humphrey was a talented full-back - and those three signings just took us above that."

Promotion followed but Dougan, conscious that all was far from well behind the scenes, maintains the club would have been better missing out. "You wouldn't believe the problems I inherited from the previous regime," he says. "I had a direct line to the Bhattis and we'd talk up to 20 times a day. They'd ring me about everything and anything, if they saw a snippet in the papers. They got carried away with the excitement of being top of the table and would come to a board meeting practically every Monday, which was always professionally run. But the problems I had to deal with off the pitch... unsecured creditors, people coming in late for the money owed to them. The club had been very badly run.

"Harry Marshall had £1.5m in assets. The funding of the new stand was based on average gates of 28,000 and, of course, crowds were on the decline. Even so, I thought the £2,000,050 had paid the debts but the Football League, through their stupidity, never put a time-scale on the repayments for secured creditors so I was on the back foot from the start. It [the take-over] all happened so quickly, I didn't have time to look into the Bhattis' family background. It took me six months to walk round the ground. I was in from 7.30am, the adrenaline flying, and I spent more time with Eddie Clamp's mother, the cleaner, than anyone else, as she would offer me a cup of tea after everyone else had gone home.

"Mahmoud would tell you everything in the garden was rosy. Akbar, at 20, was chairman of Allied Properties. They didn't actually say they were from the Middle East. They didn't say they were well connected in Saudi Arabia. But, when you went to their offices in London and saw all these pictures on the wall of princes and King Faysel, and heard talk of friends in Saudi, you assumed that's where they're from. Basically, they were a couple of Pakistanis from Manchester. They'd bought Allied Properties for £10,000 a year before and blew it up [expanded it rapidly] through a couple of property deals in London. They sweet-talked Lloyds Bank into getting a £2m overdraft, so it was pretty convincing. I started getting bad vibes about Christmas."

While the Bhattis pinned their hopes on getting planning permission to build a supermarket, where Asda now sits, to fuel the club's recovery, Molineux started to fall into disrepair. "We patched it up," Dougan said. "We had to be very nice to the surveyor to get the ground certificate, I remember. The whole place was painted, the debris cleared away, the rewiring done. I did a deal for a fleet of Japanese cars for the staff - the criticism I got for not buying British! One of the big problems I had was that the new PA system cost £30,000 but the suppliers weren't happy with Allied Properties so I had to give a personal guarantee because our owners had no track record.

"This feeling of uncertainty grew when we fell out with Lloyds and I went to my own bank, NatWest, for an overdraft of £100,000 to cover a shortfall in staff salaries. They did a search on Allied Properties and I had to give my bank a personal guarantee for that overdraft. In all, over two and a half years, I must have lent them between £150,000 and £200,000. I'm still fighting for the last £50 grand." For all the off-field troubles, a team still including Gray, Palmer, Hibbitt, Eves and Wayne Clarke staggered over the finishing line, second to Queens Park Rangers, to earn immediate promotion. That summer, Rowland left and Dougan, who was not getting paid for his troubles, wishes he had followed.

"If I had resigned that summer, it might all have turned out better," he muses. "I was chairman and chief executive, working for nothing but the promise of a five-year contract that never materialised. You can't have any greater devotion to a club than that. Of course people say: 'But what did you get out of it?' At the end of the day, it was bloody hard work. My role was to get resources for Graham Hawkins but that experience taught me that you can have all the enthusiasm and energy in the world but, if you don't have the resources to do the job, it's like swimming against the tide.

"It was unfair of Allied Properties to say I had £1m to spend on players when I didn't. I financed that promotion season through my own sheer endeavour and ability, generating money to buy those three players. I ran the club without losing money in that first year and I'm proud of that. But the more I was into it, day in, day out, the more I realised that, however hard I dug, I wasn't in an Aladdin's Cave. The council didn't give us the support we needed to develop the ground. The supermarket was the big earner to help us redevelop but we were turned down. The plan was to get about £8m in grants then another £8m from the supermarket. The whole development would have cost £22m.

"The worst thing that happened was getting promotion, then having to finance that jump up. History has repeated itself this year with Dave Jones doing wonderfully well getting this Wolves team into the play-offs. Then, after promotion, he needed at least six top quality Premiership players. I've been there, designed the t-shirt and still wear it. You've now got a situation where Wolves are swimming against the tide because there's simply not enough proven Premiership quality in this side.

"Likewise, we had a team who wouldn't have been outside the top six in the old Second Division. Frankly, it would have been in our interests to finish third." Instead, Wolves were bottom of the top flight in 1983-84, the year of Steve Mardenborough's off-the-shoulder winner at Liverpool (his lone goal for the club) and Danny Crainie's two-goal blast in the only pre-Christmas win - the disproportionately gratifying 3-1 success away to West Bromwich Albion.

Troubled times at Molineux - a 0-0 draw with Albion just before relegation became a certainty in 1984. The crowd was 13,084.

Wolves' impending relegation hardly improved their credit rating and Gray, rated at £1m, was sold on the cheap as the club scrambled round for a shilling for the meter. "I dealt with Ron Atkinson when Manchester United came in," Dougan recalls. "I said they could have him for a million but, because of our cash flow crisis, we sold him to Everton for £180,000." Gray finished the season by scoring at Wembley as his new club won the FA Cup. Wolves went down, with only 27 goals from 42 league games.

From time to time on a Monday night in games at Wirksworth's Astroturf, I still wear the striped socks of that Molineux era; it's as narrow as the playing gap between me and a top-division Wolves side ever came. If I'd turned up, I might have had a game. "You can't convince yourself this is real," Dougan adds. "You keep believing, wanting to believe, when the Bhatti brothers tell you another bank is coming in. I wasn't party to the appointment of Tommy Docherty, either. I voted against him."

Hibbitt joined Coventry and, with the old guard practically gone, Docherty's team - a mix of young and old but predominantly cheap - fared no better in Division Two. Dougan had almost had enough. "It came to a head when, fobbed off for months and with debts of about £100,000, we realised it had all gone pear-shaped. The Bhattis were always out of the office, out of the country, out of earshot. So, unbeknown to the other board members, Eric Woodward, the general manager, Starkey and I entered into negotiations with a Swedish bank to buy the club for £2m.

Derek Dougan in 2003: "If I hadn't convinced a group of strangers that a famous old club of 105 years' standing were worth saving, I would have been unbelievably disloyal."

"Typical of Bhatti, he asked £8m. That was December, 1984. I've got the minutes. I stuck it out until January 16, 1985, when Starkey and I resigned. We were in the boardroom and phoned to inform them of our decision. It was sad." The monthly wage bill was about £18,000 and Dougan had to find the interest payments for the bank. "I left 18 months before they went back into receivership, when the club were still in Division Two. The Bhattis somehow hung on until May, 1986." It was the lowest point in Wolves' history but Graham Turner, Steve Bull and co turned things around after Tony Gallagher, a property developer, and the council did a deal to build an Asda store.

The nowhere land between the exits of Dougan and the Bhattis was a grim, desolate place, a footballing Hades. But Dougan maintains he was right to become involved in 1982. "If I hadn't used my initiative and convinced a group of strangers that a famous old club of 105 years standing were worth saving, I would have been unbelievably disloyal," he says. "It was my duty. I'm reading in the papers that the deadline for the club's closure is getting closer and closer and, to this day, I'm not sure what might have happened.

"Looking back, I didn't need all the hassle, especially with not getting paid. But the adrenaline was flying at 100 miles per hour and here were a club who meant so much to me. I'm still Wolves' highest goalscorer for a season in Europe, a record that I'm sure will never be passed, and my goals helped keep the club in the First Division for eight years."

Perhaps it needed someone with the Doog's ego, charisma and presence to breathe life into Wolves even as they spiralled towards their nadir. And, while the Bhattis did little for business at Molineux, at least they helped spawn one of the most idiosyncratic songs in the club's history: "Everywhere we go, people want to know, where the hell are *you* from, we're from Wolverhampton, sunny Wolverhampton, lovely Wolverhampton. *Sack the Bhattis*, buy a corner shop, sell the cheaper lager...

Derek Dougan

Born:	January 20, 1938, in Belfast
Signed:	March, 1967
Wolves appearances:	323
Goals:	123
Left:	May, 1975
International recognition:	43 senior Northern Ireland caps

November 2003

> *Back to reality. Wolves should have nicked all three points from the 1-1 draws at Molineux with Birmingham City (how did Steffen Iversen miss in the last minute?) and Newcastle United (when Nathan Blake produced his best performance (Ed: correction, his only performance) of the season). The 2-0 defeats away to Middlesbrough and Everton, however, showed that the team were struggling to come to terms with going to Premiership strongholds. Even if Danny Mills is the most obnoxious footballer around, Lee Naylor and Paul Ince should have concentrated on stopping Gazieka Mendieta and Juninho. Dave Jones told me later he would have liked to knock Mills' head off. That was tongue-in-cheek, I'm sure. Perhaps.*

Evening Mail MONDAY, DECEMBER 1, 2003

THE MONDAY AFTER

WOLVES TOON IT AROUND

WOLVES 1
NEWCASTLE 1

BY PAUL BERRY

■ MUSCLING IN: Newcastle's Lee Bowyer tries to force past Alex Rae in the action-packed draw at Molineux

IT is a measure of this strange, fluctuating season that seven days on from a truly miserable display at Everton, Wolves should troop off the pitch against Newcastle unhappy with a point.

Despite what appeared to be a gulf in class from the names on the teamsheet, the spirit and determination which has characterised most of the season almost contrived to send the Geordies away from Molineux empty-handed for the second time in a year.

As good a point as it was, it soon started to drop in value as news filtered through from elsewhere on an afternoon where victories for other strugglers left the comfort zone above the bottom three now frustratingly out of

Portsmouth, Bolton, Fulham, Blues - from all of Wolves' other draws this season they could also have come away with strong claims to taking all three points.

What a difference if just two of the five had been converted into a maximum haul.

Still, nothing should be taken away from this performance in which Champions League-chasing Newcastle, even in the wake of their UEFA Cup tie just 38 hours earlier, boasted the likes of Shearer, Woodgate, Dyer, Jenas and Speed.

Squandered

And ultimately it was just a lick of paint which stood in the way of Wolves and all three points as they pressed forward in the last 10 minutes.

First, Joev Gudjonsson, who

chance in first-half injury time, almost capped an industrious return to the side with a curling free-kick only to see his effort thud off the post.

Then, as the game drifted into injury time at the end, Henri Camara met Alex Rae's cross with a powerful header which had Shay Given flailing before bouncing to safety off the top of the crossbar.

Given had earlier produced a more costly moment of panic to gift Wolves their 27th-minute lead, charging out of his area only to be beaten to the ball by

nerve to slot home his first goal of the season. Unfortunately the lead was short-lived as Alan Shearer, who had already struck the crossbar, finished off the best move of the contest by latching on to Lomana LuaLua's pass and beyond Michael Oakes and into the bottom corner.

Although Wolves failed to hit the dizzy heights of their marvellous FA Cup success over Newcastle at the turn of the year, they did display enough attacking intent to put the Toon Army into retreat.

Camara once again showed a

of defenders on their toes, Gudjonsson and Keith Andrews deputised to good effect in midfield and Rae was everything you'd expect him to be.

At the back the imperious Paul Butler and Jody Craddock once again called on all their reserves of strength and character to shackle Shearer for all but a couple of fleeting moments.

It was Craddock who featured in the second instalment of the 'Tale of Two Penalties', handling Olivier Bernard's late cross when diving to try and head the ball away.

Yet that wasn't the only inci-

Steve Bennett, Blake's tumbling under the challenge of Titus Bramble just prior to half-time easily a free-kick at worst, penalty at best and sending-off for either.

The challenge for Wolves now is to take this sort of display into two monumental away-days at Tottenham and Villa over the next two Premiership weekends.

WOLVES (4-3-2-1): Oakes 7, Irwin 7, Naylor 7, Butler 8, Craddock 7, Camara 7, Rae 7, Ince 7, Gudjonsson 6, Blake 6, Miller 7. Subs: Marshall, Sturridge.
NEWCASTLE (4-4-2): Given, Hughes, Woodgate, Bramble, Bernard, Dyer, Jenas, Speed, Bowyer, Shearer, LuaLua. Subs: Ambrose, Lee Bowyer, Caldwell, Ameobi, Viana.

106

Paul Cook

A CULTURED LEFT FOOT AND A FEW REGRETS

December 15, 2003: The players' bar, Accrington Stanley

The pitch is frozen white, an iced Christmas cake, as 14 players leap on top of Paul Howarth, the defender who has just scored the penalty that clinches Accrington Stanley's place in the third round of the FA Cup. They twirl and they tumble, their joy unrestrained, as they meld with supporters in the roofless Crown End of this higgledy-piggledly ground. They have, via this shoot-out, slain Second Division Bournemouth; it is an unprecedented giant-killing for a famous old club re-formed 35 years ago.

Never before, in their latest incarnation, have Accrington advanced to such a glamorous stage of the competition, the one at which all the big names join in. So 15 part-timers party like there's no game until January, never mind a tomorrow. Fifty yards away, surveying the scene from the middle of the otherwise empty pitch, the wise old pro laps up the moment, a wide scally grin etched on his wizened features. He claps his begloved hands, his breath funnelling out in the sub-zero temperatures.

Paul Cook is probably too tired to join in. He has just played a full part, over 120 minutes, in helping his new club earn a home tie with Colchester United. He thought his days of FA Cup glory belonged in the past after he captained Burnley in their quarter-final against Watford the previous season. Now here he is, at 36, stretching out his career, enjoying his Indian summer in the bitter cold of winter.

"I'll get you a drink, Pete, sit yourself down, don't worry about me, I've only played for two hours," Cookie laughs, an hour later, as he invites me into the compact players' bar. "The question is: when to call it a day? That's what I'm wondering," he says, buying me a coke. "I don't want to let the lads down. But if I can still contribute, if I can add something, then I want to. I still love playing. It's in my blood and when you get a night like this, when you see the younger lads sniff a bit of glory, and the guys who have been in non-league all their lives, like John Coleman, our manager, getting a piece of the limelight, you don't want to stop."

Coleman comes in to join the celebrations, with John Durnin, the old Portsmouth striker, Lutel James, an exciting, pacy young forward, and others. Banter flies fast. The night ahead starts to take shape. Cookie is in his element, his pint of lager on the table next to the hot pies. It is clear that he is rationing himself, relishing the single sample of golden nectar, or pacing himself at least. It is perhaps surprising he has managed to play so long, considering his love of a drink in earlier years when, he admits, he wonders if his social life got in the way of helping Wolverhampton Wanderers into the top flight.

Cook played for Wolves for five years in the early 1990s and, although he is and always has been a die-hard Liverpool fan, his sons support the club in the area where they were born and with whom their Dad maintains a close bond. He was with his own father at Molineux as a nine-year-old when he witnessed at first hand the kind of theatre the place could stage. "I was in the paddock of what is now the Billy Wright Stand the night Liverpool won the title in 1976," he recalls. "We were 1-0 down - Steve Kindon scored, I felt sick - but won 3-1. You never think then you'll end up playing there.

"I knew when I joined them from Norwich (for £250,000, in 1989) that they were a big club, with a big support and a lot of tradition. I was aware of the Steve Bull/Andy Mutch partnership, and I spoke to Mutchy before I joined because I knew he was from Liverpool. But the thing that struck me when I made my debut, away to Leicester (a

Welcome to Wolves, Cookie. In front of a baying crowd, Steve Bull is sent off in the 0-0 draw at Leicester on November 1, 1989 - the night of Paul Cook's debut.

goalless draw on November 1 in which Bull was sent off for an incident involving Steve Walsh) was the supporters. There must have been 3,000 of them at Filbert Street and they made this incredible noise." The following Saturday, Cook made Bull's goal in a 1-0 win over West Ham United with the kind of defence-splitting left-footed pass that became his trademark. It was a combination that would threaten, for half a decade, to lift Wolves into the highest division.

Wolves were still a club in flux, Graham Turner, the manager, attempting to upgrade his lower-division champions while Molineux was awaiting its facelift. "It was a bit eerie, playing in a ground with the North Bank derelict," Cook admits. Without prompting, he volunteers another factor as a potential reason why a good team failed to capitalise on the momentum gained by winning successive titles and leap into the pre-Premiership First Division. "With the drink culture in football at that time, without giving any players stick, we did get dragged into it," he says. "You think today that we should have been more dedicated then.

"We were no different to other players at other clubs, probably, but, looking back now, I just think I could have been more committed to the cause, in the way you ran your life. There was no such thing as re-hydrating. After a match, we'd be straight out drinking. Graham Turner was great, don't get me wrong, but, in those days, no-one spoke to us about food and drink. It was a level playing field, as far as I could tell, in that the Wolves lads were no better nor any worse than any other team but you look back and think: 'If I could turn back time…' It is the biggest disappointment in my career, by some distance, not getting Wolves up."

It is a footballer's idiosyncrasy to switch from the first person to the third when speaking about himself, as if uncertain where responsibility or credit should be awarded. The flip-side of this candid admission is that Cook tapped into one of the best dressing-rooms Wolves had had for many years. Through the intense adversity of the mid-1980s, when the club diced with the liquidators, to the two title-winning years in which the likes of Bull, Mutch, Keith Downing, Andy Thompson, Robbie Dennison and Mark Venus became such popular and successful players under Turner, Wolves became established at a respectable level again.

"The team spirit was phenomenal," says Cook, who contributed more than his fair share to the esprit de corps. "You don't get that no more, with a lot of nationalities in a dressing-room. We'd go the Goal Post after a game, or the Foaming Jug on the way home, with Stowelly (Mike Stowell, the goalkeeper who joined in 1990) or Veno. We'd regularly go out and people knew you. You don't see that nowadays, and that's a mixed blessing. The drink culture was heavy in football and we were no different to other teams. Tuesday, knowing we had our day off coming up, we'd all go out. Wednesday was less a day of rest, more a day to sober up. That was the case whatever club you were at then. If you weren't playing Tuesday night, you'd have a running day to set you up for a drink."

December 4, 2003: Billy's Bootroom, Molineux

K eith Downing backs up his former colleague when he pops in for a chat with him as we reconvene at the club for a photo session involving some of the characters in this book. "Graham Turner would tell me that the amount of phone calls he would get from the public was staggering," Downing, then a member of Dave Jones' coaching staff, says. "We were, like, The Tuesday Club. We'd run our socks off, then go to town for a few ales. He'd get the calls saying: 'What's going on?' But we weren't hiding. We were a winning team most of this time. Graham knew how to be fair with us. I remember stopping at the Goal Post after a match to have a couple of pints. If you'd been playing away, the fans would have got back too, and they'd come up and say: 'You were crap today.' I'd say: 'Yeah, I was mate.' That's how football was."

When they did overstep the mark, Turner's man-management skills came to the fore. Rather than dropping an errant player, he would ensure he got more out of him. "He was just a genuinely fair man," Cook says. "That's why I liked him. I remember before a game away to Notts County, me and Shane Westley had been out on a bit of a session on the Thursday afternoon. The gaffer pulled us in on the Friday and let us know we'd let him down, let ourselves down and let the club down. 'You're in the public eye, not looking after yourselves before a game,' he said. The message was that we owed him a performance next day. Not that that made it right; he pointed out the punters were waiting for us to fail. I think Shane scored in a 1-1 draw."

Turner, under whom Downing and, briefly, Bull went on to play and coach at Hereford United, was revered by his players. "I think his success was partly down to the simplicity in his instructions," Downing says. "He didn't over-coach us but we had basic principles we all knew to stick to. We pressed together, we got things forward to Andy (Mutch) and we worked hard for each other. His selection of players was very good. We had good combinations around the field."

If Mutch and Bull provided the best example of this, the midfield axis of Downing and Cook was ideal. Downing worked his Black Country backside off, his team ethos unrivalled, while Cook had a rare ability to see and execute the perfect pass. "A good player will know his weaknesses," Downing points out. "I knew I couldn't hit 60-yard balls." "I needed Keith as much as the team needed me," Cook agrees. "Me without Keith was a bad player. Successful teams have the right blend, both in characters and the combinations required to bring the best out of each other."

Then the old banter kicks in. Cook: "Keith used to go in for a pay rise, saying he was overworked, having to do all my work." Downing, all mock indignation: "He finished my career at 32. It was all that running. Anyone running past him, Cookie would say: 'Keith, have a look after him for us.'" Cook: "The best one was: 'Watch them two coming, Keith.'" Downing: "Ah, mine and his. He could pass it, though, couldn't he? I'd get it, give it him, he'd lose it, I'd have to get it again."

Cook's inconsistency came to rival that of the team. "I remember we had a meeting on a Sunday after we lost at Oxford," he recalls. "Graham Turner drew a line for acceptable level of performance. Keith, who'd been our best player, was just below it. Then Graham turned to me and said: 'You don't even get on the page.'"

Flicking through the Wolves scorebook I maintained religiously - in green ink, in the smart sixth-form exercise books Dave, my eldest brother, would 'borrow' for me from Regis Comprehensive School in Tettenhall - Cook acknowledges he was player of the year in 1990-91 (when Wolves finished 12th) and was among the goals again in 1991-92 (11th). He scored his eighth in a 6-2 rout of Newcastle United. "That sums us up," he says. "We'd go from that to losing 1-0 at Oxford; world-beaters to hopeless. That was synonymous with the Wolves team I played in.

Author's personal 1991-92 records.

		Venue	Score	Scorers
Newcastle United		Home	6-2	Mutch 3 Bennett Cook Bull
(11) Oxford United		Away	0-1	
Ipswich Town		Away	1-2	Mutch
(11) Cambridge United		Home	2-1	Ranking Mutch
Blackburn Rovers		Away	2-1	Bull Birch
(10) Swindon Town		Away	0-1	
(10) Southend United		Home	3-1	Bull Mountfield Birch
(10) Barnsley		Away	0-2	
(11) Middlesbrough		Home	1-2	Mutch

Top scorers:
S. Bull - 20+3+0+0 : 23
A. Mutch - 10+0+0+0 : 10
P. Birch - 8+2+0+0 : 10

Top appearances :(51)
M. Stowell - 46+3+1+1 : 51
M. Venus - 46+3+1+0 : 50
K. Ashley - 44+3+1+1 : 49

Finished: 11th	Pl	W	D	L	F	A	W	D	L	F	A	GD	Pts
Wolves	46	11	6	6	36	24	7	4	12	25	30	+7	64

Player of the Year:

Manager: Graham Turner

"Every year, we thought: 'This is the year.' I played 50 games the next season but was in and out with my form. I was disappointed with myself, felt I should have done better. Physically, I could have been better. Your social life was great and people still remember me as quite a good player but you think to yourself: 'Imagine if I'd done the job properly, how good could you have been.' The sad truth is: you'll never know."

It is no coincidence Cook's favourite Wolves games were in his debut season: the 4-1 win at Newcastle on the first day of the new decade, when Bull scored four and Mark Kendall saved Mick Quinn's penalty, and his first derby with West Bromwich Albion, when he "scuffed" the equaliser before Bully got the winner "as per normal." With ten games to go in 1989-90, Wolves lay sixth; a third consecutive promotion was possible. They fell away to tenth. "Just to add two players to your squad then, just before the transfer deadline, when you're sixth, might have been our best chance of getting up before big money changed the whole face of football," Cook says wistfully.

"The momentum was with us that first season after a poor start," Downing adds. "I don't know how much Graham Turner had for transfers but perhaps he was too loyal to the likes of me. By '93, it was time to break up the team. Thommo was out of favour, Mutchy went, Robbie Dennison was bombed out, I was disappointed to leave." Downing went to Birmingham City on a free transfer. Cook lasted another year.

"The fact we never got promoted meant the players changed around, the pressure increased year after year, more money was invested and, the next season, Graham was on his way," Cook recalls. "I was sad to see him go. He stayed loyal to the team to the end." Cook had lost his place as Chris Marsden and Darren Ferguson were signed and he only appeared as a substitute in an FA Cup quarter-final defeat at Chelsea in March, 1994, before playing all the remaining games as Graham Taylor took over.

It was not a marriage made to last. Cook, the free-spirited, play-making cavalier, a terrace favourite, keen on a drink; and Taylor, the work-loving disciplinarian, eager to regain credibility after troubled times with England. Perhaps it was surprising they lasted even five months together. "Graham Taylor wasn't my greatest cup of tea," Cook says, with a hint of understatement. "My contract was up that summer and, although I was offered a new one, I felt he wanted me out, wanted to change the club around. If you had an opinion in the dressing-room, he didn't want to hear it."

Cook tried discussing tactics in the final game of the season. "We were at home to Leicester, live on the telly, and, when we came in at half-time, I thought I'd played really well. He said to me: 'I want you to go and play wide on the left.' I just looked at him in disbelief. So he said: 'Why, do you not think you should play there?' I replied: 'No, I think I'm playing quite well where I am.' So he replied: 'Well go and

"I'll spray the passes, you pick up the runners." Paul Cook (right) leaves the tidying up to Tom Bennett in Wolves' damaging 3-0 defeat at Sheffield United in March, 1990.

Paul Cook: "I felt we let Graham Turner down so badly, not getting promoted. Not to get Wolves up always kills me."

get a shower then,' to which I had a reply that's not printable in a family publication. Clearly, my days were numbered. I knew then that if he was going to be a top manager at Wolves, then I wasn't going to be a top player for him."

Cook moved to Coventry City in August, 1994, for £600,000. The First Division campaign had already kicked off with Wolves, as ever, among the favourites. "On the morning of the first game, he had us here on the pitch," he recalls, pointing out from Billy's Bootroom, where Frank Munro and Derek Dougan have joined us over sandwiches. "We were doing shadow play, only with no ball, no opposition and you had to shut your eyes and walk yourself through it." ("Did you win?" Munro pipes up.) Cook laughs and continues. "You think to yourself: 'What am I doing here?' You end up opening your eyes to see if the other lads are opening theirs. Then he says: 'Hold your ears, imagine you're winning 2-0 and the crowd are chanting your name. I want you to feel the vibe.' It was time for me to go. I felt we let Graham Turner down so badly, not getting promoted. But, with the meteoric rise he had instigated, I felt he should have been given a bit more time to reassemble the side."

Cook took a pay cut to leave Wolves, where he was earning £1,500 a week. "I remember meeting Phil Neal with my father. He said he could offer me £1,200 and Premier League football, take it or leave it. With Phil Neal being Graham Taylor's right-hand man with England, you wondered about a conspiracy but I couldn't foresee a future under Graham Taylor, so there wasn't a better move I could have made. I held my own in the Premier League, making 50-odd appearances, including the highlight of my career, when we won 3-2 at Anfield. At the time, you didn't know whether you could play in the Premier, so you were a lot more serious about teams. If you had Tottenham away, for example, you had to be spot-on, whereas with Wolves at Grimsby, you knew you could play comfortably. Personally, that's sad for me. Not to get them up always kills me. I was a good player for Wolves but could have been better."

That comfort zone became a prison for Wolves but it was one in which a character who could have followed Cook to Coventry preferred to dwell. Whether it is an indictment of Steve Bull's lack of ambition or a rubber-stamping of his unswerving loyalty to the cause depends on personal interpretation. Taylor, having shipped out Cook, was quite ready to offload Bull as well but the player ultimately declined Ron Atkinson's offer. "I was involved," Cook recalls. "Big Ron wanted him so I spoke to Bully and the deal was nigh-on done. Then, he (Bull) pulled out at the last minute. Bully was happy here, he was comfortable, his status was assured and, when he was with England, he was on a lot of money here. Why put that at risk? He's like these lads," Cook says, nodding in the direction of Munro and Dougan, "part of the folklore here. If you go down the road to Coventry and back, you're on a slippery slope."

Dougan points out that Robbie Keane stopped off at Highfield Road en route to higher stations. But Cook counters: "Bully made himself such a hero here in the years the club were coming back up, though, with his 100 goals in two seasons. The Scotland goal summed him up. The ball hit his shoulder, bounced between two defenders and he just hit it. It could have gone anywhere but he fizzes it right in. Whether he was playing on a Sunday park or in an international at Hampden, he'd look the same player.

"If you played with Bully, you appreciated how special he was because he wasn't

"If you played with Bully, you appreciated how special he was."

that good a footballer, technically. But anything that dropped over his shoulder gave defences unbelievable problems because he was that strong and that aggressive. If you were playing against him and he was in front of you, no problem; but the minute the ball went over your shoulder and he turned you, you were history, honest to God. If teams even then would have said: 'Okay, Bully, we'll play 20 yards deeper and let you have the ball in front of us,' they'd have solved half their problems. But over their shoulder, he was scary." It was a place Cook planted the ball a thousand times.

Dougan has criticism of Bull. "His percentage of chances taken was not great," he says. I ask whether that team relied too heavily on Bull, whether perhaps the strategy became too predictable, for all his goals. "It was all a bonus," Downing counters. "Every good side need a goalscorer, although, as Bully says, Mutchy was a big factor in his success. They played well together. Even after Andy left, the unselfish running Bully did, the goals he scored for the team... you'd be 0-0 at Portsmouth and he'd nick you one and you'd be two points better off." Tell us about it. In a demanding 2003-04 season in the Premiership, Wolves have played well enough, at home especially, but drawn so many games. What if it had been Bull at the near post, instead of Steffen Iversen, in the last minute against Birmingham? "We're talking about different eras," Downing points out. "The game's changed, even in these five years."

"You have to enjoy your time," Cook says. No-one could accuse him of doing otherwise and Wolves' fans have shown their appreciation of his style and personality when he has returned with Stockport County, Tranmere Rovers and Burnley. His kids were mascots when he played there for Burnley in 2002-03 and he spent more time with them there than he had envisaged. "They were still making their way off the pitch when I ran past them," he jokes. "I was sent off inside three minutes.

"We'd been on a bad run so we worked all week on playing with a midfield five,

See you in a short while. Paul Cook is pictured with his children - Burnley mascots for the day - back at Molineux in August, 2002. The smiles didn't last long, though, a red card cutting short the player's farewell game at the stadium.

keeping it tight and trying to get the crowd to turn on Wolves. Then, after 30 seconds, the ball bounces off the big Greek - our keeper, Nic Michopoulos, was having one - and Nathan Blake scores. All our preparations, all our formation talk, had gone. Alex Rae trots past me and says: 'You might get past the half-way line soon.' So when he went past me on the outside a few moments later, I took him. Hands up, it was a bad tackle, but never a red card. 'Thank you very much, Jeff Winter,' I said as I caught my kids up, 'that's a fine way for me to leave Molineux.'"

January 3, 2004: The players' bar, Accrington Stanley

It is not quite the end for Cook, though. We meet again three weeks later, back at the Interlink Express Stadium, where Colchester secure a replay when their goalkeeper makes a fine save to prevent Cook heading the winner two minutes into stoppage time. "It was there, you're off and running to the crowd with your arms up," he says as the TV cameras and national press surround him outside the changing-rooms. "But we've done ourselves justice and played really well. That's the beauty of the Cup. We live to fight another day."

The draw throws up the incentive of a trip to Coventry, which doubtless would have brought Cook another 15 minutes of media spotlight. He has a lot of history, still playing at 36. Accrington, beaten at Layer Road, have history, too, of which he is particularly aware. It provides a contrast with their reawakened reputation.

Did the Wolves who Cook played for suffer from forever having their illustrious past held up in their faces? "No, that wasn't a millstone," he says. "Because of how low the club had fallen, I always felt that whatever we'd done was moving Wolves back in the right direction. When they went bankrupt before my time - after the building of the big new stand, the Andy Gray transfer, the crowds going right down - that was, like, the end of a road. After that, the team I played in were on an upward spiral. Trouble was, we bumped into a ceiling, just couldn't get promoted. I started thinking that this club would never, ever have a team in the Premier League. I'm so glad they did it. I just really hope they can now stay up."

Paul Cook

Born:	February 22, 1967, in Liverpool
Signed:	October, 1989
Wolves appearances:	214
Goals:	21
Left:	August, 1994
International recognition:	None

December 2003

Wolves stay bottom for the entire month. A second-half fightback away to Aston Villa fails to earn a point against a team briefly considered relegation rivals but the manner of the 3-2 defeat at least offers supporters some pride, which was in scarce supply during two losses - in the Carling Cup and in the Premiership - at Arsenal. A festive win over Leeds United revives hope, as Steffen Iversen scores twice after the kind of own goal from Alan Smith that makes you believe in Father Christmas. Four points off 17th place with a game in hand suddenly sounds less like a lost cause.

Alex Rae

HE'S GOT NO HAIR BUT HE CERTAINLY DOES CARE

January 23, 2004: Wolves' training ground, Newbridge, Tettenhall

Dreamland. This is how we imagined it back in our summer beach kickabouts. Kenny Miller scoring dramatic goals, internationals buckling under the strain of our midfield's pressing, Molineux rocking to its very foundations. When you watch the highlights on *The Premiership* - opening slot, 1-0 against Man United - and the camera pans to Dave Jones near the end, all of us in the upper tier of the main stand are standing, punching arms towards the heavens. On the day the bottom team beat the leaders, it is clear: Neanderthal Man is alive and well and living in Wolverhampton.

It is the euphoria of the giant-killer, the crazed jubilation where hope crashes through into reality. Later, by the Billy Wright statue, Simon has tears in his eyes as he kneels to celebrate with Tom, our eldest son. Dad, who stood here on the days when championships were won, can't stop laughing. An *Express & Star* reporter asks Tom if Wolves will stay up. "No," the realist deadpans back. But the elation is worth bottling. It is up there with Cardiff. At least we half expected to beat Sheffield United. Dave Bellingham, Si's brother-in-law and the Alan Hansen of Wolves analysts, compares it with the comeback against Leicester City. Like Tom, his Megan hasn't seen Wolves lose this season. Molineux is a happy place.

Tom's face, eyes wide and bright as I pick him up after Miller has gone through to score the winner and send Molineux surging towards meltdown, is a sight to behold. By the time Wolves rally to equalise deservedly in the last minute at home to Liverpool four nights later, callers to BBC 5Live's *606* are starting to wonder whether Dave Jones' team might actually, despite all the evidence, avoid relegation.

In the wake of this rabid reaction, Alex Rae cuts a laid-back figure as he returns from training a couple of days later. He has been absolutely immense. But, after meeting the media and laughing off speculation that he is on the verge of a Scotland debut at the age of 34, he provides a reflective response to the hullabaloo of the week.

Player of the year two seasons previously, Rae has been scoring for fun, throwing himself into challenges with scant regard for self-preservation, and keeping possession composedly. Confidence and fitness high, he has taken to racing back while a team-mate jockeys an opponent and stealing the ball from the blind side. When United took a quick free-kick in the closing moments and others were pre-occupied, Rae spotted the danger, hurled himself into Paul Scholes' shot and helped keep the sheet clean.

"You're just trying to hang on," he says modestly. "They're pressing, wave after wave of attacks. It's a case of trying to earn a wee bit of respite." Scholes, Roy Keane, Steven Gerrard: bring 'em on. Rae just played his natural game. "I find it a privilege to be on the same park as those guys. I'm not being patronising, I really love facing players of that calibre. I've spent enough time in the lower divisions to know they are top-drawer. You want to pit your wits against the best and these guys are the best."

Rae heralds it as a glorious week for fans, one of redemption for the players. Wolves have shown the football world they can compete at this level. Even if they are to be relegated, they can ask the pundits to tone down the mockery. There would have been no high jinks for Rae, though, on returning to his wife and two-year-old daughter, Alexandra. "It was fantastic in the dressing-room afterwards," he adds. "It was such a big occasion and no-one expected us to get anything. It was really important to keep the home form going as well, and we managed to do that."

Before the match, talk among fans had been about damage limitation, hope that we would score this time after all the chances at Old Trafford in August, and keeping spirits high so we might then take something off Liverpool in midweek. "Everyone was excited at the prospect of playing United," Rae says. "It's like a circus when they come to town, with all the razzmatazz. A euphoria spills into your dressing-room. We thought we could get something but it might have been a bit far out to expect to turn the champions over. We're absolutely delighted. We had such a lot of chances at their place, I thought that, if we could keep it tight, then maybe…"

When Scholes nodded wide, when Darren Fletcher fell under Michael Oakes' grope, and when Ruud Van Nistelrooy headed over from a yard, big danger threatened. "We rode our luck in the first half," Rae concedes, "but, if you keep a clean sheet, you have a chance." Vio Ganea was on the touchline stripping off when, mid-way through the second half, Miller cushioned Denis Irwin's header beautifully and glided inside Wes Brown with a burst of acceleration that persuaded Rio Ferdinand's replacement to slip. Shooting early, Miller surprised Tim Howard and was the main man again.

"I'm absolutely delighted for him," Rae says. "Like all good strikers, he thrives on goals and he's been really buzzing this week. The two goals against Kidderminster [in the FA Cup third-round replay] kick-started his season. No-one could have imagined a fortnight ago he would be the man of the moment. It's absolutely great. He's always got goals and has a wee trick up his sleeve, so he can cause problems."

While I was off to play at Wirksworth on Monday night, clad gratuitously in gold and black, Rae says training has remained orderly, not cock-a-hoop. "It's been pretty low-key," he says. "We played two games in five days, so it's a case of ticking over. Kenny's always bright and bubbly. He's Scottish. Scots tend to talk a lot."

The equaliser against Liverpool was not unexpected. Rae says: "We were looking for a result." That's football-speak for harbouring a chance of winning. "Liverpool have blown hot and cold recently and we were hoping to get them on an off-night. We worked very hard, and kept pressing and knocking on the door. It must have been a good match to watch. I thoroughly enjoyed being involved in it."

If promotion was the equivalent of Advent, being in the Premiership is football's answer to Christmas. Even if you don't get all the presents you want, it still has a hallucinogenic glow, treats like being on *The Premiership* and in the national papers, and your own page in sticker albums. We completed our Merlin pocket-size album set in October - how Alex Rae was not featured is beyond us. It is good to see he is in the FA Premier League Official Sticker Collection '04 (autograph edition). He's No569 but, with Euro 2004 looming, we might have to hold fire on collecting this lot.

On page 122 of it is a clock showing when Wolves scored their goals in 2002-03. By far their most productive time was the final 15 minutes. Miller's sweet half volley

Alex Rae: "I've been on the wagon since I left the clinic and it's been going pretty well. I've got that time behind me." Picture courtesy of Shaun Fellows/newsteam.co.uk.

against Liverpool came just as the board for added time went up. Rae himself has come up with some late strikes: the killer at Reading in the play-off semi-final second leg, the face-saver at Kidderminster, what looked like a winner against Blackburn Rovers. "Timing's everything, isn't it?" he says. "It just shows the importance of keeping going. I've noticed that a lot of goals are scored late and, against Liverpool, that steely determination never to give up has nicked us a point. When we're losing, I can afford to throw a bit of caution to the wind and move forward more."

Wolves have also been stung late on. Rae scored what most describe as the goal of his life - certainly *The Premiership's* September goal of the month - away to Bolton Wanderers. After three early pastings, Wolves' fortunes looked set to turn when Rae, who had just netted in a Carling Cup win over Darlington, thundered a 30-yard volley into the top corner. But Kevin Davies equalised near the end. Six months in, Wolves still seek their first away win. "That Bolton one choked us," Rae admits. "We were fighting for our lives and to concede so late was painful. They were just humping the ball in the box and it seemed we had weathered the pressure.

"My goal was one of those that either goes into the net or Row Z. Where's it rank in my career? Around 50th or 60th?" He laughs. "I've scored a lot of good goals over the years but that was a sweet strike. I got an identical one for Falkirk when I was 18. I'll never forget it because a guy came up to me in a pub in Glasgow seven years later and said: 'I was there when you scored the best goal of your career.' By this time, I'd scored plenty for Millwall, so I asked which he meant. He said: 'For Falkirk against Clyde.' I said: 'Why, were you there?' And he replied: 'I was the goalie.'"

His mention of a hostelry is as far as we go for now on what is almost a previous existence for Alex Rae. He has been clean for five years and, while he does not ban the subject of his recovery from alcoholism, he has tired of it. We have been here before.

February 20, 2002: The press office, Molineux

W hen Rae and I previously met, on a day he was suspended but Wolves remained on course for the promotion-that-never-was by beating Bradford City, he had reluctantly allowed me to raise the issue. His chaotic past was the remit for a piece I was doing for *The Times Football Handbook* at a time some Leeds United players were on trial for drunken behaviour. Rae had become as famous for his spell alongside Paul Gascoigne in the Priory as for his sterling, immensely popular efforts for Sunderland.

"I've been on the wagon since I left the clinic three and a half years ago," he said as he sat in his baseball cap at John Hendley's desk just after Molineux breathed a collective sigh of relief at Dean Sturridge's two late goals. "That time's behind me and the fact things are going well on and off the park should tell people all they need to know. I recall senior players saying: 'Take it easy.' But you need to be willing to listen. I sure wasn't. I thought I knew more than the next guy and came well unstuck. Players are guided a lot better now. Look at the Man United boys who have come through to provide the core of the England team. The backing they have from their club is second to none. You rarely see them in trouble. There's a lot more support, with psychologists and nutritionists. The game has moved on." Echoes of Paul Cook's words...

Rae returned to the Priory for a different sort of help in May, 2000. "I got sent off for Sunderland against Tottenham for elbowing Ginola two minutes from the end of the season. I got a four-match ban for the following season. It was stupid, destructive behaviour and I realised I had problems with my aggression. I went back to get an understanding of why I was lashing out."

Rae, a born-and-bred Rangers fan, who started his career at Ibrox before moving to Falkirk via a non-league side called Bishopbriggs, was groomed in an environment where aggression was the norm. "It was lash out first, ask questions later, because of a fear of getting hurt. It was quite rough in the east end of Glasgow and you've got to be able to handle yourself, especially as a kid playing football. You have to sand-dance. There aren't many tanna' ball players left in Glasgow. You had to be wired in, always, otherwise you were dead. It's like the dressing-room, a very tough place to grow up. Through getting an understanding of this fear, it doesn't have the same control over me. Don't get me wrong: there are still times I'm going to lose it but it becomes more of a controllable problem."

While there is a serenity about Rae, there's no sanctimony. He shudders at the cliché of a reformed character preaching to younger miscreants. He wants to leave the old image behind and, although he would help anyone in need, he does not publicise his availability. Fans have always loved his bellicose nature, his goals, his style on the park and his approachability off it. "He was our midfield engine, like Timmy Cahill now," said Paul Welch, chairman of the Millwall Supporters' Club. "He was a loveable rogue in a team containing Terry Hurlock and Keith Stevens. We're going back ten years and there was a drink culture among players then. Meeting him, you didn't think: 'He's getting a drink problem.' You'd just think he was one of the lads. He'd have a laugh and buy you a drink back."

Paul Kinsella, editor of the *Lion Roars* fanzine, added: "His last three games for us sum him up. We were top of Division One in 1995-96 yet got relegated. Alex was sent off against Oldham, scored twice against Stoke then, when we needed to beat Ipswich to stay up, we drew 0-0 when he was suspended. All we needed was his goals. He'd certainly be in most fans' all-time Millwall XI."

They cherished him at Sunderland, too. He was "a cult hero" to their fanzine, *A Love Supreme,* while Richard Hakin, author of *A Sunderland Football Odyssey*, said: "Lacking Alex's bite in midfield has cost us dear. His time at the club was certainly eventful. The battles with the booze and his temper cost him more than a few games, yet last season [2000-01] he seemed to mature and finally came good, playing some of the best football of his life, with talk that he might make the Scotland squad. Very much a man of the people, his do-or-die style made him a Mackem favourite, although

I think he had to curtail his public appearances after conquering his booze demons. He turned up among our supporters at Anfield and was instantly hailed with a rendition of his old chant."

Rae's first season at Wolves, 2001-02, peaked with a run of high-scoring victories in February that made promotion appear a formality. "I really enjoyed my time with Sunderland," he said then. "The Premiership's the place to be. You're going to big grounds and you're up against World Cup winners every other week. It doesn't get any better. I'm desperate to get back. I don't want to be sat here in the summer with regrets."

Back to the future, I remind Rae of his words as we chat in the tennis club at Newbridge, with promotion finally won, Manchester United beaten, the survival effort boosted. He has a sense of perspective, perhaps borne of the troubles he has been through; maybe aided by Alexandra's arrival. There is more to him than meets either the eye or the page. He likes to conduct himself with consideration for others.

I wonder if he felt Wolves were due for a fall in 2002, whether he assessed West Bromwich Albion would finish stronger or whether he suspected complacency had seeped into the camp, with talk of expanding Molineux to meet Premiership demands, even rumours of a squad holiday in the Bahamas. "I just know football has a history of teams coming back," he says. "In February, you can't say: 'We've won promotion.' It's hard to say why it went wrong. You can go round in circles but you just have to accept it." Perhaps Wolves peaked too soon and ran on empty after Easter. Rae and Colin Cameron, both attack-minded midfielders, had so much space behind them in the final games when, ideally, one might have been replaced by a defensive enforcer.

"There was never any one point when I thought we'd blown it," he recalls. "You go into every game thinking you're going to win but we had a tough run-in: Burnley, Manchester City, Norwich City, Millwall away on a Friday night." I talk of Dean Sturridge hitting the post near the end at The New Den. "Aye, he did," Rae acknowledges. "I missed a chance as well.

"It was obviously disappointing because we had such a lead and promotion was in our hands." Weren't Wolves 11 points clear of Albion late on? I recall swapping text messages with Simon, frantically trying to agree which game we should meet at for the party. "When you throw it away like that, it's always a bitter pill to swallow. It was a difficult summer. I went away to Portugal, played a bit of golf, but it was hard, the thought of going back to all these grounds that you'd been trying to get away from.

"I think we came back bigger and stronger for the experience, though. We showed character when a lot of teams would have suffered hangovers. A group of people grew up a bit and the benefit is seen now

RAE OF HOPE

because we've all got our sleeves rolled up." There: if we'd beaten Millwall, we might not have had this win over Manchester United.

Rae's hollow consolation that spring was his Wolves player of the year award. Yet, as the promotion dream finally unfolded, he was something of a fall-guy. After the team's poor run towards Christmas, he lost his place as Cameron and Paul Ince became the midfield axis. "When Incey came here, I knew there were only two spots available. I'd just picked up the award, though, so I never thought my place might be in jeopardy. But it shows you can never get complacent. If there's one thing I've learned from my years in the game, it is that you're guaranteed nothing."

Rae had scored twice in a 4-1 win away to Derby County, fresh out of the Premiership, to go top of the division in August but, as Mark Kennedy and Cameron regained full fitness and Wolves failed to maintain top gear, he dipped out. "To be honest, I found it difficult," he says. "There's no getting away from it. It was hard to take and I went to see the gaffer. But it's not just about one player. There's a bigger picture and you have to understand the manager's point of view - and the team's."

When he deputised for Ince in a crucial win at Reading in March, just after the disappointment of not being selected for the FA Cup quarter-final at Southampton, Rae was inspirational as the anchor-man. When Wolves returned to the Madejski Stadium, protecting a fragile single-goal lead, for the second leg of the play-off semi-final, he came up trumps in spectacular fashion, scoring the clinching goal nine minutes from time. Was that the night we struck up the loudest rendition of: 'Alex Rae, Alex Rae, Alex, Alex Rae, he's got no hair, but he don't care, Alex, Alex Rae?'

"It was critical because they had us on the back foot that night, just as they'd been ahead at our place before we got a couple of quick goals to turn the tie on its head," Rae recalls. "Matt Murray had a nervy night, they hit the post early on but, once we got our goal, it was great. There was a Reading supporter having a go at Incey when we were doing our warm-up and that's why, when we celebrated, we went over to remind our friend of what he'd said. The finish wasn't too bad. It was nice and came at the right time because it killed the game a little bit."

It is one of my favourite goals of recent years, partly because of the style with which Rae, on as a substitute, ran into space, swivelled and shot home,

Strength in adversity: Rae says Wolves responded this time when the going got tough

Wolves silently hunting end to 16 years of play-off failure

By Peter Lansley

partly because of the occasion. Finally, Wolves had gone beyond the semi-final and, at the fourth attempt, were in the First Division showpiece game. Reading was my old backyard, and Si and I were behind that very goal, free to go mental with Wolves' fans. It was a delirium we had not experienced since the late '80s. Travelling back to the curry house with Reading fans among my old neighbours was a curious affair but Graham, Ken, Robert, Mark and Gary were good sports. Rick and Doug, neutrals, knew what it all meant to us. Russell, however, couldn't face it. He rang in with toothache.

Rae reckons he made his presence felt in the final, although he was a non-playing substitute. "I was fighting Phil Jagielka for the ball when it came out for a throw-in," he says, laughing. "The referee had to have a word. That was my contribution. Of course you want to play in these games but I'm old enough and wise enough to know there's more at stake than just me. We only lost three games in 28 from the turn of the year, so I knew the team was picking itself. I couldn't have any grievance with the gaffer. What could I say? 'We've only won 3-0 this week, give me a game.'

"I had to bite the bullet. It wasn't easy because I'm very passionate about what I do. I didn't see any point arguing the toss, so I bit my tongue, went about my business and I've had chance enough this season." And taken it, with both hands. Scotland, Blackburn Rovers and Rangers have all taken note. When Graeme Souness, who showed the teenage Rae the door at Ibrox, now talks about needing players at Blackburn who are willing to get hurt blocking a ball, you can imagine he is thinking

Alex Rae beats his man in Wolves' home game against Sheffield United early in their promotion season. He missed out on facing the same opponents in the play-off final.

about Rae. "I'm fighting for my future here, because my contract's up in the summer. It's important to try and do everything right," Rae says. Would he want to stay to the end at Molineux? "Without a doubt, why not? If things are right, I'll carry on. Incey's been an inspiration for me and I'd like to continue playing as long as possible."

Wolves fans hope he stays. No three-season spell has been as enthralling as this since Steve Bull came on the scene. Rae has played a major role. Even if he disappears over the horizon and into the sunset, though, he has done his bit and more for this club.

May 11, 2004: Wolves' training ground, Newbridge, Tettenhall

Rae approaches me in the week I am in Tettenhall to meet Dave Jones and asks if *The Times* would be willing to do a piece before he left for Rangers. "It's signed and sealed, I'm going to meet Alex McLeish tomorrow after my grandmother's funeral but don't print it until next week. It's a dream come true. But there's a guy at Wolves who's been brilliant and deserves a lot of credit for the way our heads are still held so high." Jeremy, my boss, is keen on the idea, so I agree to meet Rae before his final Wolves game. In training, primarily for the reserves, he throws himself into challenges like there is no tomorrow, still less a two-year Rangers deal on the table.

No wonder he has such admiration from the manager he is leaving behind. "Alex does certain things to keep himself in check because of his history and that's all credit to him," Jones tells me over a cup of tea. "He's had to re-educate himself after all the problems he had. He set up his own rehabilitation. We've benefited from that and he's earned his contract at Rangers. I don't think anyone can have any complaints over what we paid for him or the service he's given us. He certainly goes with my blessing. He's been a fantastic servant. There was a good battle between him and Colin Cameron for the shirt last year, with Cams winning it at the death. Alex is a very likeable person. I've become friendly with him outside football. We play golf together - he's crap, mind - with Peter Baker and Jeremy Nicholls, the professionals round these parts. The friendships Alex has made with everyone at this club are testament to him as a person."

Winning your own psychological battles helps teams win theirs. Two days earlier at St James's Park, there was a sad Geordie up in the gods - Alf Garnett in black and white stripes - who could not understand why Wolves supporters were so damned jolly. His side, on the verge of missing out on the Champions League, had just lost a UEFA Cup semi-final. We were about to have our relegation confirmed yet our singing lifted the rafters and our manic Mexican Wave only bumped to a miserable halt every time it reached the Newcastle United seats. Alf eventually stood up and danced a jig while sticking his fingers in his mouth and stretching the corners to ape the demented smile he could see on every Black Country face.

Newcastle were leading at this stage but Rae, on as a substitute in his penultimate Wolves game, and co picked up the baton of positivity flowing down from the seats, and the equaliser was deserved. Talent, organisation and determination help but, without wishing to sound too much like a scout leader or a social worker, I find it true that a smile begets a smile. Positive thinking can take a team a hell of a long way.

May 15, 2004: Back in the press office, Molineux

"It's partly down to the players," Rae says, two hours before the home game with Tottenham Hotspur, ushering Tom, Joe, Shaun the snapper and me into a vacant office. "It's admirable that, when you're almost relegated, with games to go, you still show depth of character. That's what fans appreciate. No-one could question the effort we've put in."

Jones has worked hard on eradicating a state of mind he coined 'Wolfism' - 'It's bound to go wrong sooner or later, it always does for us' is the gist of it - but Rae adds that a seldom-seen character behind the scenes has contributed to the feel-good factor. Tim O'Brien is a psychologist who worked with Birmingham City in their promotion season before making a low-profile transfer to Molineux. A 45-year-old with a PhD in psychology from the University of London, where he became principal tutor in emotional and behavioural needs, he spends half his working week with Wolves and freelances on a one-to-one basis with other professional sports people. Protecting clients' confidentiality means he does not speak publicly.

"He's amazing," Rae says. "What I've achieved, and how he's helped other players I speak to, is fantastic. It's not just football, it's all aspects of life. He comes here on Fridays and Saturdays before games and is on the phone if you want him."

Rae's performances and eight goals this season have earned him his dream move to Rangers, where, as a wild child, he was released at 17. Rae overcame enough demons in the 1990s to provide an entire study for a psychologist's PhD but O'Brien enjoys working with him. "Alex has dealt with Tim a lot," Jones says. "He's there if players need him. We don't force him on anyone; he probably deals with no more than 30 per cent of our players. He is a vital member of our off-field team but Alex feels the need to talk through a lot of things because of his past."

Rae's present and future also provide challenges. "I had a lot of fear to do with getting forward and getting goals," he explains. "As you grow older, getting from box to box becomes harder and I had this mental block about it. I literally didn't believe I could do it any more. So Tim brought some material in, broke down my record in recent seasons and we eradicated the fear. The day after we'd worked specifically on it, I scored two goals at Derby. It's about breaking down barriers."

It is true, however, that injuries take longer to heal with age. As Rae moved towards the end of his three-year deal with Wolves, his next move became a concern. "I've spoken to Tim in depth about contracts because the future was a big issue for me," he admits, expanding on our discussion four months ago. "There was a fear of getting injured, losing form, having nothing ahead of me. So we analysed it logically, looked at my injury record and realised it had been years since I'd had more than a minor injury.

"Tim has taken the whole squad, set up team meetings where we'd break down problems and help shape where we were headed. At its most basic, he was keeping us positive and that attitude has been a major factor even as we've gone down."

With that, we have reached 1.30pm, time for my boys to meet their grandparents for the afternoon while I work, and for Alex, who is to be named as runner-up to Henri Camara as Wolves' player of the year, to avoid being late. "I don't want you getting in trouble on my account," I say. "Don't worry about me," he says, laughing. "I can't get fined. I'm out the door on Monday."

Alex Rae

Born:	September 30, 1969, in Glasgow
Signed:	September, 2001
Wolves appearances:	119
Goals:	21
Left:	May, 2004
International recognition:	Scotland under-21 caps

January 2004

> It was not pretty but the manner in which Wolves survived the squalls and winds of Fratton Park to take a point off Portsmouth was a harbinger of brighter times ahead. Having your woodwork struck four times to avoid defeat might sound like luck but we'll take it; we've been on the other side of the story enough times. Look at the defeat away to Charlton Athletic when Jason Euell's goals both contained elements of fortune. The win over Manchester United, added to single points off Blackburn, Liverpool and Portsmouth, add up to a superb month, leaving Wolves one off the bottom but only three points off a cluster of more talented but less united teams in the potential safety spots.

George Berry

THE BEST AFRO IN THE BUSINESS

February 3, 2004: The Little Chef, Uttoxeter

E ven a cursory glance at the picture cover of the major 1980 hit single, *Wonderful Wolves,* will tell you there could only ever have been one lead singer from that line-up. With all due respect, it was not going to be Norman Bell, stomach ever so slightly bulging, nor Willie Carr, the diminutive ginger-topped Scot. Like Jimi Hendrix on a good hair day, it had to be George Berry.

"I was the front man because of the Afro," says Berry, now balding, bespectacled and somewhat stockier than in this team shot, snapped on a freezing winter's day 24 years ago. We did a bit of a promo session for the single and I had these big old-fashioned BBC cans on my ears, squashing my hair down, so you can imagine how ridiculous I looked, with my guitar, trying to give it large. Sorry, but this was Jimi Hendrix on a bad day." The song was released, in football's time-honoured tradition, to mark Wolverhampton Wanderers' achievement in reaching Wembley for that year's League Cup final. To say it was a huge success might be stretching the stricter definitions of veracity, unless you focus on very specific areas of Wolverhampton. But a generation on, having received a Wolves compilation CD for Christmas, Joe Lansley, aged four and three quarters, rates the song right up there with the best of The Beatles and Busted.

While the song has by and large been forgotten, Berry has not. "The hair keeps me in footballing memories," he acknowledges, ordering a hot chocolate in the road-side restaurant between our homes. "In that era, with the Jackson Five and everything, Afros were happening. It just so happened I had a great Afro and was one of very few black players playing. But a lot of the white boys had curly perms too - Alan Brazil,

130

Kevin Keegan, Bryan Robson, the boys at Liverpool - and we've been immortalised in a dodgy little book about footballers' worst hair cuts.

"Then there were the other boys at West Brom - Brendon Batson, Remi Moses, Laurie (Cunningham), bless him, though Cyrille (Regis) was more of a dry head. But mine was the biggest and the best. It was a huge thing. I did toy with having dreadlocks and put it in plain row over the summer holidays but some friends in Handsworth, true Rasta men, said it was a religious thing for them and, for me to do it for fashion, would have been disrespectful.

"The Afro was very heavy in winter when it rained and, if we were playing in snow, I'd look like a burnt matchstick. Black geezer, big Afro, white on top. It didn't affect my game at all and it was useful at the near post to obscure a forward's view from corners. But one thing's for sure: any mistake I made was swiftly identified." I mention a vague memory of the ball sailing over said hair in the FA Cup semi-final against Arsenal at Villa Park in 1979. "It did go over my head but I couldn't get it because it was a fantastic ball," Berry says in mitigation. "Alan Sunderland (who had left Wolves for Arsenal the previous season) went through to score and we lost 2-0.

"The best it ever looked was for the pre-season photo shoot but, to be fair, there were a lot with big hair in those days. Look at Phil Parkes - hello? Alan Sunderland? Geoff Palmer?" We are studying a team photo from the start of 1977-78, the summer after Berry had made his first-team debut at home to Chelsea the day Wolves clinched the Second Division title. It was also Frank Munro's last game at Molineux.

"That was a massive game for me," Berry, who had been captain of an impressive youth team also containing Martin Patching and Bob Hazell, said. "I played alongside Frank, who was a fantastic footballer. He caused me a lot of heartache, did Frank, because he was so good. His timing, his heading, his skill, his awareness - he would go to head a ball, and then duck and leave it for the goalkeeper. I looked at him and tried to emulate him because I thought he was brilliant. Trouble is, there are certain things that some people can do and others can't. So if I went to dribble out of my own penalty area, like he used to, guess what: I'd get caught, 1-0.

"I learned very quickly that you have to be your own man. Do what you're good at and enjoy other people's talents. He was a good man to me as well, Frank was, took care of me when I was young, as did the likes of John McAlle and Derek Parkin. I used to clean Frank's and Derek's boots when I was a baby and, at Christmas, I'd get a fiver or tenner off them. That was like my week's wages when I was an apprentice.

"When you got to train with them, you'd pick up lots of wisdom and I'd try to take it on board. Players like John Richards were fantastic professionals, the way they trained and conducted themselves. I'd look at the first-team players and try to emulate them. I was good under pressure. If I was busy, I was a good player. If we had nothing to do, if we were battering teams, I'd have a problem with concentration."

This ties in with John Barnwell's assessment. Berry was player of the year in 1978-79 as Wolves staved off relegation after Barnwell succeeded Sammy Chung as manager. "I liked George," Barnwell recalls. "He could head it, tackle, he was quick, he'd listen to what you said. He'd have three tremendous games - heading, tackling, passing - and then have one game overplaying it, taking risks in bad areas and that's when Richie (Barker, the assistant manager) would come in and get on his case. I'd say: 'Don't worry, George, I pick the team.' Later on, George responded well to Emlyn Hughes' arrival. I said to Emlyn: 'Make sure you can see George's number, right in front of you, so you control him.' The pair of them were good for us."

"Barny was good in training," Berry recalls. "Richie was a massive influence on my career: straight, honest and, if anything, lacking diplomacy. He wouldn't care about personalities. He'd say you were crap if you were, never mind who you were. Barny had loads of stories and would float in and around training and you could have a good laugh with him. They played good cop, bad cop pretty well. John was good but we lost him for about eight months. He had a car crash and Richie basically took over."

That was the season Wolves reached the Villa Park semi-final. "They didn't think I'd survive," Barnwell recalls. "I signed Emlyn Hughes when I had no hair; I covered my head with a woolly Wolves hat. I'd had three meetings with Roy McFarland (at Derby County) but, when he couldn't make his mind up, I went for Emlyn. It turned out to be a major move for us. We had George Berry and Bob Hazell there, both young boys, at relatively early stages in their careers, so the combination wasn't ideal. When Tommy Docherty (at Queens Park Rangers) offered me £300,000 for Bob, I took it."

Berry recalls that semi-final as a major opportunity missed. "We didn't play well," he recalls, "but Arsenal played crap as well. The occasion must have got to us. If we'd played as we had been doing, we'd have taken them because Arsenal had a bad day at the office and that was the worst thing. I didn't watch the final. I'd rather have got knocked out in the third round than lose at the last hurdle like that. I've seen the goals since (Sunderland, who had big hair of his own, went on to score the Wembley winner against Manchester United in a thrilling finale) but I couldn't watch at the time."

On a personal level, Hazell's departure to London was a disappointment for Berry. "We were like brothers," Berry says. "We lived together, we married a pair of cousins. He was my main man." The two had grown up together and endured some trying times

Brian Greenhoff appears from behind George Berry's hair in pursuit of the ball in Manchester United's 2-1 defeat at Molineux in April, 1978.

when racism was far more prevalent than today. "We were a great partnership as well as best mates off the pitch. We were the only black defensive pairing in the top flight of English football and we did take that on board, by the way."

Berry, born in Germany of a Welsh mother and a Jamaican father, is proud of his disparate heritage. He was as honoured as could be to become an international, making his Wales debut against Germany in 1979. Having spent his first years in Mountain Ash, north of Cardiff, where his mother had 12 siblings, he had Welsh relations up to his ears. Later, the family - George was the youngest of three children - moved to Blackpool, where Berry acquired his Lancashire accent. At the same time, Barry, his father, was a cricket-loving West Indian. "My mum's white and my dad's black," he says, "but I've never been called a white bastard. I've never gone down the route of saying I'm half-white. I've never been acknowledged as being white at any level. I wasn't bothered."

Some neighbours in Wolverhampton were concerned, however. Racism provided an unsettling backdrop as Hazell, from Handsworth, Birmingham, and Berry endeavoured to find a base from which to launch their careers. "We had problems with digs because we were black," Berry explains. "We had a little old landlady, me and Bob, in Fordhouses, but she was getting so much stick from the neighbours because she was looking after a couple of young blacks. I went back there one day and the old dear was sitting there, crying. I thought: 'This isn't fair, we can't live here.' We had our own cultural needs, as black kids, we liked reggae and that, so it was difficult.

"We moved to Wednesfield and then on to the Tettenhall Road when the landladies were getting too much grief. Wolves weren't happy. They wanted you with a family, at home, having your cocoa, which I can understand. So we went back to Birmingham to live with Bob's parents but they weren't happy with that either, us living that far from the club. It was a problem. Eventually, what we did, once we got in the first team and could afford it, was buy our own house."

Never mind the colour of his skin, Berry, in the meantime, acquired an extra layer. He backed down for no-one; his tribulations were character-building. "They were great days as well," he recalls. "We used to go to Handsworth Park on a Sunday. If they ever knew what we got up to… but we were sensible kids. On a Sunday, in the summer, it was like being in the Caribbean. There was music, food, people cooking, playing drums, football, the dreads were there, it was fantastic. No problems, no pressure, just: 'How are you?'

"They'd kick our ass in the games, mind. They didn't give any quarter because we were young professional footballers, you were playing with the lads. They didn't say: 'We'd better go careful on these boys, it's their livelihood.' So, in the end, we had to stop playing. Me and Bob had great times together. He was a year younger, a great athlete and he had a great temperament. We had a great relationship on the pitch. Talk about protecting your back. We played some good games together, like when we saw off Joe Jordan and beat Manchester United, but it was a partnership that was never allowed to flourish because Bob left and Emlyn came in.

"We played Leeds once and they wanted to kill us, the racists. It was terrible, let me tell you. Me and Bob were outside with about 50 skinheads wanting to take us. Our team-mates were getting on the bus but it wasn't cordoned off, like it is these days. To get on the bus, we'd have to walk through the Leeds fans. Me and Bob had got our Afro 'picks,' so Bob said: 'You see the big fucker there, I'll have him, you take the one next to him. Once we've taken them, the rest will run.' It didn't happen, because my brother appeared and stepped in. 'Excuse me, you'll have to get through me to get to them,' he said. So we got on the coach. Our team-mates are saying: 'Jeeze, that was a bit hairy, wasn't it?' Me and Bob were thinking: 'It wouldn't have been quite so hairy if you'd stood with us.' People have to understand there were some serious tensions flying around in those days."

Much of the racism the black players endured in the 1970s seems to have been conditioned, a reflex verbal reaction from supporters with under-developed brain cells - Ron Atkinson without the microphone - trying to intimidate opposition players. "We were playing Albion away and I was picking up Cyrille Regis at the near post," Berry recalls. "A home fan in the Birmingham Road End shouted: 'You black bastard.' I looked at Cyrille and said: 'Is he talking to you or me?' That summed up how ridiculous it was at that time. But it motivated me as well.

"If anyone walked along the street and said that, I'd have to have them. It would obviously mean they wanted to fight me. But because it's in a football ground and I'm on a football pitch, what gives him the right to abuse me? Because he's paid five quid to get in? Hello? If he wants to say I'm crap, fair enough. But to say I'm black and crap, he's stepped beyond a certain line. You draw on it, though, don't you, and it makes you stronger. If opposition fans are slagging me, I must be doing my job right. So the more they slagged me, the more I loved it. It's about positive and negative energy when you're out there. You can be negative, not want the ball, hide. But, if I had one of their pretty boys crumpled on the floor, I'd say: 'Get up you tart.' It was a gladiatorial thing."

Berry admits there were times, hardly surprisingly, when the negative energy got the better of him. He was not only racially abused by opposing players and opposing fans, but by his own. "We played Watford at home in the FA Cup fifth round, four days after we'd won through to Wembley in the League Cup semi-final, and we lost 3-0," he says. "At the end of the game, we're beaten, when I get the ball and scuff my clearance straight to Luther Blissett, who blasts it into the top corner for the final goal. Our fans in the paddock are giving me racial dogs' abuse. There isn't time to kick off again and, as I'm coming off the pitch, this fan's giving it something large: 'You black fucker, you coon.' All his mates are laughing their heads off.

"I was passionate about my football, passionate about playing for Wolves, about having that shirt and I am gutted at this point. I've just been knocked out the Cup, just given a goal away and I think: 'I'm not having this,' so I go back up the track and ask the fan what he said. He says: 'You heard,' so I jump into the crowd and start beating him up. The police dragged us out and we were both arrested."

Working at the Professional Footballers' Association, Berry has seen the game's attitude to racism improve. "The union's massive on it," he says. "They've worked so hard to eradicate it. You get a lot less these days, with more black players and more cultures in the game, and increased awareness, but even what there is tends to be more covered up. Now, it's not acceptable and our top players are prepared to stand up and say: 'Excuse me, what are you doing?' In our day, we were in a serious minority. I reckon we'll have the same problems when Asians, third generation, start coming into the game.

"So we had to deal with the problem indoors, on the pitch, from the terraces and even in the dressing-room." In the main, the problem Berry perceived from his own team-mates was a lack of support. "If an opponent said: 'You black bastard,' it would be me and Bob who had to deal with it. It wouldn't be our team-mates coming over, saying: 'You're out of order, leave it.'

"We'd have to say something to our own team-mates if they were giving it out to other teams' black players, to point out it wasn't acceptable. If someone might have said to Remi Moses, for instance: 'You black bastard,' we'd say: 'Hang on, you're our team-mate, we need to die for each other out here, don't do it.' The white lads wouldn't know any different. How would they know they weren't being supportive, when it was new to them? It was a question of educating your team-mates, and we did all right.

"You're being told: 'You black bastard, get back to where you come from. Get back in the monkey house. Want some bananas?' We got the lot. Then you had a problem within your own team. In the dressing-room, racist jokes were an accepted part of the banter and they didn't mean anything by it but, for us, it was hard to take. Donald Gardner, a black lad at Wolves in the mid-70s, used to put up with it but me and Bob were more radical and we didn't like it.

"When you're an apprentice, you tend to get slaughtered by the pros as part of the banter. When you stand up for yourself, you get told you're arrogant. When you got in the first team, you were more on a level and, if something went too far, you'd say: 'Do it again and I'll break your face.' This made people think we had massive chips on our shoulders, were arrogant. We weren't actually. We were looking after ourselves.

"What they said behind our backs, I don't know. I'm not saying we could eradicate racism but they stopped saying it to our faces after one incident. I was at a pre-match meal when someone said: 'Pass the niggers,' as in niggers' lips, equals chips. 'Hello? Not funny,' I replied. 'I want you to say it again and we'll see how funny it is.' I won't mention names but the fact is, it happened. The personalities aren't the important thing, it's the principle of what was going on. Not that this one scene is that important and our relationship got better from that day on, so not a problem. But it was there. That is what we had to put up with. I felt we were doing our job in speaking up, paving the way for the next generation."

By the time Wolves reached Wembley, Berry was an established top-flight player. I used to deliver the *Ad News* to his house on the corner of Wood Road, up from the Shoulder of Mutton in Tettenhall Wood. As well as his Wales caps, his player of the year award, Karl-Heinz Rummenigge's shirt and a kit deal with Adidas, he traded the red Cortina all the first-team squad had for a BMW after Wolves won the League Cup. But the best day of his footballing life turned into a nightmare.

"Words can't explain how good it felt to win at Wembley but it has ended up a bitter-sweet memory," Berry says calmly, issuing no warning of the personal tragedy he is about to recall. "My Dad died on the night we won the cup. We went away on the Thursday, and on the Friday, apparently, he got rushed into hospital. But my family decided not to tell me. He died at about 8pm on the Saturday, three hours after I'd been cavorting around Wembley. They didn't tell me that whole weekend and, later, I was so angry. I had a massive guilt feeling about having so much fun when my Dad was dying, so I had to go through that mourning process coping with extra guilt.

"I wouldn't have played if I had known. They all said: 'Your Dad would have wanted you to play.' But the bottom line is it's your Dad, you only get one. Wembley? Dad, on his death bed? Hello? Drop Wembley, can do that another time, you think. I'd rather have been with my father, by his side as he was dying, than on any football pitch in the world. A cup final's nothing in comparison. I didn't find out until the Monday morning. All my family were scheduled to be at Wembley and, as far as I was

George Berry slides the ball away from Garry Birtles and out of danger in the League Cup final of 1980. But personal tragedy was just round the corner for the defender.

concerned when I came out on to the pitch, they were. But they weren't. With my eyesight (Berry played with contact lenses), I couldn't have spotted them in the crowd anyway. When I was 18, I thought my Dad was the stupidest man on this earth. By the time I was 21, I thought: 'Hello, he's learned a great deal in those three years.' In reality, of course, I was doing my own growing up."

Berry concurs with the professionals' adage that cup finals in the early stages of a career can quickly pass by. "The one thing I remember about Wembley was being inside the tunnel, and you could hear the 'clatter clatter' of studs on concrete as everyone jumped up and down, trying to deal with their nerves. Then it all goes quiet, then you walk up the tunnel, out, and the noise, as you made that final step into the daylight, was ear-shattering. I looked around and thought: 'Am I the luckiest man in the world, ever?'"

Wolves beat Nottingham Forest, the European champions, 1-0 in a poor game, Andy Gray scoring as David Needham, the defender, and Peter Shilton, the England goalkeeper, failed to deal with Peter Daniel's long ball. "The game is a blur, until after the final whistle, when I remember nearly raping Emlyn on the pitch," Berry says. "It felt surreal afterwards, going up the steps, going into the changing-room. They were on a hat-trick of League Cups, Forest, and I went and knocked on their door and asked if I could change shirts with Viv Anderson. Talk about bad timing but Cloughie (Brian Clough, their manager) was brilliant.

"The only downer at the time was they dragged us back from London to have a party 150 yards from my home, at the Mount Hotel. In the dressing-room at Wembley, everything was high, high, high and then they drove us three hours up the road to celebrate and that killed the atmosphere. The Sunday felt good, though, as we went through the streets on an open-top bus showing off the cup." My own Dad touched the cup that day as Barnwell, coming out of the Mount, grabbed it nervously to his chest as we approached him. Berry did not know at that moment that his Dad had passed away. No wonder his joy was so shattered the next day, although imagine the dilemma in which his family found themselves.

Within two years, Wolves nearly folded. Berry, having played 56 games in the season Barnwell and Barker's team won the League Cup and finished sixth to earn their qualification for a UEFA Cup adventure that lasted only one round, found his place under threat in 1980-81. Colin Brazier, Rafael Villazan and John McAlle shared the duties with him and Hughes and, as the latter departed, Joe Gallagher, acquired from Birmingham City for £400,000, and Bob Coy, graduating from the reserves, arrived the following season. That was the year Wolves were relegated and Berry, out of contract, was the cheaper option to move on as the club fell into receivership.

"Ian Greaves, who succeeded Barnwell, said he was doing me a favour in letting me go. I said: 'If that's a favour, what do you do for bad?' I was out of work for five days because Richie Barker took me to Stoke, where Derek Parkin had just gone. I loved Wolves. It was my life. Leaving them was the last thing on my mind. It felt like my world was coming to an end. I was devastated, but I couldn't grow up any more after that. I was only 24 but I'd been at Molineux since I was a baby. I'd already had

Berry (centre), Geoff Palmer and Uruguay-born No6 Rafael Villazan fail to prevent Martin Henderson scoring in Wolves' defeat away to Leicester City in October, 1980.

a career. I'd captained the youth team, got in the first team young, had great games, been player of the year, won a cup at Wembley, played for my country. I thought: 'What a life I've got here!' But at the end of my contract, in May, 1982, I was called in and I was gone.

"I was on £400 a week, having come up through the ranks, and Joe Gallagher, a big-name signing, was on a great contract. Ian Greaves said: 'I'd love to have you in my team but I've got to let you go because your contract's up. We don't have to pay you up and we're bankrupt.' I thought: 'Do I care? You're ending my relationship with the club I love. Don't wrap it up as a favour.'"

Berry went on to play for eight years with Stoke, where he was granted an early testimonial. He also faced England at Wembley before playing out his career with Peterborough United, Preston North End, Aldershot and, until 1996 at the age of 38, Stafford Rangers. Before he left league football for Stafford, he endured life with another club dicing with extinction - and, this time, not coming out the other side.

"I was there in London the day they shut the doors on Aldershot," he recalls. "That shows how a team can pull together with spirit, even though the players were being shafted by the club. I was the PFA rep and, though we never used to train together, we would never let anyone say it was the players who brought the club down. The club were gagging for us not to show up for a game, so we could be thrown out for not fulfilling our fixtures.

"I trained at Stoke, who were great for me, and, when we turned up for games, the camaraderie was fantastic. We used to go to matches in our cars, three or four of us in each, and we'd get to the car park and they'd say: 'What are you doing here?' And we'd say: 'We're the players, can we come in please?' They were good times. We had whip-rounds from fans to help pay for our petrol and I remember the standing ovation we got from the Cardiff City supporters for the last ever game [on May 20, 1992]."

There, but for the grace of God, could have gone Wolves. As Aldershot Town rehabilitate in the Nationwide Conference a decade on, Wolves are fighting a brave and thrilling battle to stay in the Barclaycard Premiership. Worlds apart, Berry has lived in them both.

George Berry

Born:	November 19, 1957, in Rostrup, Germany
Signed:	July, 1973
Wolves appearances:	160
Goals:	6
Left:	June, 1982
International recognition:	5 senior Wales caps

The best and worst of Wolves this month: after giving it a damned good go against Arsenal, who were being held 1-1 at half-time before powering through to win 3-1, Wolves looked as if all their exertions had got the better of them at Elland Road three days later. Selecting Paul Jones in goal looks a mistake and Alex Rae and Colin Cameron were out-muscled as Leeds United won 4-1. Pride - and Paul Ince - were restored as Fulham were thrashed, honestly, 2-1, Carl Cort scoring his first goal for the club and a goalless draw away to Leicester City lifted us out of the relegation zone for 24 hallucinatory hours.

THE TIMES FEBRUARY 11 2004

Viduka crowns night for resurgent Leeds

FOOTBALL /

Dickov ruffles Wolves in stalemate

February 2004

Kenny Hibbitt

CHOCOLATE, WINE GUMS AND TWO PINTS OF BANKS'S

March 20, 2004: The directors' lounge, Villa Park

It had in one sense taken Kenny Hibbitt three decades to get to the Park Hall Hotel in the Goldthorn area of Wolverhampton but it was the four-hour trek from Gloucestershire that he was cursing. It was the 30th anniversary of Wolves' first League Cup triumph and Hibbitt had kindly arranged to meet for a chat before the function; not the first time we had tried to co-ordinate our diaries.

On this occasion, however, Pam Richards, wife of Wolves' other 1974 Wembley goalscorer, phoned me on my way from Leicester City to say Jane Hibbitt had called with a traffic flash. The M5 was blocked and Ken, who did not have my number, would not be able to make our tea-time tete-a-tete. This at least gave me an extra hour to polish up my latest piece for *The Times* on Leicester's La Manga scandal. Three players had allegedly been involved in a drunken night out on the club's mid-season break and their manager and team-mates had been fronting the press. Later, I would be hearing more alcohol-fuelled footballers' tales, if of a rather different tenor.

Hibbitt, introducing me to his wife, arrived an hour before the bash and we agreed to rearrange our interview. He was one of the first characters inked in for this book. We met on the streets of Cardiff on May 26 last year as he was going to the Millennium Stadium on media duties. I was floating around with Si and Dad, bumping into friends, wallowing in the fantastic atmosphere of the play-off final. It was the most momentous day in Wolves' history since Hibbitt and Richards scored in a 2-1 win over Manchester City in the days when sideburns were long and tracksuits lurid gold.

Kenny said he was happy to meet in the summer, no problem. By the time I saw him four months later at St Andrew's, where he was working as a match delegate for the Premier League, I'd started to appreciate how much work this tome involved. "When it suits, Pete, just give me a call," he said. I realised he was on duty at Villa Park early in the new year but left it too late to schedule a meeting. So when this reunion for the class of '74 cropped up, it seemed the most appropriate opportunity.

As it happened, the Legends in Sport people arranged a marvellous 'do' and the nostalgia flowed in direct proportion to the alcohol. Richards came up to shake hands and confirmed his availability to talk through his story. Frank Munro was there - "When's this book coming out then? How long's it taking you?" - Gary Pierce, Dave Wagstaffe, Mike Bailey, Alan Sunderland, Barry Powell, Geoff Palmer, Phil Parkes. Sadly, Derek Dougan was absent. Apparently, he had persuaded Derek Parkin and John McAlle against attending as the former players, he reckoned, were being fleeced. It was actually more a labour of love for the organisers, Wolves fans who allowed their hearts to get the better of their calculators.

It has been said that nostalgia is not what it used to be but it was marvellous, if rather surreal, to see these Wolves heroes of a past generation laughing together and lapping up the echo of adulation for their efforts at Wembley all those years ago. "We all drank champagne in the tunnel to calm our nerves before the match," Bailey, the

The class of '74 are reunited 30 years on. Back row (from left): Sunderland, Wagstaffe, Hibbitt, Powell, Parkes, Palmer, Pierce. Front row: Bailey, Munro, Richards.

captain, dared suggest. Richards nodded in vigorous confirmation. Are you sure? "It was a wonderful feeling," Hibbitt said, when he took the microphone in front of 400 diners after the showing of the first-half highlights on big screens. "Looking back, I can't really remember a great deal." Cue much laughter, before he added of his goal, a sliced volley that looped in to give Wolves the lead: "It took the three stripes off my Adidas boots. John Richards tried to get a foot on Geoff Palmer's cross, I took my eye off the ball for half a second, and it hit the right side of my boot, so Keith McRae, the goalie, was left grasping at air. I've just told Willie Carr I can't remember seeing the ball hitting the net. Just look at the sideburns on McRae!"

The video confirmed Pierce's brilliant performance. He stepped in, on his 23rd birthday, for the injured Parkes. Rising from the table he shared with Richards, Palmer, Sunderland, Powell and their partners, he was overcome with emotion. "There's one thing I've wanted to put right all my life," he said. "I was too young to say it then. Phil Parkes, man of the match at Tranmere when we drew in an early round, did as much as anyone to get us to Wembley. I don't think he ever got the recognition he should have. He played for years for Wolves and, the year before, he only let in one goal in the FA Cup - and that beat us in the semi-final."

Compere for the night was Paul Franks, who often commentates on Wolves games for BBC WM. The station used to create stomach-knotting tension in our Tettenhall Wood household if we were not at matches, sounding a distinctive alarm to herald a goal in any game involving a West Midlands club, thus doubling the pleasure-or-pain anticipation. Franks asked JR if being a Wembley match-winner was better than sex. "Well, at least I can say it lasted 90 minutes," was the reply.

Hibbitt, who was staying overnight at the hotel, asked if he and I could chat over breakfast but I had to struggle back through the snow to Derbyshire, school run and day job calling. It proved unfeasible to reconvene at Molineux before the Villa game we were both attending on the Sunday. Within a week, however, we were both back at Villa Park for the Barclaycard Premiership visit of Blackburn Rovers. Finally, the honour of an hour with Ken Hibbitt was booked in...

Ever the gentleman, he is bang on time and ushers me into the directors' lounge at 12.30pm, giving us enough time and coffee before our respective jobs require our attention. When Dad used to buy us black and white player photos 30 years ago, Mark used to get Hibbitt and I got Richards. But we idolised both. They became the team's main goalscorers and played with unstinting enthusiasm, skill and a youthful zip. Hibbitt, hair long and strangly, shirt soaked in perspiration, seemed to epitomise the age, as well, in his appearance. "Hibby, with his wispy moustache, would be surging through nine inches of mud, orange

ball glued to either foot, him going one way, his hair flying the other," Robert Plant, the Led Zeppelin lead singer and a Wolves nut, recalls. Hibbitt reasons: "I could pass the ball any distance, left or right foot, I got goals but, as much as anything, the fans liked me for my work-rate. They used to see the sweat on my shirt and know I cared." This was true for 16 years.

Today, Wolves are at Liverpool, the ground where, in Hibbitt's last season with the club, they recorded their last top-flight away win in January, 1984. Hibbitt was injured but Steve Mardenborough scored a fluky winning goal. This morning's *Daily Express* has captured the moment nicely and Hibbitt laughs. "I'd never won at Anfield, used to lose ten pounds in weight chasing those European champions around. Look at Steve's goal. It was off his shoulder, not a header, but you needed something like that to win there. You go through our line-up and, on paper, it doesn't look a side that's going to go to Anfield and get a result. Sadly, that great win wasn't enough to keep us up."

Hibbitt twice featured in League Cup final triumphs and played in three FA Cup semi-finals and a UEFA Cup final in his Wolves career. He scored a load of goals from midfield, 114 in all in 574 games and earned his testimonial in 1981-82, not to mention the label of the best English midfielder of his era not to win a senior cap. He also endured three relegations, bouncing back on each occasion to return to the top flight within 12 months, albeit by joining Coventry City in the last instance. So he knows how it feels for Wolves to suffer in the drop zone.

"It's very difficult to compare the situations of 1984 and 2004," he muses. "If you look at the quality in the Premiership now, there are world-class players all round. We had great players in the old top flight but it was before the mass influx of foreign talent. There was a lot going on behind the scenes at Wolves. The Bhattis were in charge and it looked like the club would fold. It wasn't a happy place to play football. It was the only time I can recall there being a bad spirit in the dressing-room. We were in dire straits and everyone was pointing the finger at each other. We were conscious of the club's predicament and it affects players, there's no doubt about it. Look at Leeds and the mess they've been in. We did get paid, fortunately, but it was a big disappointment to see a big club like Wolves going down so quickly. Then they fell through the Second and Third, and into the Fourth. It was the worst time in their history.

"My heart thinks they'll still stay up and my head says they might," Hibbitt says, turning his attentions to the current situation. "They definitely have a better chance to build up again (should they go down) than 20 years ago. The foundations have been laid. Financially, they're more secure and Dave Jones has more stability in his job, whereas managers in the early '80s were under pressure all the time. I don't think Dave will leave even if Wolves go down, and I think they could come straight back up.

"I like Alex Rae. He's a good midfielder who puts himself about and scores goals. Kenny Miller has had injury problems but he is a clever player. Paul Ince is probably in his last season but he's done fantastically, he and Denis Irwin. I think the centre of defence has been a bit iffy, although Paul Butler was our best player against Villa last week. You suffer in the Premiership for things you get away with in the First Division. Dave has found it difficult to plug that gap and just looking at Manchester United, going out of the title race and the Champions League since Rio Ferdinand was banned, shows how a manager likes to build from the back. It was a big ask for Joleon Lescott to survive in the Premiership but we haven't even had the chance to assess him. For Dave and Wolves, losing him for the entire year was a big disappointment.

"It was a great day at the Millennium Stadium and we were all celebrating but, within ten minutes of the final whistle, I thought: 'Now the problems start.' Even as Dave Jones was parading the trophy around the pitch, he'd have been thinking ahead. Maybe Wolves should have given him an extra £10million. I really don't think he's had the full backing of the board, so it's not been easy for him. Wolves have had to huff and puff even to be within a chance of staying up. But it's wonderful to see the likes of Man United and Liverpool back at Molineux."

Hibbitt's first game in the gold and black round-necked shirt - "that was the best kit, they should bring that one back" - was at Old Trafford, where he partnered Munro in the centre of midfield in a reserve match. A Yorkshire-based Wolves scout had tried to lure Terry Hibbitt to Molineux before he joined Don Revie's Leeds but his younger brother, having broken into Bradford Park Avenue's first team at 16, was offered the chance to sign in November, 1968.

Their father, Gilbert, had recently died of a heart attack, so it was a difficult time for Ken to leave home. "It was a question of whether to leave my sister (Valerie) and mother (Mary) by themselves. They said: 'Seeing you play in the First Division is what your father would have wanted.' So it was my Mum who made the final decision. She said: 'You go.' I got on the train and, at every stop, wanted to get off. But something kept me going. When it arrived in Wolverhampton, I hadn't got a clue where I was.

"We were brought up in back-to-back houses. We had no money, so, when someone wanted to pay £5,000 for me, it seemed like millions. Wolves paid £3,000 up front, another £1,000 was due on so many appearances and a final £1,000 was due if I won any sort of cap, which I did, for England under-23s. Then, within 48 hours of me joining, Ronnie Allen [Wolves' manager] had been sacked."

Hibbitt made one substitute's appearance under Bill McGarry in that modest 1968-69 campaign, in a home defeat by West Bromwich Albion in April, but had to wait almost 18 months for his full debut. Injury and some established talent lay ahead of him. "Other than Billy Wright, I think Mike Bailey must rank as the best captain Wolves ever had," he suggests. "He was a quality player, Mike was. When I first came down from Bradford at only 17, I played in a practice match for the reserves against the first team lads at the Castlecroft training ground. Mike battered me. I saw stars and he said: 'If you want my number, son, you're going to have to work for it.' He was quite right. To get past him, you would have to be pretty special. In the end, I took Peter

Knowles' shirt." Perhaps we should thank God for Ken Hibbitt remaining at Wolves for so long, then.

It was at Chelsea in September, 1970, that Hibbitt celebrated his inauguration to the top flight with a memorable goal. "I remember walking out the tunnel into a total downpour. We were soaked before kick-off. For my goal, Waggy took a corner, Peter Bonetti punched to the edge of the box and I drilled it back into the bottom corner."

Hibbitt became a regular in the No8 shirt, playing in midfield alongside Bailey and Jim McCalliog, and earned a Texaco Cup winner's medal ("it's gold, on a little wooden plaque") in a campaign when Wolves finished fourth in the First Division. The next season, as Richards graduated from the reserves to join Hibbitt in the team and the young duo scored their first European goals, McGarry's developing side reached the UEFA Cup final. In between the two legs against Tottenham Hotspur, Leeds came to Molineux needing to win to lift the championship and so complete the double. They were the team Hibbitt supported in childhood and all the rumours of attempted bribery made the Monday-night game even more intense. "I remember biting into a tackle with one of their players," Hibbitt recalls, "and he said: 'What are you doing? We're on 15 grand a man to win this game.' I said: 'We're on £40 a man and that counts to me.' It's fair to say we were well wound up after everything that had been going on.

Peter Knowles, whose Wolves jersey passed to Kenny Hibbitt after his retirement, finds roles reversed as he is sized up for a shirt for the latter's testimonial game in 1981.

"We had a great team spirit and camaraderie in those years. Bailey was a terrific captain, Waggy on the wing, Dougan up front, Richards coming through. Six or seven of us stayed there for many years and that helped maintain the bond. We finished equal third in Division One, had the FA Cup semi-final against Leeds in 1973 when we lost 1-0 after Richie's shot hit the post, we got to the UEFA Cup final. Then, after reaching the League Cup semi-final the year before, we won at Wembley in 1974.

"I was the same as every kid, I used to watch all the Wembley finals on telly and to play there, score the first goal and go on to win, was a dream. Mike was taking the mick about the champagne the other night. We just had juice in the dressing-room. Nervous? Listen, in the tunnel, you've got me, John Richards, Geoff Palmer, Alan Sunderland, Barry Powell. All kids. Opposite, you've got Francis Lee, Rodney Marsh, Mike Summerbee, Colin Bell, Denis Law. They've all played at Wembley so many times, it's like a home ground for them. There they are, tossing balls in the air, spinning them on their fingers; there's us, with our hands down our fronts. I have to say, it was frightening - but a nice frightening. As soon as we walked out and saw all the gold and black, we felt fine. We had some crap tracksuits on, mind. We looked like bananas."

The words style, '70s and Wolverhampton don't mingle easily. The long hair, sideburns and lurid tacksuits - sorry, tracksuits - were a combination to trouble fashion historians, if they can bear to look. This is where Slade came from, after all. There is a photo of Wolves' players lined up in luminous trousers leaning on equally orange VW Beetles. "We could have had them for a £5 a week," Hibbits confirms. "I didn't get one, though. I couldn't get my golf clubs in the boot.

"I remember seeing my boots by the No7 shirt when I walked in the dressing-room at Wembley an hour before the game. That was a nice moment, the first time I realised I was playing. Barry Powell, a great young player, had been in the side because I'd had thigh strains left, right and centre, and I felt for him. I was glad when he got on, when Waggy was snipered." Wagstaffe's twanging hamstring gave Powell his opportunity moments before Richards was due to be withdrawn; a moment of fate that allowed the young England forward to snatch the late winner and Wolves to lift their first major trophy in 14 years.

"I just wish my Dad had been there to see me," Hibbitt says. "That year, I played in the League Cup final and Terry played in the FA Cup final, when Newcastle United lost 3-0 to Liverpool. Dad would have been so proud."

Later that summer, after Dad had taken me, Mark and Dave (Simon, not yet two, had stayed with Mum at Auntie Beat's place) to Wembley, we got our first pair of season tickets to share. I was so excited about 1974-75, fresh from Wolves' triumph and watching the World Cup on television, yet, within a week of it starting, we went on holiday to Cornwall, just as Hibbitt scored all Wolves' goals in a 4-2 home win against against Newcastle. Dad, sort your diary out!

Hibbitt the younger always enjoyed playing against his brother and Newcastle,

Fashion victims 1974 style. Kenny Hibbitt (far right) receives a hug from Geoff Palmer in this happy team gathering as part of a VW Beetle promotion in the months following the club's first League Cup triumph.

who were the only club he considered leaving Wolves for in his hey-day. "That 4-2 was one of my favourites," he says. "I was brought up watching Bobby Charlton, scoring his goals in the 1966 World Cup and the 1968 European Cup final, and I was always told: 'If you don't shoot, you don't score.' He was my inspiration. I had a decent shot in both feet. Terry and I used to work for hours as kids on our weaker side.

"For the fourth goal against Newcastle, I remember cutting in from the right on my left foot, Iam McFaul in goal, and lashing it. Because I'd already got three, I could go for it. It went in the top corner. I just wish someone had it on video. Terry was so hurt but, as we walked off, he said: 'Well, if we had to get thrashed, I'm glad it was you that scored them all.' We had a fantastic relationship. There was a 1-1 draw at Molineux (February, 1973) when we both scored and one at St James's Park when my goal got us a replay on our way to the semis in 1979. Bill McGarry was at Newcastle by then and I had the opportunity to join him.

"I thought about it very seriously. I remember sitting on the staircase in Penn, and Bill ringing, asking if I was interested. 'If I could have had Terry on the left and you on the right, it would have given me a nice balance,' he said. It was tempting because I knew from Terry what great support they had but I knew deep down my life was with

Wolves, nobody else. I think Bill heard the tone in my voice. I was settled. Our daughter was six and our son two. It would have been a big upheaval."

Hibbitt was devastated in 1994 when Terry died in his mid-40s, from cancer of the pancreas. "Twelve months prior to that, we had a wonderful time at his son Richard's wedding," he says wistfully. "I remember him running around, we had a few drinks, argued about football. He was a wonderful person. I missed him most, more than my father really, because I'd known him longer. I didn't go to see him when he was ill. I wanted my memories from that wedding to remain freshest. His wife told me how he was lying on the sofa one day, looked up and said: 'I want my life back.' He was never to get it. I still miss him, of course I do. My family's important to me, like anyone's. Our son is the professional at Cotswold Edge Golf Club, where Jane and I play regularly. It's good we all play together. It's a sport you can play at whatever age."

The climax of Hibbitt's football career came under John Barnwell. Although he played for eight more years until a broken ankle forced him to retire, the 1980 return to Wembley was the highlight. He top-scored for Wolves in 1974-75, again two years later when Sammy Chung's team were promoted and was selected for an England B tour in 1978, only to be ruled out by another broken ankle, sustained when scoring in a 3-3 draw with Norwich City. "That was the closest I got to an England call-up after my one under-23 cap as a kid," he adds. "Although I was disappointed at the time, I'm not now. A lot of people said I should have got a full cap but that's their opinion. I was happy playing first-team football. I had to work tremendously hard to keep my place. I played over 550 times for Wolves and you have to work hard to do that."

Hibbitt posed his management team a tactical dilemma on the eve of the League Cup final against Nottingham Forest in 1980. Brian Clough's team were the European champions and in line for a hat-trick of triumphs in the League Cup. They had Trevor Francis up front with Garry Birtles, Martin O'Neill (the No7 with whom Hibbitt swapped shirts afterwards) on the right and the best left-winger of his day, John Robertson. "We sat up until 1am the night before deciding where Ken Hibbitt and Peter Daniel were going to play," Barnwell recalls. "We had to eliminate John Robertson, a tremendous player, if we were going to win. We had to cut out the service to him, so we marked him front and back, made him the meat in the sandwich, with Geoff Palmer sticking tight and Daniel in front of him.

"Richie [Barker] wanted Ken on Robertson, with Pete inside. But, because of the size of Wembley and the occasion, Ken at his age might not have lasted. I wanted Ken on the ball as much as possible and you're not going to get that with him out wide. Eventually, I said to Richie: 'That's it, Kenny's playing inside, Daniel out on the wing, doing the running.' Richie said: 'Just tell me one more time and I'll go to bed: why?' I said: 'Because I'm the friggin' manager, that's why.'" As fate would have it, Daniel played the pass from which Andy Gray, capitalising on Peter Shilton's ill-judged run, tapped in David Needham's back pass. "He doesn't miss those," Richards laughed.

"Tactically, we did very well," Gray said. "We changed Peter to the outside, where he wouldn't normally have been, and from where he knocked the ball in for me."

Watching the DVD now, I hear for the first time that the band, as the players emerge from the tunnel, played *Hi Ho Silver Lining* - an anthem at Molineux in recent years. The tracksuits are much more toned down, although the silkiness of the kit itself suggests another job for the style police. The Umbro diamond runs down the shirt sleeves and the side of the shorts.

"We got battered that day and came off picking the cup up again," Hibbitt admits. "Forest were the in-form team, we were underdogs, like six years before, and I recall we played with that red and white ball that made you dizzy as it turned over. It was another wonderful day. Andy scored the winner from three yards. He was lethal from that range. We had to work extremely hard, especially once we scored. I wouldn't say I had a great game with the ball but I worked my socks off for the cause, like all the players did. If anyone had not pulled his weight, we'd have got murdered."

Either side of that triumph, Wolves went close to reaching the FA Cup final. They lost 2-0 to Arsenal in the 1979 semi-final on the pitch just outside where we are now chatting, and 3-0 to Tottenham Hotspur in a replay at Highbury two years later after a controversial 2-2 draw at Hillsborough that brought Hibbitt's long-standing good name into question. With Wolves trailing in the 89th minute, he went down under a tackle from Glenn Hoddle, Clive Thomas awarding a penalty from which Carr scored.

"I didn't dive," Hibbitt says, laughing, when asked if anything stands out from that 1981 semi-final, in which he had scored the first equaliser. "Well, it wasn't a penalty, put it that way. From where Clive Thomas was standing, it looked a clumsy tackle by Glenn. If Clive had been in a different position, he'd have seen that Glenn played the ball out for a corner. When I was laid out on the floor with my socks down and I heard that huge roar, I thought: 'That's a big cheer for a corner.'

"I was the penalty-taker and that's the only time I've bottled a spot-kick. John

The tickets for two of Wolves' big days out.

Richards came over and said: 'Get up, it's a penalty, you're taking it.' I said: 'Get out, I'm not taking that one,' and Willie Carr stood up and planted it in."

At a time when Gerard Houllier, the Liverpool manager, and Michael Owen have revealed they have been receiving death threats, Hibbitt does not wish to elaborate on the nature of the hate mail he started receiving. But he had an unexpected opportunity to set the record straight a year later.

"I got a lot of letters from Tottenham supporters but I don't want to get too deep into that," he says. "After the game, John Barnwell told me not to talk to the national press but they picked up my quotes from the local media. In answer to a question, I said: 'I had to go down because I was knackered.' The locals asked if I realised it was the last minute and I replied that I thought it was pretty late on. By the time the nationals reported this exchange, my words had become: 'I had to go down because I knew it was the last minute.' We always got the *Express* and the headline next morning was: 'I dived.' I got letters from Spurs fans wishing I'd break a leg.

"In the warm-up at White Hart Lane the next year, I was knocking the ball to the keeper when I pretended to trip over. That got them laughing. After the game - I scored from a free-kick in a 6-1 thrashing - I was sitting on a wall waiting for the coach when about ten Tottenham fans came over. We talked it through and I explained that I hadn't dived, that the press had glued together the bits of quotes they needed to fit their story. One by one, the fans shook my hand and accepted I was telling the truth."

Hibbitt had always been known as one of the gentlemen of the game and would have loved to finish his playing career at Molineux. He left, though, in the summer of 1984, disappointed, at the age of 33, to be offered no more than a single-year contract by Jim Barron, the caretaker manager. "After 16 years, it was a big wrench to leave because I had a fantastic rapport with the supporters," he says.

Following two more years in the top flight with Coventry, he joined Bristol Rovers as a player-coach and it was when he came back to Molineux late in the 1988-89 season as part of the West Country club's backroom staff that he was left in no doubt as to his standing there.

There had been stories that, despite having left without a £5,000 loyalty bonus that was due to him, he had been willing to return and play for the club for nothing in their darkest hour. Graham Turner had by now turned Wolves around and they were on their way to the Third Division title when Hibbitt strode out along the touchline to take his place alongside Gerry Francis in the visitors' dug-out, and 20,913 supporters let him know they had not forgotten him. "Ken Hibb-itt, Ken Hibb-itt, Ken Hibb-itt," the old chant went around Molineux again. "I knew I might get a reasonable reception but it seemed the whole crowd were on their feet clapping," he says. "It was quite emotional. Ian Holloway was playing for Rovers that afternoon and he was choked by it all. The only disappointment is that there's no video of the game I'm aware of. I went round afterwards to say thank you to the Wolves fans and got a few choice words from some of them! Dennis Bailey scored and we won 1-0. It was the only home game Wolves lost all season."

Hibbitt became manager of Walsall the next year and we used to think it natural that, one day, he would return to take charge at Molineux. There was a lot of talk when Graham Taylor became manager that Hibbitt would become his assistant. Instead, his coaching career took him to Cardiff City and, latterly, to Hednesford Town, with whom, ironically, Barry Powell is about to win the FA Trophy as manager. Although Hibbitt loves his golf and his media duties, he is itching to get back into a dug-out. "It's difficult to get back in," he confesses, "but I feel I've still got a lot to offer."

At this point, Andy D'Urso, referee for the match between Villa and Blackburn, comes over to say hello. Contrary to preconceived notions up and down the land, he is convivial and courteous, urging us to relax and finish our interview. On the pitch, Derek Dougan is helping hand out some prizes; centre stage as ever. I think to ask whom Hibbitt roomed with at Wolves: for seven seasons, he tells me, it was Carr and herein lies another tale from the gold and black country.

The secret to their midfield partnership lay in the pre-match drinking sessions. "On the Friday night before a game, we'd have two pints of Banks's Mild, a big bar of chocolate and a box of Lions midget gems wine gums. We'd sit up in bed watching television and talking football until we dropped off. The ale was to help us sleep because we both suffered from nerves. Willie used to be sick before a game and my shirt used to be wringing wet with sweat.

"We never drank five or six pints, just two, as a ritual. The other lads would walk past our door at half past ten and go: 'Puck... slur' (insert own noise for the sound of a ring-pull being tugged) and say: 'They're at it again.' We wouldn't go to sleep before 1am."

With that, we shake hands over the fact that we have finally managed our interview. Hibbitt goes to join D'Urso and the other match officials to receive the team sheets. Phil, Ken's golfing pal, clears away our coffee clutter and we agree that you will struggle to find a nicer character than our mutual acquaintance. Ken Hibbitt - there's a name worth raising a glass to.

Kenny Hibbitt

Born:	January 3, 1951, in Bradford
Signed:	November, 1968
Wolves appearances:	574
Goals:	114
Left:	August, 1984
International recognition:	England under-23 cap

March 2004

There are lots of different ways of losing and Wolves tried three of them this month. The varying degrees of pride and pain endured in holding Liverpool goalless at Anfield (only for Sami Hyppia to score in added time) and deservedly leading Chelsea 2-1 at Stamford Bridge (before capitulating to a late Hasselbaink hat-trick) were largely undermined by the numb horror of being humiliated 4-0 at home by Aston Villa. How could Wolves start with such sloth for a derby, knowing victory would have pulled them out of the bottom three? It was the day the logical portion of my brain accepted relegation, and the fates were not arguing. I'd pranged my car on the way to seeing Leicester City win at Birmingham City the previous day. Tom, enthralled by victories over Leicester, Leeds and ManU, could not believe how bad it felt and begged to go home at half-time. Marginally lifted by the promise of a McDonalds - on the proviso he stuck it out for 90 minutes - we knew it was time to give up when, having nipped from our table to the toilet, we returned to find our barely-touched meals had been binned, along with our match-day programme.

Hyypia's late strike lacking in conviction

WHENEVER DISCUSSION centres on Gérard Houllier's job tenure or Wolverhampton Wanderers' Premiership status, the words "slow lingering death" spring to mind. It was no great surprise, therefore, that neither cause was helped in this first Anfield meeting of the two clubs for 20 years.

The points went Liverpool's way, courtesy of Sami Hyypia's towering header in the last of three minutes of stoppage time. But the satisfaction of regaining fourth place, on goals scored, was overshadowed by just the sort of witless, sterile performance that is turning the screw on their manager.

Whether or not they limp into the Champions' League, they will need to play a whole lot better than this. The Frenchman

BY DAVID INSTONE

Liverpool	1
Wolverhampton Wanderers	0

admitted as much before delivering his latest hard-luck story.

"I just hope it's an honest mistake, it was a blatant penalty," he said of Jody Craddock's unpunished 28th-minute challenge on Emile Heskey. If deemed illegal, the desperate recovering tackle would have made the defender the referee Rob Styles' ninth red-card victim of the season.

The overriding impression, though, was familiar. Only Steven Gerrard rose anywhere near as high as the winds, Michael Owen's subdued contribution putting to flight notions that he was buzzing again after two goals against Portsmouth.

The plaudits belonged to Wolves, who made an even game of it for 70 minutes and ensured that Jerzy Dudek was the busier goalkeeper. They have failed to score in their last three games and, after dusting themselves down from their humiliation against Aston Villa, now have to pick themselves up again - at Chelsea on Saturday.

At least they produced a display worthy of more. With Paul Ince relishing his return to a club where he felt kicked out by Houllier, they were in sight of completing an excellent afternoon's work when they were struck by a double blow.

Not only did Liverpool's 14th and final corner prove one too many, but at virtually the same moment Marcus Bent's equaliser at the Walker's Stadium meant Leicester City, not Wolves, benefited from a one point swing on the drop-o-meter.

"I don't think we deserved that," their manager, Dave Jones, said. "They weren't causing us any problems in open play. Unfortunately, we invited pressure by giving away silly free-kicks and one led to a corner that we didn't defend well enough."

Ince, Alex Rae and Paul Butler were Wolves' best performers, as they have been for most of the season, but their combined age is 101 and all three are out of contract in the summer. But boyhood Liverpool fan Mark Clyde impressed after being preferred to Denis Irwin, and Vio Ganea and Kenny Miller stretched Hyypia and the errant Igor Biscan.

At the height of Wolves' survival effort two months ago, Miller struck the winner against Manchester United and hit a brilliant last-gasp equaliser against Liverpool. On this occasion the clock would not tick round quickly enough for a side still without a top-flight away win since beating Liverpool's all-conquering side of 1983-84. Alas, in the bigger picture, time is beginning to run out.

Goal: Hyypia (90) 1-0.

Liverpool (4-4-2): Dudek 8; Carragher 6, Biscan 5, Hyypia 6, Riise 5; Murphy 4 (Diao ...), Hamann 6, Gerrard 7, Kewell 6 ...; Heskey 5 (Baros 5, ...), Owen 4. **Substitutes not used:** ...

Wolverhampton Wanderers (4-4-2): Jones 8; Clyde 6, Butler 7, Craddock 8, Naylor 5; Camara 6, Ince 7, Rae 7, Kennedy 6 (Cort, 61); Ganea 6 (Newton 6, 70), Miller 5. **Substitutes not used:** Oakes (gk), Cameron, Irwin.

Referee: R Styles (Hampshire) 5.

Booking: Wolverhampton: Newton.

Man of the Match: Gerrard.

Attendance: 42,...

Hasselbaink ignores mixed messages to show Ranieri the way

CHELSEA are temporarily employing the former editor of The Sun newspaper, Stuart Higgins, to advise them on public relations. But they could do a lot worse than offer the job to Claudio Ranieri. He is brilliant at it.

On Saturday he did an extraordinary thing. Twenty minutes to kick-off against Wolves, and he strode stern-faced on to the Stamford Bridge turf. Suited and booted he turned to all corners to salute the fans. Maybe he is taking this Roman gladiator imagery a little too far but the Chelsea faithful loved it. He is certainly up for the fight. His job at Chelsea may have gone - hawked around behind his back - but his dignity, his reputation, remains intact. Indeed, for a man who has won very little, it is visibly growing.

Ranieri had the fans eating out

BY JASON BURT

Chelsea	5
Wolverhampton Wanderers	2

of his hand - not that many of them know what to think at present as minutes later Roman Abramovich appeared, in his box, to another warm ovation. It all made for a strangely uncomfortable atmosphere - a sort of musty sense of decay, of rottenness, as if the foundations being put in place are not quite true.

It should not be like this. Just as they should be pulling together, they are pulling apart. Second in the Premiership and with a fighting chance of the Champions' League semi-finals, Chelsea appear to be doing their best to beat themselves. Indeed, the team is a microcosm of what is going on. Wolves, as committed and as limited as they are, should have been kidded, but Chelsea made slip-shod work of defeating them. It very nearly turned into a famous victory for Dave Jones and his players who, for the most part, were in the ascendancy. If only they had not lost their heads once they got in front. The scoreline masked a multitude of sins.

But for Sven Goran Eriksson, the afternoon should have belonged to Jimmy Floyd Hasselbaink who - on his 32nd birthday - scored a hat-trick after rising from the substitutes bench with half an hour to go. The goals took his Premiership total to 102 - becoming only the third foreigner, after Thierry Henry and Dwight Yorke, to reach a century. But the fact he had to come on as a replacement - along with Damien Duff - added to Ranieri's infuriating tactics. The mess surrounding his departure should not overshadow that, granted in trying circumstances, he has made some strange decisions.

Players needed to be rested after the astonishing exertions in midweek against Arsenal. But he rested the wrong ones. And so Eidur Gudjohnsen, who had run himself into the ground, started and, inevitably, got injured. Marcel Desailly was excluded - even though after his dismissal he is ineligible for the return. It went on. But the biggest indictment was the omission of Hasselbaink - a bull of a player suited to trample over a team like Wolves - and Duff whose pace shredded the visitors once he did come on. Instead Frank Lampard again shouldered the burden.

Within four minutes Lampard and Joe Cole had made a chance for Mario Melchiot which he accepted. But then nothing. Wolves, encouraged, edged forward and Henri Camara intercepted a lax pass by John Terry to prod the ball between the goalkeeper's legs. Jones' players grew, Ranieri's unravelled. None more so than Marco Ambrosio who, after the break, flapped at a corner only to be beaten by the head of Jody Craddock.

It was now Wolves' turn to panic. They sensed their first away win. Adrenalin was pumping and it went to their heads. As they poured forward they were caught on the counter. Lampard started and ended a move - with a right-foot shot from 35 yards - after linking with Duff. As space opened up, Hasselbaink exploited it. First he crashed into the penalty area to thump a shot past Paul Jones, then he collected Duff's flick to roll the ball into the net and finally, in injury time, he steered another shot around the goalkeeper from Lampard's clever pass. Afterwards Jones vented his frustration. "We made the mistakes," he said. It was a common theme.

Goals: Melchiot (4) 1-0; Camara (...) 1-1; Craddock (...) 1-2; Lampard (...) 2-2; Hasselbaink (...) 3-2; Hasselbaink (87) 4-2; Hasselbaink (...) 5-2.

Chelsea (4-4-2): Ambrosio 6; Melchiot 6; Terry 6, Gallas 4, Bridge 6; Gronkjaer 3 (Hasselbaink 8, 60), Lampard 7, Makelele 6, Cole 6 (Parker, 80); Gudjohnsen 4 (Duff 6, ...). **Substitutes not used:** ...

Wolverhampton Wanderers (4-4-2): Jones 8; Clyde 6, Craddock 7, Butler 6, Naylor 6; Camara 6, Ince 6, Rae 6 (Cort, 84), ...; Ganea 6, 70), Miller 6 ... **Substitutes not used:** Oakes (gk), Irwin.

Referee: ...

Bookings: Wolverhampton: ...

Man of the match: Duff.

Attendance: ...

Andy Mutch

THE ARTFUL DODGER WHO KEPT BULLY ASKING FOR MORE

April 6, 2004: Calling Southport

Dave Jones has figured at some pivotal points in Andy Mutch's career: at Southport, where the Everton reject was prevaricating over a move to Wolves; as Stockport County manager ten years later, when the striker was entering the twilight of his playing days; and in the summer of 2003, when Morecambe, the Nationwide Conference club where Steve Bull's one-time attacking partner had become assistant manager, took on the newest entrants to the Premiership and thrashed them 6-1.

If the pre-season friendly proved an ignominious day for Wolves, Mutch took no special pleasure in humiliating either the club he served for seven years or the manager who has been behind some of his better career decisions. "The boys enjoyed it more than Jim (Harvey, the Morecambe manager) and I did," Mutch says, when he has eventually been strapped down next to a telephone at an agreed time. "We had been back (from the close-season break) a couple of weeks longer than Wolves and were a little bit fitter. It was like a training session for them in one respect and they didn't perform on the day while we put on a scintillating performance and were three ahead in half an hour. They were a bit shell-shocked, I think. Ince, Irwin, Butler, Luzhny, Naylor, Sturridge were all playing and, while it looks as if we're going to miss out on the play-offs this season, on that performance we should be winning the league.

"I met Dave afterwards and he was fine. He was disappointed with the application of his players on the back of their promotion, as a manager would be. But I've worked with him over many years and he's a good fella. I knew he wouldn't accept that kind of performance. He'd have let his players know as much in his own sweet way."

That idiosyncratic managerial manner was one to which Mutch became accustomed at either end of his playing career. "He was assistant manager at Southport when I left for Wolves, after I'd been released by Everton, but I was probably a bit young to make any observations about his coaching potential at that time. I just know he was good for me, as a young player trying to make my way in the game," Mutch says. "I think he went on to become assistant manager at Morecambe for a while before he got the youth-team coach's job at Stockport and it was when he had stepped up to manage the first team that he signed me from Swindon.

"At Stockport, I got to know more of what he was like, as far as knowledge of the game is concerned, because I was at an age when you start to take more interest in management methods, and I realised what a very good man-manager he was. He was marvellous. He got the waifs and strays in from around the league: good players who had lost their way. He put them together, treated them like men, got their respect in return and the rest is history. Stockport were very successful over that period and that leapfrogged Dave into the Southampton job."

Mutch, at 33, helped Stockport reach the semi-final of the League Cup - playing in a 1-0 second-leg victory at the Riverside Stadium that could not quite prevent Middlesbrough reaching Wembley - and to win promotion to the First Division before leaving the full-time game to finish at Barrow and Southport. This provided a neat circularity as the Liverpool-born striker had started his first-team days at the latter.

Impressing in the Northern Premier League, Mutch came to Wolves' attention by accident and his purchase in February, 1986, was ultimately sanctioned by a Molineux great. Sammy Chapman, manager as Wolves plummeted towards their nadir, recalls: "Southport lost six at Kidderminster and everyone was watching Kim Casey (a Harriers goal machine) whom we'd have loved to sign but simply couldn't afford, what with his job and his football. I asked a Southport lad I knew whether Mutchy ran like that all the time, very quick and with wonderful energy. He said he did.

"I thought if we could get a few shillings together, I might go for him. We mentioned it to Dot Wooldridge (the club's long-time manager's secretary) and she liaised with Jimmy Mullen, a lovely man, who was on the Wolves Development Association. They had £9,000 in their kitty so I got £7,000 down to sign Andy. Because of the turmoil the club were in, the WDA agreed to sign the cheque direct to Southport. Andy took some persuading. He wanted to sign but I could only offer him £150 a week plus appearance money of £100 a game. Dave Jones drove him down to talk to us."

Jones, whose professional playing career had been prematurely ended by a knee injury at Preston North End, takes up the story: "I joined Southport part-time and did a bit of coaching there. They had a pretty good team, with the likes of Shaun Teale and Andy Mutch. I came down here with Mutchy when Wolves wanted him. The deal wasn't going through because he was looking for assurances and this and that. I said: 'Mutchy, you're a carpet-fitter, don't be looking for assurances. Just go.'" Actually, Mutch was a trainee engineer with a refrigeration company, but you take Jones' point.

"The awful thing was," Chapman continues, "that I forgot to tell him to run up to the bank when the pay cheques were issued because it was only the first ones that were guaranteed to land. Eventually, he took his in and it took a nasty bounce."

"The club were going through a period of bad financial problems," Mutch concedes, "but I got paid in the end, it wasn't a problem. I'd have been on more money for my day job than for my non-league football but it was the opportunity to prove yourself that we all wanted. If money were the reason for going, I wouldn't have signed. I found it very difficult adapting in the first instance. Physically, it was very demanding because I'd got out of the rhythm of full-time training, but fortunately for me, because of the state the club were in, I seemed to be chosen every week. I started to achieve what I wanted, which was to play regularly and contribute on the goal sheet.

"I knew Wolves were a big club. I remember watching Ken Hibbitt and Willie Carr on telly on Sunday afternoons. I remember Liverpool, the team I supported, going to Molineux to win the championship in 1976. I was listening on the radio: Steve Kindon scoring for you, Kevin Keegan scoring for us. The place was run-down when I went there and Sammy Chapman was trying to hand-pick the good young boys who had been laid off."

Chapman added: "It was smashing, getting Mutchy in. He lifted people. Then when Graham Turner came in and signed Bully, they became the ideal front pair. Jon Purdie was starting to look like he could become a player, Micky Holmes scored a few, they got to play at Wembley. These were lads who were brought to the club for nothing and earned next to nothing. But do you know the nicest thing? They knew they were playing for Wolverhampton Wanderers. They weren't the best players in the world but they knew they were playing for a great club.

"People have no idea what was going on at the club then. The place was a health hazard, for a start. You couldn't use the baths. Some of the away teams refused to get changed in their dressing-room. They'd get into their kit on the bus or back at a hotel. If you'd switched on their bath taps, sewerage would spew out. They had the washbasins but, afterwards, a lot of teams preferred to put their tracksuits on and clear off back to their hotel to clean up. It was all so very old, the drains had collapsed. It wasn't the best place for young players to start their careers but they got on with it and did their best."

Relatively speaking, Mutch proved an immediate hit, scoring seven times in 15 games - finishing joint second top scorer in 1985-86 - as Chapman's own waifs and strays were relegated to the Fourth Division. The next season, with Brian Little in charge, did not start too brightly either and, by November, there was an ominous sign that Wolves could not even claim to be non-league standard. "Chorley was certainly a big disappointment in the history books," Mutch says of the notorious FA Cup saga that saw the four-times winners dumped out by sub-Conference opposition. "It was non-league against a big famous old name but the reality was Wolves had dropped right down through the divisions and we were a bad team by then. Chorley deserved credit for their victory, in a second replay at Bolton Wanderers' ground, I think it was, but it had no significant bearing on me individually. You think either you'll drop down to that level personally if you can't stand out, or work hard, improve and progress individually; or maybe the team will."

Mutch lost his No9 shirt after that night at Burnden Park as Turner, who had succeeded Little in October, had just signed another young striker. The lowest point in the club's history coincided with the arrival of a West Bromwich Albion reject who, in tandem with Mutch and the best of the rest, was about to ignite a renaissance that will never be forgotten at Molineux. Yet Mutch does not remember Bull making an initial impact in the camp. It is easy to ignore what an uncertain place the dressing-room must have been with all these young newcomers coming and going; their subsequent success makes it seem as if this fantastic spirit was sparked as soon as they were introduced to one another.

"Steve was a very raw player, no doubt, but the one big thing he had in his favour was his ability to keep getting into goal-scoring positions," Mutch says. "He probably missed more than he scored but he could get 15 chances in a game, even if he didn't take a very high proportion of them. His technique in converting chances was very erratic in the early days. He's very much his own man and, like myself, he turned up at a new club, kept himself to himself while he tried to find his feet. He wanted to be a player; you could tell he was desperate to succeed. There wasn't a massive team spirit at the very onset of Graham Turner's reign. I don't remember much about Chorley at all but I do know Graham was still getting to know the players."

The lowest ebb: Ally Robertson, David Barnes and Vince Bartram on damage-limitation duty away to Chorley.

"Most of us have now blotted Chorley from our memory banks," Turner says with a wry smile. "It was just such a horrible occasion. We had a good opportunity to beat them at Molineux on an abysmal night when the rain was lashing down. I do believe a linesman mistook a ball boy, who was wearing a yellow anorak, for one of our players and gave a Chorley forward onside when he was miles off. They scored from that, we went up to Bolton and we got murdered. The following day, all the national press were hanging around, like vultures, thinking it was the final nail in the club's coffin. With hindsight, it was probably the catalyst for better times.

"I never thought of chucking it in, not even after Chorley. The one mitigating factor for me was that I was always a Wolves supporter as a lad. I was brought up in Ellesmere Port, on Merseyside, but Billy Wright was my idol and I'd always go and watch them if they were playing at Everton. It was terrific for me when Billy came on the board in my time there.

"So to get the opportunity to manage them, irrespective of what state they were in, was a real attraction for me. I felt we could pull it around and felt there was an opportunity to build something. Gates were down to around 2,500, yet I've since met about 15,000 who tell me they never missed a game in those days! Two sides of the ground were shut and the club were in a desperate state. There was an air of despondency and you could sense defeatism was in the very fabric of the club because they had dropped from the top division to the bottom in successive years. Not only was the whole ground falling to bits but the equipment, the balls, the training kit - you wouldn't have handed it out to a pub team.

"You could understand the despondency among the players but the fortunate thing for me was having a few characters, Andy included, who helped lift us. Ally Robertson and Floyd Streete were a great help. You could count on one hand the number of players you could hang your hat on but those two were very experienced players who did not shirk the challenge. It would have been easy for Ally, having played at the top level for many years, to soft-pedal at a club like Wolves but he was a very good professional, even in his twilight years, and his presence helped people such as Andy, keeping a steady hand on things."

Not that Turner immediately rated Mutch as part of his hoped-for renaissance. "No," he says. "My initial reaction was that his first touch was not that clever, he had a funny style of running and he tended to lose the ball when it was played up to him. Anything into his feet wasn't his strength. So initially, I thought he would do well to make a living at lower-league level. But gradually, as we played to his strengths, and he did have terrific pace, I was forced to change my view. He formed the partnership with Steve Bull and you started to realise how good he could be.

"If he got the ball down the side of him, no-one could stay with him and, of course, he developed into a very good goalscorer. He was a confident character who always had a view on things. From his early days, he had an opinion and sometimes you want characters who will express themselves. He was never shy to put his two-penneth in and very often they were valid points. That's why I think he has a chance in management now. He's an intelligent lad, knows what the game's about, and is learning his trade with Jim Harvey."

Chorley did prove the low point, Wolves picking up in exhilarating fashion to reach the inaugural play-offs by dint of winning 11 of their last 12 games, with Bull and Mutch's partnership starting to click. "Time moved on, eventually the strays moved on, stronger players came in and results improved," Mutch recalls. "From that, confidence inevitably grew and the camaraderie improved. Steve's a very private lad. We got on fine and, as time went on, we got on better and better and, to this day, we still speak regularly."

It was Bully who told me how, as defenders in the late 1980s would testify, Mutch could be difficult to pin down. From my experiences in trying to set up this interview, I have sympathy with them. We were going to meet six months ago just off the M6. I was due to travel to Blackburn Rovers for a game, so arranged post-school childcare in order to leave early after spending the morning on my exercise bike watching the 1988 Sherpa Van Trophy final on video. That takes a certain kind of dedication. Mutch called to cancel just after lunch. Then, otherwise engaged when invited to join Paul Cook for a photo session at Molineux, he planned to scout Morecambe's Christmas opponents a month later, when Accrington Stanley agreed to lay on pre-match tea for us as I was reporting on their FA Cup replay with Bournemouth. Again, he rang, just about the time the afternoon temperature hit zero, to postpone.

I remember meeting Mutch in 1990 when spending a week at Paper Plane Limited to try for a job with the company who used to produce the Wolves programme and match videos. He was injured for a game against Ipswich Town and, before climbing to the gantry on commentary duty, we retired to the bar for a quick snifter. Mutch was a gentleman, chatting away to put me at my ease. I'd already got my Andy Mutch mug and fully appreciated the support role he offered Bully, taking much of the physical pressure and providing the flick-ons and hold-ups integral to the team's style. After he moved to Swindon but was out of the team, Keith Scott, whom I knew from Wycombe Wanderers, invited me into the players' lounge and was ribbing Mutch when I reminded him that he was in the company of a Molineux hero. I told Scotty about my Andy Mutch mug; I don't think they ever got round to making a Keith Scott mug at Adams Park.

The last time I met Mutch was in 1998 after a Stockport County game and, again, he was affability personified if a bit non-plussed when I made a bid for his telephone number. Why would I want to ring him? I told him I was thinking of doing a piece on the ten-year anniversary of the Sherpa Van triumph. I'm still awaiting *The Daily Telegraph's* response to that particular idea. So when, five years on, I did call him, it was with the idea of getting together, face to face.

Mutch keeps his old friends' numbers. Bull has been speaking to Paul Jones, their old team-mate, who is dividing this season between Southampton, Liverpool and back with Wolves. "You can go two years without speaking then take off again as if it was yesterday," Bully says. "It was like Jonah said to me: he hadn't heard from Mutchy for years, then he rings up and says: 'Jonah, have you got tickets for Liverpool at

Molineux?' so Jonah says: 'Hello, Mutchy, how you been?' He rang a fortnight ago and said: 'Bully, I'm coming down to see Liverpool, how are you?' I said: 'Fine, I'm on a beach in the Caribbean,' and he said: 'Ta-ra then,' and that was it. The phone went dead."

He did get his tickets from somewhere. "I took my lad, George, down and was rooting for Wolves by the end," this die-hard Liverpool fan admits. "I was delighted when Kenny Miller equalised. Wolves needed the points more. If Liverpool had needed to win for the championship, I'd have been cheering them as usual."

In seven years together, Mutch and Bull shared 310 goals. Mutch initially lodged in Aldersley with an elderly couple, Edna and Fred, before settling in Ironbridge. "We had some very successful times and not only did Graham Turner get together a strong squad, we were fortunate not to get too many injuries. A good spirit grew. Although we had ability, it was more to do with how well we gelled," he says.

"Graham Turner chose his players well, he got a good discipline into the club and he worked us hard. He treated us well and it all came together. The fact that we had a few key players in the side helped, of course, particularly in Steve. Once you get on the crest of a wave, you want to keep riding it. My time at Wolves was fantastic. It was a privilege to play for a club of that stature and I was very well received by the supporters. All the players, the fans, the staff were cracking people who all wanted one thing. That was for Wolves to do well."

Mutch scored 23 goals in each of the promotion seasons, laying on a good number of Bull's 100-odd in that period. Either modest, forgetful or contrary, he cannot pick out a favourite. The most memorable for me was at Wembley on May 29, 1988, in

Lethal from four yards. In the shadow of the emerging Billy Wright Stand, Andy Mutch (second right, next to Robbie Dennison) touches in the only goal at home to Newcastle United in April, 1993. It was the last of the striker's 106 Wolves goals.

between the two championships, when Bull hooked a ball back across the penalty area for Mutch to head in. "I remember the occasion more than anything else," Mutch says when pushed. "I recall going to the game, seeing all the supporters going down Wembley Way. Then to see 50,000 of our followers in the ground itself was absolutely fantastic. They proved that day that if the club could keep climbing back up, then the support base would be incredible. They are very passionate supporters who can be tough on you at times but, if you're giving it all you've got, get right behind you.

"I'd been to Wembley many times to watch Liverpool and it was the same, except with gold and black instead of red and white. Being part of that was marvellous. I have a video of the game, since you ask, though I can't remember watching it. I was pleased to score, it felt like an achievement, but to win was even more of one. Truth be told, we were a class above Burnley and had beaten them twice in the league that season.

"Scoring goals is always a tremendous feeling. The fact that it's at Wembley gives it more profile but, at the time, you're focused on the game. The significance of it all hit me more before the game, when you walk out and look at the surroundings and the supporters, and then, in a funny kind of way, afterwards, when you walk out there and it's all empty and quiet. You can reflect on the excitement then. It's nice to look back on but it's the supporters' day. We enjoyed the day, don't get me wrong, and enjoy the memory now. But, if we turned up and you lot hadn't been there, what would it all have been about? What would we be doing it for?"

Winning the Sherpa Van Trophy was a benchmark for the revitalisation of a grand old club. "Having already won the Fourth Division title, to go in front of 50,000 fans at Wembley was something very special," Turner remarks. "I remember being at an early meeting of the former players' association - all these fellas who had won titles, cups, international caps. Dick Homden, then the chairman, invited them all to Wembley and it was staggering to see their reaction, as if all their Christmases had come at once. Ron Flowers, Bert Williams, Billy Wright, Bill Shorthouse, they all went. I scoffed at the idea of an open-top bus ride, for a club who had won so much in their heyday, but we agreed to it. There must have been at least 100,000 in the town centre that May Bank Holiday. That gave the lads a fresh hunger for success."

Bull and Mutch played together for the England B team the next summer, on a tour of Iceland, Norway and Switzerland. They collected under-21 honours as over-age players around the same time. A strong B squad included Paul Gascoigne, David Platt and Gary Pallister. "I didn't feel out of my depth, that's for sure," Mutch recalls, "but I got an injury in the first game against Switzerland, so only came on for half an hour against Iceland. I really enjoyed the experience and felt I could get used to that level but the B team didn't play regularly enough for players to bed in."

Mutch agrees with Paul Cook's contention that, having reached the old Second Division, Wolves' best opportunity to rejoin the elite was in their first season up. It was, with hindsight, perhaps a chance missed, although Turner's team deserved great credit for stabilising at the higher level following their lower-division heroics. Mutch continued to reach double figures for three of the next four seasons but admitted that his form levelled out after a back injury. "I lost a bit of spark," he says. "Players came into the club to try and kick us on and, back then, if you could spend a fair bit of money on players, you were expected to get up. When better players were brought in and didn't perform as well as hoped, that would have been why they changed the manager."

Mutch himself was supplanted by David Kelly and yet, although he did move into the top division with Swindon, he suspects he could have made a better career switch. "I don't know what the difference is between turning up for work at one club and another," Mutch says. "Yes, Wolves were a big club, but you turn up, you train, you play. You can't manufacture situations. You go out and play to the best of your ability and if the club want to keep you, you stay. If the club don't want you, you leave. Certainly, in my case, I'd always move on straightaway.

"I know a lot of clubs came in for me but, in those days, transfer inquiries were always a lot more cloak and dagger. I just felt if I was good enough for the top grade then clubs would eventually come in and pay the money. No-one wanted to come in and pay what Wolves must have been rating me at, so I stayed for seven years. I know Tottenham Hotspur, West Ham United and Aston Villa inquired about me but it's immaterial now because nothing came of it. I had great times at Molineux and my only disappointment was the way in which I left."

Out of contract in the summer Sir Jack Hayward handed Turner his first hefty transfer kitty, Mutch was left at home when the club went on pre-season tour. "I wasn't in Graham Turner's plans by this stage," he adds. "I was on a month-to-month deal and, although I didn't want to leave, I went to Swindon early the next season. I didn't feel Graham Turner gave me the respect I deserved for what I'd done for the club. It wasn't about playing in the Premier League, it was about being part and parcel of a club. Wolves had gone to Sweden and I hadn't been invited, so it was clearly time to look elsewhere. I was told Swindon had come in for me and I should speak to them."

Turner says: "I didn't have a price in mind that I wanted to sell Andy at. One or two clubs were interested - Terry Venables, at Tottenham, was very complimentary, and Aston Villa were supposedly about to bid for him - but I can't recall any concrete offers. There comes a time when people need fresh challenges. The Bull-Mutch partnership had been successful for so long but we were beginning to stagnate at Second Division level and we needed to change one or two things. I brought David Kelly in from Newcastle United, where he had just scored 27 goals in their title

Andy Mutch shapes to turn an Oldham Athletic defender on the first day of 1990-91.

triumph. Perhaps I could have dealt with Andy's departure differently, with hindsight, but all good things come to an end. I felt the partnership had run its course."

Swindon lasted but one season in the Premier League and, while the former Wolves man managed eight goals by early January, they conceded exactly 100 in the league. "Defensively, as a team, we weren't good," Mutch says, "so we got some right drubbings. We could cause problems going forward but, at the other end, there were days when it went horribly wrong." Oh dear; this is starting to sound horribly familiar.

"I wouldn't say there's a comparison with Wolves this season," Mutch says. "The majority of Premier League teams ten years ago were a lot stronger than Swindon. Now, while the top five clubs are obviously a lot stronger than Wolves, there is very little to choose between the bottom eight. It's how you fare in those games that determines who goes down and who stays up. Regardless of who comes up, whether they're as big historically as Wolves, they must break the bank just to stay up, spend millions and millions. That puts the club in jeopardy, on a financial cliff edge. When Norwich go up this year, they should be able to spend right through next season, not just in the transfer windows. It's a restraint of trade, as far as I'm concerned.

"Liverpool, Arsenal and the majority of Premiership sides have been establishing their squads over a period but newly-promoted teams have next to no time to adapt their squad to a new grade of football. So the odds are stacked against them, when surely it would be more competitive and more in the interests of the game if they were given a leg-up, to be able to compete on a level playing field.

"Wolves got up and, before they know it, the August transfer deadline is hurtling towards them. Even if you had £12million to spend, you couldn't spend it on one player because you need to convince him of the calibre of other players coming in. But if you're spending that type of money on five or six players over the whole season, you can realistically bring in better players.

"Wolves were forced into signings, in my view, that, given more time, they might not have made. It becomes very difficult for the new team to compete. Wolves have got plenty of lads who were top First Division players, some of whom were equipped to climb up to the Premiership, and some of whom have struggled; the additions have not really been of a higher quality. The only difference now is that the squad who are going down should be well primed - if they keep the spirit and some key characters - to challenge for an immediate return. Then it's up to the club to see how they've learned from this experience."

It is a frustration most Wolves fans share. This team have gone one step better than that of Mutch's day but Premiership status, 19 years in the finding, is slipping away and a formula for a longer, stronger return is not easy to find. Following the latest heavy defeat, Jones, Mutch's old mentor, answers his phone to me just when his own annoyance is spilling over. "It's so frustrating because, if we had three or four more players of top quality, it would have made all the difference," he says. "We outplayed Chelsea for 70 minutes, then they send on £40m of talent. It was 0-0 after 90 minutes at Liverpool. At Molineux, we haven't had a spare seat for three years, they can't sell any more executive boxes. Our wage bill is £16m, the lowest in the Premiership. The board can see it but they're chasing their tail now, the horse has bolted."

We agree to do a piece for *The Times* next month. I suggest Wolves fans are grateful to have at last experienced the Premiership, which had eluded players of the quality of Mutch and Bull, Mike Stowell and Mark Venus; that everyone appreciates the phenomenal attitude that Alex Rae and Paul Butler, Paul Ince and Lee Naylor have produced. Jones is not convinced. "They are starting to ask questions on the streets. They want to know why we did not give ourselves a fighting chance." I insist Wolves should be better set for promotion than ever in 2004-05 - and trust that Jones fancies the challenge. "We'll see," he says. "A lot of issues need to be addressed."

Andy Mutch

Born:	December 28, 1963, Liverpool
Signed:	February, 1986
Wolves appearances:	338
Goals:	106
Left:	August, 1993
International recognition:	England under-21 and B caps

April 2004

T.S. Eliot must have been a Wolves fan, for no month has been as cruel as April. We have been equal to or better than opponents for most of a game, only to be stabbed in the back at the last. I write after Bolton Wanderers yesterday became the fifth team in succession to score against us in stoppage time but it was Uriah Rennie who played Brutus. I've watched The Premiership - oh, ephemeral joy, to be on telly every week - and both Mark Kennedy, in the first minute, and Kenny Miller, in the last, were clearly fouled in the box when the scores were level. No penalty on either count. We're adrift of the safety zone by nine points with five games left. Yet I was on a high on Saturday night, having seen us outplay Manchester City, only to be done by a stoppage-time equaliser. We out-bombed Bolton before being afflicted by the same outcome. Not going Saturday, despite booking time off for Tom's eighth birthday. He said he'd prefer to be happy. To turn round from the press box yesterday and see Joe playing with his Action Man as Mum chain-fed him chocolate eggs made me remember not to take it all too seriously. Maintain this attitude and we're going to rock the First Division to pieces.

Robbie Keane

THE IMPISH GENIUS WHO CARTWHEELED THROUGH MOLINEUX

May 4, 2004: The West Lodge Park Hotel, Hertfordshire

The Nigerian taxi driver explains that we are in the heart of Arsenal country. Turn off Cockfosters Road, into a palatial estate, and we'd find Kanu and his mates, ensconced in millionaires' row. Not that Kanu is the age he says he is. Apparently, he's closer to 37 than 27. Some footballers seem to defy their birth certificate like this. Take Robbie Keane. Can he really be only 23? It is almost seven years since he exploded into Black Country minds with that spectacular debut for Wolves away to Norwich City. Yet here he is, £38million worth of transfers and a World Cup finals later, impudently scoring a last-minute equaliser for Tottenham Hotspur to dull Arsenal's title celebrations.

If Keane has a habit of pooping parties, it is simply because he scores so regularly. Arsenal did not so much mind him netting at White Hart Lane a week earlier; at least they maintained their unbeaten run for the season. Not even Wolves begrudged him his hat-trick six months previously, especially as he had the class to acknowledge who gave him his break by refusing to celebrate with his trademark cartwheel. Everyone says what a chipper chappie Robbie Keane is but, clearly, he also possesses humility.

He may live only a few minutes away from this well-heeled seat of Hertfordshire, presumably in similar opulence, but he actively remembers his Molineux pals. From the days when he used to nip next door for tea at Carl Robinson's on the outskirts of Telford, from when they used to go on lads' package tours to Cyprus with Matt Murray and Lee Naylor. Keane's has been a nomadic existence - five clubs already - but, for all that, feet remain firmly in contact with terra firma.

Somewhat larger than I expect, compared with the darting image espied from the distance of television and the press box, Keane cuts a reserved, almost shy, figure as he enters the hotel reception with Simon Bayliff, his agent. This is the only interview for this book that has been orchestrated through the endeavours of the secretary of the agent of the player. Our 45-minute chat has taken six months to fix up and when, at 1.45pm, Helene from SFX rings, I fear it is to cancel. However, with the utmost professionalism, it is merely to say Robbie is running 15 minutes late from training.

Everything else about his career has been ahead of schedule. From the tour of top English clubs he made in his early teens as he chose whom to sign for, to breaking into Wolves' first team a month past his 17th birthday; from becoming Ireland's youngest scorer to taking the tag as English football's costliest teenager in moving to Coventry City for £6m; then the premature, if lucrative, £13m move to Milan, followed by an £11m switch to Leeds United and a memorable stint in Japan, where he scored in three successive games in the World Cup, including last-minute equalisers against Germany and Spain. Nothing, yet, has fazed the lad from the sprawling council estate in south Dublin. So tackling a putty-in-your-hands Wolves obsessive should be a breeze.

"When I first came over, I'd never heard of Wolves," he admits. "In Ireland, it's all Liverpool and Man United. I was a Liverpool fanatic and thought Wolves, as a First Division club, would have this little ground. But when I went and saw Molineux, it took my breath away. It was fantastic. The people who walked in gave it a magnificent atmosphere, so I had good feelings as soon as I got there."

Chris Evans, the Academy director at Molineux, deserves much credit for persuading Keane and his parents that Wolves were a better bet than Nottingham Forest, Liverpool, Leeds and Manchester United. "Chris came to my house, with Eddie Corcoran, their scout in Ireland, and Rob Kelly, who's now the youth-team coach at Blackburn Rovers," the player recalls. "They made me feel Wolves were my club. It was just how welcome they made me feel. Chris Evans looked after me, from day one to when I got into the first team and even now we get on really well, speak to each other all the time.

"He got me a sponsored car from a local garage, a Fiat Bravo, when, as a young lad just passing my test, I had expected to be buying my own. Getting one for free? I thought it was the best thing in the world, with my name on the side. I wouldn't do it again, to be honest, but it felt fantastic at the time."

Before this interview, I rang Evans, an amiable Welshman who has introduced a conveyor belt of top young talent at Wolves over the past decade. "I told the club I was going to look after him, on and off the field, and I've done that," Evans says. "He had 20 agents after him but I wouldn't let him near them. I knew Tony Stephens from when he had produced a marketing strategy for Wolves ten years earlier. He had Beckham, Yorke, Shearer, Owen and Platt in his stable and I said: 'I've got a boy for you who's in our first team at 17.' He hadn't heard of him but I said: 'Believe me, it's worth a conversation.'

Wolverhampton Wanderers
Football Club

Molineux Stadium, Waterloo Road, Wolverhampton WV1 4QR
Tel: (01902) 655000   Fax: (01902) 687006

Our ref: CE/DMW

18 September 1995

Master Robert Keane
26 Glenshane Grove
Brookfield
Tallaght
Dublin 24.

Dear Robert

We hereby present the financial terms in respect of our offer to sign you with Wolverhampton Wanderers Football Club:-

1. <u>Length of Contract</u> – 4 years (July 1st 1996 – June 30th 2000)

   a. Year 1: ▉▉▉▉▉▉▉▉▉   ▉▉▉▉▉▉▉▉
   b. Year 2: ▉▉▉▉▉▉   ▉▉▉▉▉▉▉▉
   c. Year 3: ▉▉▉▉▉▉   ▉▉▉▉▉▉▉▉
   d. Year 4: ▉

The formal offer, with sensitive bits blacked out, that Wolves sent to the Dublin home of 15-year-old Master Robert Keane during Graham Taylor's final weeks as manager.

"He pulled up on my drive in David Beckham's Landrover. He was immaculately dressed, crisply turned out and a great orator. After our conversation, I rang Robbie and said: 'This is the man for you. Do you want to meet him?' They met at my home. A top player needs a top agent, psychologist, manager. They teamed up and I'm sure neither party regrets it."

SFX handle Keane very carefully, as they have the aforementioned superstars. It is easy to dismiss agents as money-making leeches but Keane values the more low-key support he is given. "It's handy for me because they take a lot of stuff off my shoulders. There's no way I'd be able to sort all this out. They've been magnificent for me, ever since I was 17, and I'm sure we'll carry on together until I finish."

It was the pre-season in which he turned 17 that Keane could no longer be left out of Mark McGhee's first-team squad. "Robbie had been scoring goals for fun in the youth team at 16," the Scot recalls. "He went off for the summer and, when he came back, looked as sharp and good as anyone we had. I said: 'Let him train with us so we can have a look at him.' When he joined in the five-a-sides, he was the best player. We had to give him an opportunity, so we took him to Scotland in pre-season. We used him in the 'hole' and he was the best player on the field. It didn't matter that he was 16 or 17. He was a good player. By the start of the season, we decided he was playing."

Robinson, four years older, had broken into the team at the end of 1996-97. "I only

168

played one reserve game with Robbie but you just thought: 'Wow!'" he says. "He was a bit lightweight but his was such a talent. I came from a quiet background in Wales and probably didn't speak to anyone for three months when I got to Molineux. As soon as Robbie arrived, he was chirping away, chatting, full of confidence. He had two fantastic years with the youth team before he and Mark Jones, who both scored about 30 goals for the juniors the previous year, joined us for pre-season.

"I was a substitute against Norwich when Robbie scored two of the best goals you'll ever see. One was a left-footed volley from the edge of the box, the other he dribbled past about three players before sticking it in. I was delighted for him. Chris Evans and Rob Kelly had put a lot of work in with him and, when they saw youngsters coming through and succeeding, they realised their efforts were paying off."

The Norwich game, unsurprisingly, is the first Keane nominates when asked to recall his Wolves favourites. McGhee was brave enough to build the team around him. Selected in the No7 shirt in front of a midfield of Mark Atkins, Darren Ferguson and Steve Froggatt, Keane played off Steve Bull and Don Goodman. "It was my debut, my parents were there and to play was absolutely magnificent," he says. "But to score two good goals just rounded it off. I didn't get nervous before the game, don't generally, I just get excited. There were a few butterflies but they went once we kicked off. The club flew my parents from Ireland for the match, which was great. They still had to drive about five hours to East Anglia, mind, but I could see them up in the directors' box and, when we met after the game, they were just buzzing."

Naylor, the same age as Keane, also made the first team that season. "I wasn't at all surprised when he got in," the Bloxwich-born left-back says. "Everyone knew he had the ability. It was just a question of when it was going to come out. It came out early. I was so chuffed for him when he scored those goals at Norwich. When one of the youth team goes into the first team and does so well, all the young lads are just thrilled for him. It's something you want to happen for a mate."

McGhee is modest concerning the faith he placed in his prodigy. "I have never had any fear of putting young players in," he says. "I gave Emile Heskey his debut at 16 with Leicester. It wasn't a hard decision, it wasn't a brainwave. If you were standing watching the training session and didn't know their ages and I asked you to pick the best player, you'd pick Robbie Keane. It wasn't rocket science."

Keane kept his place for a dozen games, netting his first competitive home goals in a 4-2 win over Bury. Although rested at times, he ended as the team's leading scorer in the First Division, with 11 goals. "It was evident he could handle first-team football," Colin Lee adds. "We didn't need to wait. You needed to look after him, put him in and bring him out, but he was very confident, knew he was a good player, so mentally, he could handle it. In training, he could do things others couldn't. His improvisation was excellent and gave us another dimension."

Lee, then McGhee's assistant, had been a centre-forward of no little promise

How Wolves' match-day programme heralded the sensational arrival of the young Robbie Keane on the opening day of 1996-97. The Norwich keeper, Andy Marshall, had a short spell at Molineux in 2003-04.

himself, scoring four times on his debut for Tottenham Hotspur 20 years before, and was eager that Keane be left to express himself. "If you've got exceptional talent, you don't want to stifle it," he says. "Robbie Keane knows now when to play it simple and when to try his tricks. You become a better player if you work that out for yourself because you do it naturally, rather than having a coach ranting and raving, and risking inhibiting you. The players around him will demand a certain amount of simplicity at times but Robbie's skill in tight areas in the box is something every team looks for, so we encouraged him to work it out for himself."

This brought its frustrations as Keane's precocious talent took him dribbling up some blind alleys or attempting outrageous flicks that would come off once every other game. Like the best kid in the school team, he probably sensed he would do better on his own than pass to a lesser-skilled colleague. "Keaney was very good," Bull says. "He was a bit cocky but that's the way he was. He was young and knew he had something others hadn't. He was very skilful but, to me, quite frustrating as well. He would try nine tricks as I'd do nine runs hoping to get the ball slipped in and then the tenth time, I wouldn't go, and he'd play the perfect pass. It was like Graham Turner in my early days. He'd yell: 'Pass the ball, Bully, pass the ball, pass the... oh, great goal.' You can see Robbie's learned since he left Wolves. He scores for fun and more of his touches come off because he's learned from the players he's played with."

Bull's last two seasons coincided with Keane's first two and it is left for Wolves fans to dream about what the pair could have achieved had they played in harness when the older man was younger. John Richards and Derek Dougan had the better part of four years together and who is to say Bull and Keane would not have helped take Wolves up a grade if time had been more generous? "I mostly played alongside Bully and his experience was second to none," Keane recalls. "You know the way he plays, liking the ball over the top, and the way I like to drop off and link the play. It worked well and I see no reason why we couldn't have done it in the Premiership. Bully's a goalscorer and he'd have scored in the Premier, no problem; I've been lucky enough to do OK, so I see no reason why we couldn't have done well in the Premiership."

As it was, their partnership received scant opportunity to flourish as Bull's knee problems hastened the end of his career. With Keane having played all but two of the first 30 league games of the season, however, it was still a surprise when the duo were left out of the starting line-up for the FA Cup semi-final against Arsenal.

Perhaps it was because of the success Wolves had in winning their quarter-final at Leeds, where Keane, still only 17, had gone on as substitute to make a near-calamitous contribution. "That was a great occasion," Robinson recalls. "We were underdogs, of course, as they were at the start of some great times, with Harry Kewell and everyone, while we were on the fringe of the play-off places. Late on, I put Don Goodman in and he put a fantastic finish on it. We were so close to a semi-final."

Keane takes up the story. "I was on the bench and went on for about 15 minutes. One of the first things I did was take Jimmy Floyd Hasselbaink down in the box. I don't know for the life of me what I was doing back there. I haven't been that far back since. I think he made a bit of a meal of it but my heart was pounding away. I was panicking, a young lad, quarter-finals of the FA Cup, and I've given it all away. The other lads didn't say 'owt. A big fight was brewing as Hasselbaink and Keith Curle squared up to each other, with Kevin Muscat (Robbie chuckles at this point) not too far away. Luckily, Hans Segers saved Hasselbaink's penalty. It's a good memory now because we won."

Arsenal were one of the powerhouse clubs tracking Keane very closely. "You never think: 'One day I might be playing for them,'" he says now. "But of course you want to do well in such games because you want to be judged against the very best. I was gutted I wasn't playing. Mark McGhee said he was saving me for the final, which was a polite way of saying he preferred me playing in the league. Most of the season, me and Bully had been playing and doing well. I got the last five minutes on the wing. Steve Claridge played, didn't he? To play all season and then be left out for such a big game…was Claridge on loan? It was hard but I had to be strong and get over it."

Robinson adds: "I think Mark McGhee was concerned not to go all out from the start, so maybe he set up cautiously, but no-one knows why Robbie and Bully were on the bench. When two of your best players, your best goalscorers, are left out…but managers are paid to make big decisions. I know how disappointed Robbie was. He had helped us reach that stage but a manager has a plan." With Christopher Wreh scoring in the 12th minute at Villa Park, Wolves' intention to stifle Anelka, Overmars, Vieira and company backfired. But, hey, hindsight is an unfair advantage.

Claridge could have been a chapter in this book. You have my publisher to thank for talking me out of including him. I recognise he is reviled by most Wolves fans but he had that maverick quality that either sticks or busts with you. Look at his time at Leicester City, when he volleyed in a Wembley winner with the last kick of the 1996 play-off final, and with Portsmouth, where he is a legend. With his rolled-down socks, Worzel Gummidge appearance, non-league background and gambling habit, his ability to hold the ball up one minute and stick it in the back of the net the next, Claridge is one of that disappearing breed in football, a character. Okay, he is no marketable icon, but an interview with him can involve a car race from the burger van outside Fratton Park to tea and cake with his mum at home in Fareham, an opportunity to get to know the person inside the player.

"Right club, wrong time," he says, when asked why he lasted only six games with Wolves before scuttling back to Pompey. Only once did he wear No9. He didn't want to be seen as the man who tried to replace Bully. Ironically, he could have been a good foil for Keane. "Robbie was a fantastic talent," Claridge says. "He didn't listen to a word I said. No, seriously, he could take advice on board but he did some silly things as a kid. Some lads would take the mickey and he'd take the bait. He was a typical spotty teenager and it took him a while to get used to the dressing-room banter but I think it showed the respect all the senior pros had for him, that they involved him and didn't hold back. You know what it's like when you're young. But as he's matured, it's clear he knows how to look after himself. I think Wolves were trying to use him sparingly but he came on so much that they had to unleash him. I remember him playing up at Middlesbrough and he was absolutely brilliant. He was a good lad, I liked him."

March 5, 1998: A hotline from Reading to Molineux

I t was during the Cup run that I first spoke to Keane, for a *Daily Telegraph* piece. Lorraine Hennessy, Wolves' press officer, got him to the phone when Wolves were drawn with Leeds, his father's favourite team, and he talked about his trial at Elland Road. "When I was 15, I went for a week at mid-term with two other Irish lads, Stephen McPhail and Alan Maybury. We each scored in a trial game, but they clearly weren't interested. No-one from the coaching staff really spoke to me." He also went to Liverpool. "It was lovely to go and see Ian Rush and Robbie Fowler, who were my heroes, but my parents said: 'Don't just sign because you support them.' It was good advice. If I was there now, I probably wouldn't be doing as well as I am here."

The next time I was reporting on Wolves, ten days later, I sauntered to the touchline at Swindon Town to introduce myself to Keane. "I mustn't talk to the press, you must go through the gaffer," he said, coming over all panicky after a 0-0 draw in which he had not even played. I explained I just wanted to say thanks for the interview. We shook hands but it struck me under what pressure he must be operating.

Back in the here and now, rain lashing against the hotel window in Hertfordshire, I show a few cuttings to the maturing superstar. He is wearing a brown zip-up cardigan, jeans and a day's stubble. Simon sits next to him, minding us, minding his client's schedule. *The Telegraph* article for the Leeds tie had carried Robinson's picture by mistake. "Everyone got us mixed up," Keane laughs. "He's a good lad, Carlo. I lived on my own when he was living with his girlfriend, Laura, and Kevin Muscat was round the corner. It was nice to go for meals sometimes, it saved me cooking for one."

Keane even went to the Robinson household in Priorslee for Christmas dinner, courtesy of his friend's Mum, while, with Muscat, they socialised and drove together to and from training. With Murray and Naylor, Robinson and Keane went to Cyprus for three successive summer holidays. "Can't say too much," Keane says archly, "but we had some laughs." Naylor expands on the theme, with a family audience in mind. "We were playing in the pool, just messing about with a ball, and there'd be a forfeit if you had a goal against you. Robbie had to do these star jumps on the side. Everyone recognised him, so that added to his embarrassment."

In the club's best start for two decades, Wolves led the First Division after winning their first four league games of 1998-99, Bull and Keane linking superbly. The pair scored all the goals in a 5-0 rout of Barnet in a Worthington Cup tie at Molineux. Bull plundered what turned out to be his last hat-trick that night, and afterwards I bumped into John Richards, then the club's managing director as well as their previous record goalscorer. He was purring in admiration of the combination.

McGhee had cleared the decks that summer, with Claridge, Dougie Freedman, Mixu Paatelainen and Goodman moved on, and hung his hat on Bull and Keane. Two months in, however, Bully's knee injury flared up again and he never started another senior game. McGhee was succeeded as manager by Lee in the November. Keane, partnered by David Connolly or Haavard Flo, manfully took on the mantle of terrace favourite and chief scorer, leading the charts with 16 goals in a season in which Wolves finished seventh. Second top scorer was Robinson.

"We had a bet who could score the most," recalled Robinson, who is on loan, as we speak, from Portsmouth to Sunderland. "He gave me five start and I was getting a lot of chances. We had a couple of quid on it but I couldn't catch him. Bully was the big star and, as he went out, Robbie became the new idol, although everyone acknowledged there would only ever be one Bully. Having a great young player helped Wolves fans cope with his departure. Robbie liked the attention but could handle it. If they ever got on to him, he was one of those who could cope, would keep running with the ball, keep trying things. You could see he had the temperament to succeed."

"You look at the Norwich game, and away to Manchester City," Lee adds, "and you thought then: he can handle the big stage. It doesn't surprise me he's gone where he's gone. A lot of players out there have ability but not the mental strength to produce it on every stage. He had that belief. I've played with Glenn Hoddle and Ossie Ardiles and they had that same self-belief that they have something special.

"I've been to a couple of the Ireland games and met him afterwards. He's a terrific lad, Robbie, and he won't change. I don't think he'll ever forget where he's come from. The minute you start getting carried away with yourself, you can forget the work ethic. I don't think that'll happen with him. That's another asset. We know he's always looked after his family closely. Unfortunately, he lost his father last year. I know what it's like to go through that because my Dad died when he was 59. He saw me make my debut for Tottenham, was always with me, every step of the way when I was a young player, so I know what a test it is to cope with that."

Chris Evans had seen at first hand how close Keane was to his family. He flew to Dublin to see Robbie senior and Anne, his parents, when he heard Forest were putting every incentive available in front of the schoolboy in an effort to sign him. Evans earned the family's trust and recalls: "Robbie's first £1,000 from Wolves was sent home to put the family on gas for the first time. He doesn't forget his roots."

The jury was out on whether Wolves, under pressure to downscale after several big-spending years, could reach the Premiership stage Keane needed. The board were divided but Lee felt he needed to rebuild the team, post-Bull. This was around the time that Sir Alex Ferguson said he would pay no more than £500,000 for the young forward - and then name him only for Manchester United's reserves. Aston

One of Keane's Irish shirts, presented to Wolves' Academy director with the simple message: "To Chris, thanks for everything."

Villa, who made an offer of around £5.5m and then Middlesbrough, with whom Keane held talks, were more serious. "We had a major decision on whether to sell Robbie," Lee admits. "In my period of management at Wolves, there was no money available for transfers. We were struggling when I took over, so we had a discussion at board level and, as he was our only major saleable asset, if there was going to be a way of rebuilding the team, it would be through selling Robbie."

"Colin and I were fully aware of Robbie's market value," Richards says, "but we were only able to spend on new players what we could bring in. Kieron Dyer went that summer for £6m from Ipswich to Newcastle, and we felt Robbie was of similar worth. I know questions were asked later about sell-on clauses but 'jam today' is what Wolves needed then. We turned Villa down at £5.5m and stuck to our guns."

"There was talk of him not being worth that," said Lee, who went on to manage Walsall for two years. "John Richards and I were confident. There was never any talk of needing a sell-on clause and there were directors who were prepared to take a lot less. We had a blueprint for spending the money, which had to incorporate wages of the new players as well as transfer fees. We bought Michael Oakes, George Ndah, Ade Akinbiyi, Ludo Pollet and Michael Branch. We had to try to build a team to give us a better chance of winning promotion."

Hindsight has persuaded fans that Wolves should have made more from selling Keane but McGhee, who was then out of the game, suffering the consequences of talking Wolves up too much during his spell in charge, points out: "You have to remember the circumstances. Robbie Keane is a particular type of player and people weren't banging down Wolves' door to buy him. One of the reasons I think Gordon [Strachan] bought him was that, as a pal of mine, he'd been to a lot of Wolves games and probably seen as much of him as any other Premier League manager, so he had become more convinced about him than others were. There weren't queues and queues, so it's supply and demand. Wolves got what they could."

Keane scored in his final two league games for Wolves, cracking goals both: the winner at Manchester City and an equaliser in a home draw with Portsmouth (one of his favourites for the club) before moving to the Premiership. Although Akinbiyi came in and scored goals, Lee was dismissed just before Christmas the following year. "I've been back a couple of times and been well received," he says. "I think the fans recognised the job I did and the restrictions I was under. Sir Jack came to Walsall's first game of 2003-04 and left a note on my windscreen saying: 'Well done, good luck for the season. Keep up the good work.' We'd just beaten Albion 4-1."

There were fond farewells for Keane from his Molineux mates. "I knew he was on his way," Robinson says. "He was close to going to Middlesbrough before Coventry came in. He chatted it through with his family; I tried to stay out the way. I wanted him to stay, as 90 per cent of Wolves folk did, but the club saw it as a financial opportunity and Robbie wanted to play at the highest level. If it hadn't been Coventry, it'd have been someone else and it was only a year before he went to Milan. He'd been at Wolves for four years and it was the right move for him. It was just down the road, so he stayed living next door to us for a while." "I knew he was going on to bigger and better things," Naylor says, "and I want that for my mates. I just said: 'Go and do your stuff. It's a stepping stone and you're only going to go on from there.'"

Not that Keane says as much, but he was not initially eager to join Coventry. Meeting Strachan changed his mind; the personal terms helped seal the deal. Two of his 12 Premiership goals that season came in his debut in a 2-0 win over Derby County and it was not long before his fame spread. "He rang me a year later," Evans recalls with a laugh, "and said: 'Inter want me.' I said: 'Interflora?' He said: 'Milan, I've got to fly to Lake Como.' Two days later, I was in Poundstretchers in Bridgnorth with my wife Elaine, and he rang and said: 'Chris, I've signed for £13m.' I said: 'They've paid Coventry £13m?' He said: 'No, that's for me.' He was joking, of course. I think."

Keane keeps in touch with friends. He was in Newcastle at Michael Bridges' wedding as Wolves won the play-off final, rushing around to find a pub with Sky TV. The week before we meet, he has been staying with McPhail. "Friends are friends," he says. "Just because I leave Wolves doesn't mean the end of that friendship." Not only was he a constant mate to Matt Murray when the goalkeeper, whom he still backs to play for England at full level, was out for an entire year, but he retains affection for all the players he has befriended at his various clubs.

So has he been counselling his pals from Wolves and Leeds after relegation? "No, because we were down there as well," he says, wryly. "I've had to counsel myself. There was not a lot I could say, except: 'Unlucky, I hope you bounce back next year.' When I was with Stephen in Leeds last week, he and Gary Kelly were chatting about what a difficult season they've had. I heard Wolves saying - is it Rick Hayward, the chairman now? - that they can hope to keep their players because their salaries are linked to the division the club are in. So with the players there now, I see no reason why they can't bounce back. With Leeds, you can't tell because they're talking about players going and it's difficult to say who'll be left. But they are a massive club with massive support that deserves to be in the Premiership.

"Of course I can understand Wolves fans' frustrations. It was a long time coming, the Premiership. I remember when I first broke into the team, it felt like the club had been in the First Division forever then. So when eventually they do achieve their goal, to go down in the first season is gut-wrenching. But full credit to them as well. They took a lot of points in the second half of the season and, if they'd matched that in the first half, they'd probably have stayed up. I think Dave Jones has done a tremendous job, especially considering the limited amount of money he had last summer."

Keane, like all Wolves fans, was surprised the club did not follow their promotion with a big-name signing to put down a marker, a statement of intent. "I'm sure they must have tried to get some big players in but who was available? And a manager can

only do the job to the best of his ability and work to the confines of his budget."

For all of his professionalism and his status as an experienced international, Keane remains a fan. Tom and I met him at Molineux before the FA Cup classic with Newcastle United in January, 2003, and he was back for the game against Liverpool 12 months later. "It was a great atmosphere," he says. "Sitting in the executive box, looking at the gold scarves, flags and shirts, it was terrific. When you're playing, you can't appreciate it the same because you've got a job to do. But, as a fan, you can take it all

Linking the past, the present and possibly the future. Robbie Keane leaves Molineux in a Wolves shirt again in May, 2004.

in. When we scored (that is, Wolves), the whole place erupted. I was on my feet, jumping up and down. I'm a Wolves fan, really. That's the way I look at it."

This, of course, did not stop our hero pummelling a hat-trick past Michael Oakes in December. He usually performs an elaborate goal celebration, a somersault followed by a pistol-slinging impression, but on this occasion walked back to his own half with barely a smile. "Wolves' fans were magnificent that day," he says. "They sang my name nearly all game, even when I scored. It was: 'Keano is a Wolves fan.' I went to clap them afterwards and they gave me a standing ovation, which really got to me.

"Supporters like that you never forget. I've got a soft spot for Wolves because of going there as such a young lad, and the memories that I had there, from 14 years of age, the friendships I made, going through from the youth team to the first team. All of that will never leave me. To throw the supporters' appreciation back in their faces would not have been nice, so when I scored, I didn't want to rub it in."

Tottenham are due at Molineux a week on Saturday and, as Wolves' form gathered momentum recently, there was even the bitter-sweet prospect that Keane could mark his first competitive return by determining whether they went down. We all know what would have happened then. "Wolves 0 Spurs 1, Robbie Keane," is how Bully envisaged it when we'd been glancing over the fixture list. "I'm relieved that's not the case," Keane says. "I'd hate to have scored the goal that would confirm the relegation of my old club but I've got a job to do for Tottenham and I would not shirk my professional responsibilities. I'm just glad I'm not in that situation."

With that, Simon having given me my two-minute warning, time is up, and they prepare to move into the bar area for the young superstar's next appointment, with a production company. Robbie asks if I have enough material, poses for a quick photo, signs some pictures for my family and offers a warm handshake. He seems genuinely pleased to hear a copy of the book will be sent to him. You wouldn't rule out the possibility of Robbie Keane playing for Wolves again at some point.

May 11, 2004: Wolves' training ground, Newbridge, Tettenhall

L ee Naylor, shivering in his t-shirt, shorts and flip-flops, confirms as much the following week as he awaits his turn on the treatment table. "You never know," he says with a chuckle. "I'm sure he wouldn't mind coming back at some point." Naylor, substituted because of a dead leg in the tremendous performance away to Newcastle United, is determined to be fit for Saturday; not only for the reunion with Keane but to finish the season as Wolves' only Premiership ever-present.

"Just to come up against some of these players, like Thierry Henry and Keaney - it's what I live for," says another of Chris Evans' protégés. "This is where I've wanted to be from the start and, to play every game in the Premiership, against these players, is more than a dream. I haven't found it difficult, having to respond to heavy defeats, maybe because I've been going on adrenaline: the prospect of the team we're playing against has got me through the disappointment of losing the last game."

Naylor is the club's longest-serving player. He has been castigated for lapses of concentration - handing Bolton Wanderers the ball back so that they could take a quick throw-in over his head and equalise with five minutes to go was not his canniest move - while his distribution is still erratic. But his commitment, as he has surged forward, willing to run through brickwalls for the cause, deserves credit. The cheerleader at the Millennium Stadium after the play-off final, he understands how much Wolves fans care and bottles that for every time he goes on the pitch.

It is more than a job, you see. Sure, players come and go, their careers may have many ports of call. But while they are at Wolves, a certain level of commitment is the first requirement. Look how Kenny Hibbitt, John Richards, Steve Bull and Robbie Keane took up the torch. It was not through sheer talent alone that they are still beloved at Molineux.

"I should be fit for Saturday," Naylor says as we watch Rae, Mark Kennedy and Henri Camara getting stuck into a training match arranged for the reserves. "As soon as the fixtures came out, I couldn't wait to face Keaney. I gave him a little call before we played last time, just said 'break a leg' and he goes and scores a hat-trick. He was chanting away in the game, as he always does. He was singing his own song: 'Keano, there's only one Keano.' Just chipping away, like. I couldn't laugh because we were losing, but that's the sort of person he is." Barry Holmes, the physio, calls Nayls in for his treatment. Robbie Keane's Wolves story has just one more postscript. For now.

May 15, 2004: Molineux

He scores, of course. And even as he walks away - his first shot, after a deft dart, saved, his second going in off the far post - Molineux rises to applaud the revered old boy, their disappointment submerged by an appreciation of a home-grown talent who has gone on to bigger and better things. The chants breaks out: 'Keano, there's only one Keano; Keano is a Wolves fan, Keano is a Wolves fan, la la la la, la la la la.' Two minutes from the end of a game Wolves threatened to win at a canter before Keane's goal, David Pleat calls for applause as he substitutes his leading scorer. Spurs' caretaker-manager has nothing but praise for his attitude and class afterwards while Jones says: "He's nothing to do with me. He plays for the other team." A tad truculent, perhaps, but maybe he's frustrated Wolves do not have a scorer of such quality.

Denis Irwin, having played his 902nd and final club game, rightly receives the day's plaudits. He has maintained a level of professionalism that Jones holds up as an example to all his players. Paul Ince scowls his way to a red card for hacking at Jamie Redknapp after his old Liverpool team-mate had gone into a tackle studs up. I can not believe Ince will sign off his career on that note. He has been a success this season, his leadership unrivalled, his will-to-win undimmed and his mobility admirable. Jones knows he will have to use him less often next season if he is to play at his best.

Keane ends the day in a Wolves shirt, traded off Paul Butler, and goes to applaud all four sides of the ground. The fans' return is immediate and warm. At least next season his goals can not deprive Wolves of six points.

Robbie Keane

Born:	July 8, 1980, in Dublin
Signed:	August, 1995
Wolves appearances:	83
Goals:	27
Left:	August, 1999
International recognition:	51 senior Republic of Ireland caps

May 2004

> The defeat by Tottenham is the only blot on the landscape as Wolves finish their Premiership season in fine fettle. Only when relegation is confirmed, on May 1, as Manchester City beat Newcastle to take them out of Wolves' reach, do Carl Cort and Henri Camara stop scoring. Camara's 30-yard blockbuster against Everton, followed by Cort's towering header, provide Wolves folk with heartfelt hope that they can storm into the next campaign. The trip up to St James's Park is made wholly worthwhile by the gutsy performance and, thanks to Vio Ganea's goal and Paul Jones' penalty save from Alan Shearer, a merited 1-1 draw.

PLEAT PLEASED WITH LEGACY

WOLVERHAMPTON WANDERERS (0) **0**

TOTTENHAM HOTSPUR (1) **2**
Keane 34, Defoe 57
Referee: S Bennett 6, Attendance: 29,389

★★★☆☆

Tottenham's failings highlighted by Keane

IT WAS A SIGHT TO GLADDEN old gold hearts, Robbie Keane in a Wolverhampton Wanderers shirt waving to all four quarters of Molineux, but as the Ireland forward was cheered from the field of his first footballing home after swapping jerseys with Paul Butler, it was to deliver a damning indictment on his present team-mates. Even though Tottenham Hotspur have finished nearer a European berth than the relegation zone, it is hard to avoid the conclusion that they have underachieved more than Saturday's demoted hosts.

Keane must have been licking his lips in anticipation when Glenn Hoddle was investing £12 million in attacking options to complement his own unquestioned talents. Yet on scoring his nineteenth goal of a personally satisfying season, he turned on the players who have hidden behind David Pleat's long caretakership as an excuse to muddle around in mid-table.

"It has been an inconsistent and indifferent season and it's very easy to point the finger at certain people but as a team, we knew the job we had to do and we now know we have under-achieved," Keane said. "We have to take a long, hard look at ourselves."

Pleat signs off as Hoddle's short-term replacement, to go and see his "lovely grand-daughters" and "terrific wife", proud of the legacy he has left his unnamed successor. "We had nine British players out there today and we

have blooded more players from our youth system than any other Premiership club this season," he said. "That doesn't win you champion-ships but if you add the right players, you should have the foundations for progress."

The identity of Spurs' new manager remains a mystery eight months after Hoddle's dismiss-al, but there appears little question that Dave Jones will be allowed to build Wolves into a stronger club despite being relegated. His team played some superb football in the opening half-hour as Carl Cort headed against the cross-bar and Denis Irwin, on the occasion of his 958th and final senior game, struck a free kick against a post but the bubble burst after Keane, played through by Mark Yeates, scored at the second attempt. Jermain Defoe capitalised on Cort's weak back-pass to wrap up victory.

As Irwin took his gentlemanly departure from a game he has served with such decorum, Paul Ince was chalking up yellow cards 14 and 15 for the season, diving in a bid to earn a penal-ty before tripping Jamie Redknapp up as retalia-tion for a studs-up tackle. The old warhorse has been surprisingly mobile this season, however, and there is still enough fire in the belly to sug-gest the former England captain wants to give first-division adversaries another hard time.

Jones was handed a measly and belated £3million last summer for squad strengthening. "We know our targets and it's whether we can land them," Jones said. "I'll know how much money I'll have to spend after Monday's board meeting. But this is a unique football club. There not many teams who get clapped all around the pitch after being relegated."

PETER LANSLEY

Wolverhampton Wanderers (4-4-2): P Jones 7 — D Irwin 6 (sub: J Craddock, 89min) I Okoronkwo 5, P Butler 5, L Naylor 5 (sub: A Rae, 71) 6 — S Newton 4 (sub: I Ganea, 90 6), P Ince 5, C Cameron 6, M Kennedy 7 — H Camara 5, C Cort 6. Substitutes not used: M Oakes, S Iversen. Booked: Ince. Sent off: Ince. FORM: LDWDW.
Tottenham Hotspur (4-4-2): K Keller 7 — S Kelly 6, L King 6, A Gardner 5, C Ziege 6 — M Yeates 7, M Brown 6, J Redknapp 5, R Ricketts 6 (sub: F Kanoute, 72) — R Keane 7 (sub: G Poyet, 88), J Defoe 6. Substitutes not used: R Burch, G Doherty, M Malbranc. Booked: Redknapp. FORM: WDLD.
Shots on target: (h) 6 (a) 9. Fouls: (h) 9 (a) 11. Offsides: (h) 6 (a) 2.

John Richards

May 10, 2004: An audience with The King in Pattingham

Those of a gentle disposition may care to look away now. If Molineux was the Hogwarts of our childhood, John Richards was more Draco Malfoy than Harry Potter. Gambling, drinking, queue-jumping, the Wolves icon of the 1970s was a tearaway in hiding, a riot inside.

Ring the *News of the World*, alert the *Express & Star*. The darling of the Molineux terraces used to spend his free afternoons dispensing his new-found wealth at the bookies at the back of the Mander Centre; sometimes as much as 11 shillings (before tax). Shock, horror, the young Richards would stay up all night, imbibing Watney's Red Barrel over a game of Totopoly until Micky Kent, his new house-mate, settled up. On one occasion, the debt escalated to what is now known as 10p. No wonder the manager, Bill McGarry, made Richards and Bertie Lutton stay behind after training to practise their heading as punishment for a lost night on the lash. Or on the sherry at least. Is it any surprise, when you consider the rock and roller lurking within, that Richards befriended Bev Bevan, the drummer from the Electric Light Orchestra?

Only joshing. It is a challenging task, though, making your way into a chapter on your all-time hero. John Richards is, after all, the Gary Lineker of Wolverhampton Wanderers. He will always be remembered among those of a gold and black persuasion as the burgeoning England forward who followed up a season as the country's top scorer by playing through the pain barrier to notch Wolves' winner in the League Cup final of 1974. He was a gentleman of the game, who went on to become captain and Molineux's leading marksman of all time before Steve Bull came along. He served the club loyally for 14 years as a player and was the ideal successor to Billy Wright on the board in 1994. A nicer man you could not wish to meet; a few hours in his company only adorns the golden reputation Richards' playing career earned him.

He was no goody two-shoes, though. In the early 1970s, finding his feet as fame found him, Richards was like any other young lad, hence my parody depicting him as Wolves' answer to George Best. "Ken (Hibbitt) and I were in the same group of lads," he says, "and we'd go to the clubs or Oliver's coffee bar, at the back of the Mander Centre. That was handy because it was close to the bookies. I used to bet quite regularly then on the horses, as a way of passing the time.

"The coffee shop was a magnet for young girls as well. Ken was going out with one, Jim McCalliog would be with another. They'd know we'd be there for a sandwich and coffee, once or twice a week. Tuesdays and Thursdays were double training sessions, sometimes Mondays as well for the young lads, so we'd have a half-day off on Wednesday and Friday. I got into betting, not very seriously, and Mick and I would bet sixpence each way. He'd pick two, I'd pick two and we'd share the proceeds.

"This was when we'd been in digs for about 18 months. Barry Powell and I lodged with Mrs Eagle near Bantock Park and three of us - Micky Spelman, Mick Kent and me - rented a house by Bushbury Baths; our escape to freedom. By coincidence, the first night we went out, without the curfew we'd had in digs, I met Pam, my prospective wife, at the Lafayette nightclub. It was only after that Ken, who had started going out with Jane, and I realised our girlfriends' fathers were brothers.

"We were all in the same age group, just breaking into the first-team squad, with Paul Walker and Jeff Wealands, who went on to keep goal for Manchester United. Micky Kent bought a Totopoly game but we needed somewhere to place it, so one night, we unscrewed a door off its hinges, put it on a table, and Mick and I stayed up all night betting on it. We just got so engrossed. Before we knew it, it was 6am and light. At the end, he owed me two shillings. We turned up in quite a state at training. If you ask why did we do it, it was simply because, for the first time, we could."

Such an inclination for wild debauchery brought the young Richards a painful lesson when Wolves were away participating in the Anglo-Italian Cup in 1969-70. "We were staying in a very up-market resort," he recalls. "The day after we played Fiorentina, we were allowed out to the beach. Later, the older lads were drinking litres of beer, with Hughie Curran leading the way, and the younger ones were allowed to stay up until 11pm. Then we went back to our rooms and Bertie Lutton, who I was sharing with, had a bottle of sherry.

"We opened it for a nightcap - and the next thing I remember is a hammering on the door. It's Sammy Chung, saying the bus is leaving for training in ten minutes. It's 10am. We're two young lads, not daring to be late for training, so we panic, rush our kit on and get down to reception. When the tinted glass doors open, we're blinded by the white marble - and promptly fall down the steps. We get on the coach and say 'sorry boss' as we walk past Bill McGarry. He doesn't say a word.

"In training, we have pounding headaches but we're thinking we've got away with it until McGarry says at the end of the session: 'Waggy, ping a few crosses in. John, Bertie, get yourselves in the middle, we're going to practise your finishing.' We had 15 minutes of heading. It destroyed us. I haven't drunk a drop of sherry since."

Richards looked up to Jim McCalliog - and not only for the Scotland playmaker's goal-scoring instincts. "Jimmy was the bachelor hero of Wolverhampton," he recalls with a smile. "He was single, an international, good-looking, drove around in a bright red Alfa Romeo Spider and, as a young lad, was the player you aspired to be. He had more gorgeous girlfriends than you could count and seemed to change for an even better-looking model every fortnight. He wasn't a gambling man - I don't think he had time. He was there to get the girls. He used to mix with the younger lads but was also very much a family man, moving his parents to Wolverhampton and opening a garage on the Penn Road that they all ran."

Richards' natural affability, intelligence, importance to the team and standing in the Wolves community later led him to succeed Mike Bailey as club captain, a role which incorporated social duties he happily embraced. Wolves' players would play charity cricket and darts matches, or attend functions, with supporters. "They didn't raise a lot of money but meeting fans away from games helped develop relationships. Come match day, they'd know you weren't having a bad game on purpose.

"The link between players and supporters is important but the game was a lot less scientific or under the media microscope then. You had a public private life: you could go out, have a drink and it would not be in the papers. That was the culture of the time. We could go out on a Saturday night and get drunk. There were times I'd drive when I shouldn't have. Whether it was with your club or with England, it was no different. Now, the foreign players bring in a discipline where everything they do is geared to becoming an athlete. We got away mostly with natural ability. But everyone was the same. It was the way of the world. It was no different from players in the 1950s going to a game on the bus and stopping for a pie and a pint with the punters beforehand."

Richards, a late starter in the pro ranks, shot to a level of stardom that

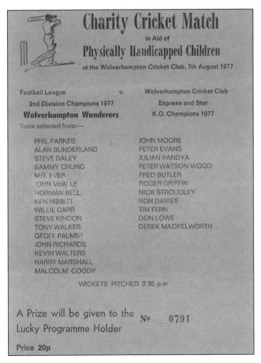

Putting summer free-time to good use...

would have tested anyone's ability to remain level-headed. No-one suggests he was a Wayne Rooney or a Paul Gascoigne but 36 goals in 1972-73 and an England debut at 22 took him beyond the stage at which the heads of Kenny Miller, Dougie Freedman or Adam Proudlock may have been turned. So did he ever find himself playing Billy Big Time? "When we left digs, there was no doubt Wolves players had privileges around town," he says. "After games, we'd go to the Lafayette and there would be queues. We'd walk to the front, knock on the door, and it'd be: 'Come in John, nice to see you, come in boys.' The regular customers must have thought: 'Who on earth do these guys think they are?' I cringe now but, at the time, it seemed natural.

"You were invited to functions, like now, but, you wouldn't charge for going. In hindsight, they were selling tickets on the back of having Wolves players there but you were well looked after. You were privileged and thought: 'This is nice.' Now, it'd probably be: 'Speak to my agent and we'll see.' There were Jack-the-Lad moments. You have that fancy-free attitude as a young player that says: 'I'm bomb-proof, I can walk to the front of the queue, I'm in the first team.' You felt the world was your oyster and was never going to change. It quickly does."

A boot deal with Gola followed - I remember being so proud when I was bought a replica plastic-coated pair - and Richards briefly signed with an agent. "He came to our wedding," he says, laughing. "Pam said: 'Who's that?' I said: 'My agent.' Because I had pelvic problems for much of 1974, there was only a short spell when I was highly marketable. The agent did a deal with a company who signed 30 emerging England players, for picture cards to be sold with chewing gum. That was worth about £1,000."

Richards, notwithstanding the grey hair, does not look so different now. A keen golfer, he remains in good shape at the age of 53 and is a hospitable but relaxed host. He reassures me that time is not a pressure, as he has cancelled his five-a-side that evening. Pity, I confess, as I've brought my trainers. I show him my Soccer Stars collection and he chuckles as he sees himself in the 1972-73 album, red-cheeked, determinedly chasing a ball down, with Willie Carr in the background in a Coventry City shirt. "This one's coming loose," he says, as George Best, rather appropriately, drops out. "You don't want to lose him."

As the sun beats down, he recommends the chocolate biscuits. The terrace, at the Pattingham home he has shared for 20 years with Pam, who is currently out on the golf course, overlooks a long, beautifully maintained lawn; no wonder, considering he is now the operations director for Pitchcare.com, a website he runs with Dave Saltman, the groundsman at Molineux when Richards was managing director.

That was the late 1990s but, in the late 1960s, Richards was an England schoolboy international, who had started out as a goalkeeper, aged eight. He was to finish up a centre-half, aged 34. He stayed on at school in his native Warrington to do three A Levels but, by the time his innate talent had helped him score five goals for Wolves reserves away to Blackburn Rovers, there was very little chance he would be going on to Chester College to train as a PE teacher. Instead, after his initial one-year Molineux contract, his education in Wolves' first-team dressing room was about to start.

"It was interesting to see how the first team prepared for a game," he says. "There was a vast age range in that dressing-room. Mike Bailey, to us younger lads, seemed a lot older, married and with kids, so while we all got on well, socially, you kept in your own groups. It was a lot more serious than I'd expected. There'd be banter between ones and twos but the atmosphere was pensive, nervy even, and people would deal differently with it. Waggy was a bundle of nerves. He'd settle down by disappearing to the loo for a cigarette at about ten to three. The manager would turn a blind eye but for me, just starting out, it was an eye-opener. It made you realise: this is serious."

Richards' league debut came at West Bromwich Albion in February, 1970. "I'd been on the bus to help with the kit a few times but they used to name a squad of no more than 15, because everyone on the list would be on half appearance money," he says. "I was on £25 a week so to earn an extra £5 was quite something. My aim was to play *one* senior game. If I'd gone back to college having done that, I'd have been satisfied. I was delighted to sign for a club like Wolves (Derby County and Sheffield Wednesday also showed interest) but, once I was in the reserves, I thought if I could play once for the first team...that was the extent of my ambitions."

With Derek Dougan injured, McGarry only told Richards he was to partner Curran as they travelled across the Black Country at about 1pm. A 3-3 draw was watched by 37,819. "I thoroughly enjoyed it," Richards recalls. "It wasn't as difficult as I thought it would be. There was not the massive difference I'd expected, probably because you were with better players. It was by far the biggest crowd I'd ever played in front of but I can't recall feeling nervous. I hadn't figured out where Waggy was disappearing to. Mike Bailey was the vociferous one and he came up and had a captain's word with me: 'Play your normal game and pass the ball to a team-mate as soon as you can.'

"I've still got very strong images of those players. I recall Hughie scoring with a header. I'd never seen anyone head a ball as powerfully; he headed it as hard as some people kick it. That was my main impression, of the quality of play. Perhaps I was fortunate I wasn't from the area because I was less conscious of the local rivalry. It was very intense even then. I know Bully spiced it up when he crossed over but, in those days, Albion and Wolves were the top sides in the region. Villa went as low as the Third Division, Birmingham came through later, in Trevor Francis' time.

"After the match, we were gutted because they equalised with two minutes to go. The big thing you'd do on returning to Molineux was wait for the *Sporting Star* at the social club. I couldn't wait to see what Phil Morgan had said about me. It wasn't so much what *you* thought of your performance, it was what other people thought. It mattered to us what the local reporter wrote. That was when it sank in that I'd achieved my goal of playing for Wolverhampton Wanderers. That gave me a lot of satisfaction."

Richards scored his first senior goal against Huddersfield Town early in 1970-71.

"I checked all the papers to see which had a photograph, then went to the *Express & Star* to order some," he recalls. "I got about six. They were big things to you as a young lad. That was a special goal to me and I remember it vividly, at the South Bank end. Jim McCalliog crossed and I hit it left-footed back across the six-yard box into the far corner." That season, Richards was named as substitute many more times than he played. "That second season was like my apprenticeship as a pro footballer. It involved helping Sammy Chung put the kit out. Within a towel, you had to roll socks, shorts, a slip, a shirt and lay them out, above the boots, in a big metal skip. Then I'd hand them to Sammy to place around the dressing-room as he knew who was playing.

"I wasn't playing much. I'd play one or two reserve games when they didn't clash with the first team and come on for three or four little run-outs; nothing significant. So I asked to see McGarry. I explained that, while I appreciated going with the first team, I missed playing and was a bit fed up. He said he understood and proved it, by leaving me out of the squad for six weeks. I got my match fitness all right - with the reserves. I was learning so much. I learned that you don't mess with Bill McGarry. I was disappointed. I was playing well for the reserves, scoring goals, but, having had a taste, you want to be back on the first-team list. He was saying he knew best and, looking back, he did. That's why it was like my apprenticeship.

"I was very raw. My skill level wasn't too high in that first couple of years. I hadn't had any professional coaching. It was more that I had speed and could score goals, so I was still developing and learning from people like Derek Dougan, Bobby Gould, Mike Bailey. When you watched them in training, you'd see how they prepared to receive a ball, backed their body into defenders, knew where their team-mates were, the way Doog would prepare to head the ball to a colleague. That was my most important season. It set me up. Bill McGarry was teaching me,

P/FL

An Agreement made the 21st

day of June, 19 72 between Philip Alfred Shaw of Molineux Grounds, Wolverhampton in the County of Stafford.

the Secretary of and acting pursuant to Resolution and Authority for and on behalf of the Wolverhampton Wanderers FOOTBALL CLUB of Molineux Grounds, Wol

(hereinafter referred to as the Club) of the one part and

John Peter Richards.

of 44 Finchfield Road, Wolverhampton.

in the County of Stafford.

Professional Football Player

(hereinafter referred to as the Player) of the other part Whereby it is agreed as follows:—

1. The Player hereby agrees to play in an efficient manner and to the best of his ability for the Club for the period of one (year/years) (hereinafter called "the initial period of employment") from the 21st day of June, 1972 to the 30th day of June 1973 Unless the initial period of employment shall either be (a) previously determined in accordance with the provisions of one or other of Clauses 10, 11 or 12 hereof or (b) terminated extended or renewed as provided by Clauses 17 and 18 of this Agreement.

2. The Player shall attend the Club's ground or any other place decided upon by the Club for the purposes of or in connection with his training as a Player pursuant to the instructions of the Secretary, Manager, or Trainer of the Club, or of such other person, or persons as the Club may appoint.

3. The Player shall do everything necessary to get and keep himself in the best possible condition so as to render the most efficient service to the Club, and will carry out all the training and other instructions of the Club through its representative officials.

4. The Player shall observe and be subject to all the Rules, Regulations and Bye-Laws of The Football Association, and any other Association, League, or Combination of which the Club shall be a member. And this Agreement shall be subject to any action which shall be taken by The Football Association under their Rules for the suspension or termination of the Football Season, and if any such suspension or termination shall be decided upon the payment of wages shall likewise be suspended or terminated, as the case may be and in any proceedings by the Player against the Club it shall be a sufficient and complete defence and answer by and on the part of the Club that such suspension or termination hereof is due to the action of The Football Association, or any Sub-Committee thereof to whom the power may be delegated.

5. The Player shall not engage in any business or live in any place which the Directors (or Committee) of the Club may deem unsuitable.

6. Unless this Agreement has previously been determined by any one of Clauses 10, 11 or 12 hereof as hereinafter provided, the Player shall not before the last day of the playing season next preceding the expiration of any further or additional further period for which this Agreement shall have been renewed in accordance with the provisions of Clauses 17 or 18 hereof or before the last d of the playing

The vital paperwork that tied John Richards to Molineux in his early 1970s prime.

making me watch. If I'd been chucked in too soon, it'd have killed me. That happens to a lot of young players now. People clamour for youngsters to be thrown in but you have to have exceptional talent to be a top player at 18 and 19. I was with Bully the other week and he said he wasn't a regular until he reached the age of 21 or 22. He wasn't a 17-year-old prodigy."

The notion of Rooney attempting to cope with his temper and the hype his sublime talent has brought him springs to mind. "It takes a while to learn, especially in the top flight. It's a special gift when people like Robbie Keane can slot in very nicely but you've still got to deal with them carefully otherwise you can destroy them. In Robbie's case, even his introduction was limited and Wolves were playing at First Division level, not in the Premiership. Too much is expected too soon by fans, and the press add to that. For every one who makes it, 20 don't even get started."

Richards, fortunately for Wolves, was the one. While Lutton, Spelman, Kent and Walker faded away, their pal made it - and then some. After four starts in 1970-71, when Curran and Gould were top scorers as Wolves finished fourth, the youngster left them trailing in his wake the season after, making 33 appearances in the league and scoring 16 times in all. The run to the UEFA Cup final, though, was followed by the most thrilling yet frustrating campaign imaginable for Wolves fans. Richards, now earning £60 basic a week with no goal bonus, played all 60 games, the only outfield ever-present, and scored 27 league goals as McGarry's team finished fifth and reached the semi-finals of both League Cup and FA Cup.

"In that spell, we didn't fear anyone," he says. "It was the only time in all my Wolves career that we were genuinely disappointed if we didn't win every match. As a young lad, you just took it all for granted.

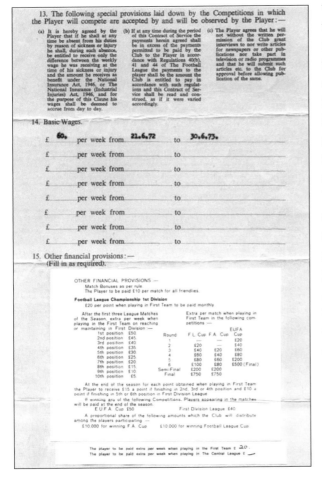

All those goals for £60 a week.

We were absolutely gutted when we lost the two semi-finals; we really thought we'd win both. It was the same in the UEFA Cup the previous season. We sailed through the early rounds, then played Juventus, Ferencvaros, some great teams. Never did we fear any of them.

"There was a game in 1973 when we beat Manchester City 5-1 at Molineux. Doog got three, I got two and it all came together. We played almost perfect football. Doog tapped in a couple of rebounds from shots I'd had saved and the *Sunday People* gave me ten out of ten. That season, we were fairly close to pushing for the title. We'd got a European final under our belt and got to the last four of both domestic cups; so near yet so far. We should have beaten Leeds at Maine Road. I remember it vividly. Two key players, Frank Munro and Mike Bailey, were doubtful and McGarry decided he couldn't risk both from the start, so Mike was sub.

"We should have won. Hitting the inside of the post late on summed it up. I turned Paul Madeley just inside the box, shot left-footed and the ball spun from the post along the line. People talk about that Wolves side and say we should have achieved more. That was the year." So why didn't they? "You might say we lacked quality in depth. We had 15 or 16 players and were very dependent on a relatively small nucleus. If we'd had two or three more of the same quality, we might have really taken off."

Childhood: one fan's perspective

I was eight, the same age our Tom is now, when I started going to Molineux. That thrilling 1972-73 season largely passed me by but I soon got into it all. It is difficult to pinpoint precisely where my hero worship of John Richards started but I remember Dad kept offering me a Saturday afternoon out, to go to watch Wolves' and England's leading young goalscorer.

I knew about football, if not as much as about Action Men, with their gripping hands and moving eyes, or safari animals. Dave, my brother, had collected an album full of elephant and lion stickers but no-one at school swapped them. This year, we were both collecting the Wonderful World of Soccer Stars. One Saturday, Jamie Scott, my chum from up the drive in Wood End, didn't want to play any more, so I took Dad up on his offer. It must be October 6 because I have the programme: a 2-1 home win over Manchester United. Richards didn't score but he could run really fast.

Inside the Subbuteo FA Cup I received that Christmas was a ticket for an FA Cup third-round tie versus Leeds. Molineux was packed and it was incredibly exciting. Dad explained that Leeds had stopped Wolves winning this competition the previous year just one game before he would have been going to Wembley, the biggest ground of the lot. Leeds were good and everyone hated them. I couldn't quite fathom that one. Still, in a couple of weeks, we were going to beat them. I'd got John Richards in Soccer Stars by now and it was all coming together. At Molineux for the tie, men were smoking their festive cigars and we had Bovril and Wagon Wheels. Disgusting combination, come to think about it, but all part of the day. Richards scored. So did Leeds, and we went out in the replay.

Thankfully, there was another cup - one Subbuteo don't make - and we were in the semi-finals of that. We drew 1-1 at Norwich City, whom I'd watched lose to Tottenham Hotspur on telly the year before, even making notes. They played in yellow but were in all red at Wolves and Dave Stringer, their defender, kept jumping on Richards' back. Richards scored the only goal, though, and we were going to Wembley for a cup final. Marvellous.

If it was going to be like this every week, I wanted in. So we went to the next home game - a 1-1 draw with Stoke City - and Munro, who lived on our estate and whose sons I'd been playing Action Men with for three years, was sent off. Not so good. Here my scrapbook starts. Next to the *Express & Star* report - "It was not a day for Richards and Derek Dougan to get on target" - are my incisive views: "Ere ar sum guod players jom ricards, alan clak, deruk dugan, petr lowimer.' Booker Prize stuff or what?

Left-over soccer stars fill the remaining pages until a gratuitous Glasgow Rangers poster and a *Tiger* and *Scorcher* pic of Burnley's Martin Dobson finish it off with a hint of wandering loyalties. That'll teach Wolves to draw with Stoke. Richards was injured for the rest of the season - not surprised after Stringer climbed all over him - and, on the Action Man front, I swapped Jamie Scott's Stoke strip for an inflatable dinghy.

I recall just one other game that season but it gave me a sufficient appreciation of what Wolves, football and the whole experience was about. Dad got tickets for the League Cup final at Wembley - me, him, my two eldest brothers. Mum and Simon, only two years old, travelled to London with us. We stayed at the aunts' house in West Ham and Auntie Beat bought me a superb heavy plastic ball, although it had Bobby Moore's name on it. Still, finders keepers is the way I saw it.

We had the Wolves pre-match brochure in which each of the players had a head shot cut out so his hair was all bouffant. They wore black tracksuit tops with gold bottoms. Oh, the glamour of being a cossetted, Wembley-bound superstar. Richards, with his pelvic problem, barely played in the weeks leading up to the final but was deemed sufficiently intrinsic to the team's aspirations that they patched him up to face Manchester City. "There was probably a doubt but everything was geared to make sure I could play," he recalls. "At Worthing in the week before the game, I had my legs strapped together at night to prevent me parting them inadvertently. I didn't train at all. I walked around the pitch, saying: 'Get on with it lads. See you at Wembley.'"

Memories of the game are clouded by TV footage. It's hard to distinguish between real recollections and those images attained subsequently. But watching it again brings back the terrific emotion: Kenny Hibbitt's marvellous mis-kick into the corner, Colin Bell equalising and then Richards, who had expected to be substituted before Waggy pulled up and had to limp off instead, banging in the winner with six minutes left. It was the quickest game of my young life, almost passing me by, and I thought there was

John Richards and Derek Dougan are joined by 'trainer' Sammy Chung for a picture opportunity at Worthing.

ages left when we went 2-1 up. A nice policeman let me jump up from our seats near the edge of the pitch to go and touch the turf at the end and we had a photograph taken sitting on the perimeter wall. Then it all becomes a bit of a blur.

That was it. I was totally hooked. On my ninth birthday, exactly four months later, two season tickets were unveiled, to be shared between us. Dad had done without one for five years but, with our interests at heart, reinvested. Dave, the most studious of the four brothers, kept mainly to hunting for snakes on Cannock Chase, and Simon, the youngest, to rolling about on the floor screaming 'Ga ga' (which the arrival of George and Sarah has allowed him to return to of late). So Mark and I alternated our visits to Molineux, altruistically chauffeured by Dad. The things he did for his family...

Games become clearer from now on. The *Express & Star* headline following an opening-day win at Burnley was 'Back with a bang' as Richards scored in his first competitive game since Wembley. Wolves had a really good programme that season and the start of our League Cup defence, versus Fulham, was marked with drawings of Mike Bailey holding the trophy. We were promptly knocked out. We were concentrating on our UEFA Cup entry, I was told. We were stuffed 4-1 away by Porto, where Richards didn't play. Portugal wasn't his favourite destination at that time after a sending-off at Belenenses the previous year, when he clashed with an over-attentive marker. I had to settle for watching the second leg against Porto (whatever happened to them?) on *Sportsnight*. It was the main game and Wolves were a whisker short of matching the result. My horizons had been broadened.

Mark and I would do 'trades' for our tickets and I did a full share of dog-walking and shoe-cleaning to see the matches that I fancied. Fortunately, I booked in the 7-1 win over Chelsea in March, 1975, when Willie Carr scored on his debut. We were 3-1 up at half-time and Richards scored twice.

Carr made his mark against us a couple of years previously when whingeing away for Coventry in the FA Cup quarter-final. The sheer acceleration of my hero, in running clear to score, is incredible, even if the play was generally a lot slower. That season, while I was still in Action Man mode, Richards made his England debut, against Northern Ireland at Goodison Park. Why he never played at full level again is a mystery, despite his cruel subsequent catalogue of serious injuries. Getting him called up again

Richards's Wembley winner, reproduced pictorially and in words, by *The Times* some three decades later.

became a crusade for me and, sitting under the quaint old gold arches in the Molineux Street Stand, I would join in the 'Richards for England' chants most vehemently.

When you listen to the early-seventies terrace songs now, it appears everyone must have been doped up to the eyeballs. Even if Richards is about to lash home from a Dougan knockdown, the North Bank seem to be just standing there, everyone in a Parka, crooning one of the dirges that stood in for encouragement back then. "Those were the days, my friend, we thought they'd never end, we thought they'd last, for ever and a day…" It amazes me that those Wolves players in their perfect round-necked jerseys didn't just sit down, pack it all in and light up.

Richards can not name his favourite Wolves song, although he does hastily nominate his worst - the *Wonderful Wolves* anthem of 1980. "Before going to a match, I'd play Queen's *Don't Stop Me Now* at home. At the ground, I liked *The Happy Wanderer*. I remember *The Liquidator* being played but it didn't make any difference to me," he says. "It was more the lift of the crowd that made me realise I was in an arena. We'd come out second at Molineux, after the away team, and that crescendo would drown out the tannoy music."

A strange phenomenon occurred in 1975-76, causing my world to wobble on its axis. I had my Wolves shirt, with black v-neck, wing collar and No9 sewn (by Mum) on the back. I'd broken my leg before the school-team trials (Stuart Wall, I forgive you) but it seemed reasonable to assume I'd follow Richards' lead. Lack of talent need not be an issue. Mid-way through that season, however, The King was left out and, when he returned, it was to wear No10 or No11. On Valentine's Day, we played Charlton Athletic in the FA Cup fifth round and he was substitute. He still bagged a hat-trick. In the quarter-final at Manchester United, he scored our goal as we earned a replay I endured from beneath the bed covers, listening to Radio 2 (sure it was Alan Parry commentating) as Mark and Dad saw us lose despite Richards' brilliant effort.

I don't know why Richards lost *his* shirt. Nor does he but it doesn't matter to him. Sure enough, Wolves were relegated, although he managed 25 goals that season. Three were against Newcastle United in a 5-0 demolition at Easter, when we were on holiday in Crantock, Cornwall. Don't know what it is about thrashing Newcastle that makes our family want to go away. I remember Dad appearing at the top of the dunes, having gone back to the car to get the results, and holding up five fingers while forming a circle with his other hand, then holding up three fingers. I knew what he meant. We were on *Match of the Day* that night but match of the century was still to come as we faced Liverpool on the season's last night at Molineux, us needing to win to stay up, them needing a point to clinch the title. It was Mark's turn for the ticket. I spent the evening with Jamie Scott, Action Men discarded, and we suffered it all on the radio.

Down. And out. I was staggered, despite Dad's assurances of fun ahead. Like now, we bought season tickets again for one year to see how it went. Richards, similarly, opted to give it one winter in the Second Division to see if he could revive our fortunes. Preposterously handed the No8 shirt in a three-man forward line with two of Steve Kindon, Alan Sunderland and Bobby Gould, he came back from career-threatening knee operations to lead the title challenge. His goal against Chelsea, in the final home game, clinched it and was banged in right in front of me. Mark again had the ticket, so I went with Stuart Morgan in the North Bank. It was brilliant to be standing, free to go bananas at my hero's vital equaliser. He came towards me to celebrate. I don't know how he knew I was there. The pitch invasion was unnerving, though, so I stood behind the net until Dad appeared and led me back to the sanity of the stands.

It was then, with Simon now able to ride a bike, that we started nipping to Castlecroft to watch Wolves train in the summer holidays. It was three miles from home but pre-season training stopped the games taking so long to come round. As we were back in the elite, allied to the fact that Mum was conspiring with my teachers at Regis Comprehensive to smarten up my academic approach, I started keeping a Wolves score-book from the executive exercise books Dave would pilfer for me from the sixth-form Cretney Building.

The manager by now was Sammy Chung, previously McGarry's trainer. Not his assistant, or first-team coach, but *trainer*, his role including running on to the pitch to squeeze a magic sponge over injured players. Chung used to go to Christ Church (Tim, his son, was in the choir with us), but not as regularly as he might. He went only when Wolves had won. I don't know what his prayers were but you can imagine him genuflecting at the altar: 'Please make sure Richards' knee problems don't play up next week at Anfield.' I know I did.

The late peak of Richards' career coincided with the glamorous three-year reign of John Barnwell that marked the onset of (without necessarily causing) the financial strains that saw the club descend into darkness. Richards' right knee led surgeons to recommend he consider retiring but he returned late in 1978-79 to score nine goals from 17 games and prevent another relegation. Transient prosperity was signalled by progress to the FA Cup semi-finals. When Barnwell yielded £1.5m for Steve Daley, who had performed out of his skin for a couple of years, and brought in Emlyn Hughes, Dave Thomas and, amid pomp and ceremony, Andy Gray, we felt we were supporting a big club again. Sure enough, Barnwell's first full year in charge saw Wolves back at Wembley and in the top six of Division One, Richards leading the way.

It was an optimistic time. The shirts were glossy, the lapels wide and Gray's perm tacky. In line with the expansive thinking and, to help finance the new John Ireland Stand, Mark, Dad and I all had season tickets and I reckoned I knew the worth of each match slip. As Regis was too far away to nip home for lunch and most of my mates lived closer, I kept a chart in my blazer pocket of how many times I was invited to each home. After a fortnight, I would check whether Mike Cox, Jon Smith or Jon Brayshaw had been the most frequent host and then proclaim to the 'winner' that he had Mark's ticket for (drum roll, please) … the next day's reserve match at Molineux. I couldn't understand why Brayshaw shut the door on me. It was a deeply trying period of adolescence on the road to self-knowledge. Please let Tom and Joe find a short-cut.

By the end of that 1979-80 season, my class-mates were buying their own tickets for big games. From the turn of the year, Richards was rampant, stuffing home 15 goals - all after a barren three months activated, in my mind at least, by the heinous actions of one Brendan Ormsby. Over 36,000 were packed into Molineux for the visit of Aston Villa and we'd read a bit about Gray, the new boy, teaching Richards a few tricks of the trade. There is a chance Richards was getting a bit of punishment in the back from Ormsby. If our man put his arms up to protect himself, can he be blamed? My theory, as Richards lay on the ground, nose bleeding after the Villa thug had lamped him one in alleged retaliation, was that Ormsby shoving JR in the back forced the victim's elbows back and they accidentally connected with the defender's face.

Mark was yelling for retribution for Ormsby's felony - "Off, off, off" - and jumped to his feet in gladiatorial celebration when he was dismissed. I was telling my brother to keep quiet. This was ominous and, sure enough, Richards, following long treatment, was also sent off. I couldn't believe it. Neither could he. He sat on the bench, head in hands, in what I perceived to be the shame of injustice. Maybe his nose just hurt. It was the only time I saw my hero sent off and my head hung low that week. The game finished 1-1 but it felt worse than a defeat. I shall never forgive Brendan Ormsby.

Atonement came with another League Cup final at Wembley. Richards scored two in the semi-final against Swindon Town and my journalistic pretensions prompted me to make my own preview brochure. It was crap, even for a 15-year-old. I was writing so much for the Regis Rag, the school newspaper, that the editor, Mr Sutherland, our economics teacher, printed apologies for conveniently misplacing reams of my copy. We walked to the Stars newsagent at Tettenhall to buy the *Express & Star's* version the lunchtime it came out. None of these efforts could compare with the levels of artistic achievement of the Wembley song, however. Nothing had ever been that bad.

It whetted the appetite as Wolves, underdogs by far despite impressive league form, took on the European champions. The side worked their wotsits off, players such as Peter Daniel and Mel Eves playing above themselves. It was not a great game and couldn't compare with the magic of our previous visit to Wembley, with Richards no longer the boyish hero but now one of the senior statesmen. Gray clocked the clownish winner, when David Needham and Peter Shilton ran into each other going for Daniel's long ball and left the net gaping. I remember Richards, having waved to the crowd as they sang 'Oh Johnny, Johnny Richards, You're the greatest, in the land' before the game, doing a seal impression when grounded on the very goal-line, the ball hanging, tantalisingly, above him and Shilton. Overall, he had a very quiet game.

"The 1974 final was very special," Richards recalls. "Getting there after all the previous disappointments was very gratifying and, although I was carrying an injury, I really enjoyed it. It was a good game compared with the 1980 final, which was fairly dour. Forest had won the two previous finals and were in between two European Cup triumphs. In Richie Barker, we had a very good tactical coach. I've a lot of respect for him and he'd worked Forest out well.

"The message was to stop them scoring and for Andy and me to battle on our own up front. It went exactly to plan. We were fortunate with the goal, then we shut up shop. There weren't many chances for either team - it was the complete opposite to the Man City game, when you had terrific saves, three goals and the promise of more."

Another of Richards' memories of '74 is celebrating at the London Hilton. "One of the people I respected most in football was John Ireland, the chairman. He was like a father figure to us young lads. We idolised him and he really looked after us. He had a wolf made out of ice and had it wheeled in as the centrepiece for the table. It was magnificent. I remember John's pride because we'd won the League Cup, as he gave a speech. Everyone of that generation revered John Ireland.

"One of the most shameful things Wolves have done in recent years is remove his name from the stand. He did more than any chairman since the 1950s, led the club to the second most successful period in its history and his name should still be associated

Richards shows the predator's instinct to pip George Burley to a loose ball and net in an FA Cup tie away to Ipswich.

with Wolverhampton Wanderers. I can't believe it was beyond the club's ingenuity to come up with something, if they wanted to honour Steve Bull, that would not have damaged the memory of John Ireland. It's wrong to recognise someone's achievements by dismissing those of another." This is the old Molineux Street Stand, renamed the John Ireland Stand in 1979 and then the Steve Bull Stand in 2003. "It's nothing against Steve Bull at all, just a sadness for John Ireland's memory and his family."

As in the UEFA Cup first round of 1974, the lights quickly went out on our 1980 continental adventure, floodlight failure holding up the return against PSV Eindhoven and a single Mel Eves goal leaving us one short. The old backbone of the team was wearing out: McAlle was not a first choice, Parkin and Palmer were no longer assured of places, Hibbitt, Carr and Richards were into their swansongs. Richards enjoyed his last year of sustained performance in 1980-81, his second successive 17-goal haul keeping us away from relegation and helping us to the last four of the FA Cup. He scored in the fourth round (against Watford), the fifth (Wrexham) and, after a 1-1 draw at Middlesbrough, in the 3-1 quarter-final replay win, the last occasion Molineux attracted a 40,000-plus crowd. Richards celebrated with a cool single-hand wave but, yet again, we were left disappointed at the penultimate stage.

It was a crushing blow and we went down the following year, with Ian Greaves replacing Barnwell. Richards was in and out of the side at first, substitute for a League Cup game at home to Villa just after they had stonked us 3-0 in the league. We went to both and my cousin Liz couldn't work out why I was so depressed in the intervening days. When Richards came on in the cup tie, he ran around demented, so worked up to prove himself, and scored a consolation - one of only four he managed that season.

The writing was on the wall. The Richards era was over. I think I was going out with Lucy the following winter and she threatened to commit suicide when I wasn't paying her enough attention. The girl could have spared a thought for what I was going through. Around the time Richards was loaned to Derby, who were struggling at the foot of the old Second Division, I took to my bed, collapsing through illness. The doctor called it glandular fever but that, surely, was symptom, not cause.

One of the sad aspects of Richards' departure as Wolves won promotion in 1983 was the deterioration of his relationship with Dougan, who had returned to Molineux as front man in the Bhattis' boardroom. As team-mates, they had been the ideal partnership; the wily old pro, strong in the air, and the pacy young tyro, such a strong finisher on the ground. "I got on very well with him in our playing days," Richards says. "I had a lot of respect for him. He taught me a great deal and, while we never socialised, we did travel together to Manchester for PFA meetings because I took over from him as Wolves' rep when he became the union chairman.

"Initially, we had Waggy, Doog and me. I was on the right as a natural right-footer but a key move by McGarry switched me to the left, and Doog, as a natural left-footer, to the right, so we were facing in on goal. When Waggy crossed and I was looking to feed on Doog's flick-ons, I'd be running in to shoot with my right. It was a subtle move and became very effective, with Kenny dinking balls from the right into space Doog would create by running to the far post, leaving me to run into the inside-right area. I would say McGarry was the best tactical manager I played under."

It was under Graham Hawkins in March, 1983, that Richards was recalled from a loan spell at Derby. "I felt I should have been in the first team at Wolves still, but I would say that, wouldn't I?" he adds. "I'd got myself match-fit with Derby, where I'd enjoyed playing again, and expected to be selected when Wolves recalled me early. Instead, I was made substitute at Grimsby, where I came on for exactly one minute. I was doing a column for the *Express & Star* and wrote: 'Rarer than a penny black, more elusive than the abominable snowman. What is it? A picture of me in a Wolves shirt this season. The Christians had a better chance in the colosseum than I've had.'

"Dougan hauled me in and asked me to explain but it was my right to say what I felt. If I wasn't in the team when they were on their way to promotion, it was even less likely I would be the following season. So, even with two years left on my contract, I couldn't see the point of sitting it out. I wanted to play. Because it wasn't resolved until that summer [1983] that I would leave, however, I wasn't given the opportunity to play a farewell game and, after being at the club for 14 years, that annoyed me."

Richards left on a free transfer for Maritimo, a Madeira-based Portuguese Second Division side, but without his due settlement. "It was ironic that Dougan, a former chairman of the PFA, withheld my payments. I had the PFA ready to take action against the club and it caused me problems and my wife a lot of upset, bearing in mind I was in Madeira. I felt the way Dougan behaved was abysmal and hypocritical. The PFA threat proved enough but the damage was done. Our relationship has never been mended."

Richards, who had a testimonial in 1982, finally had his chance to say goodbye to Wolves' fans with a 1985 match in his honour - after prolonging his career with two enjoyable years in the sun. Ronnie Allen, Wolves' former manager, had recommended him to Maritimo, who signed a player they had not seen. After some ups and downs on the field - nearly settling up and coming home six months in, scoring four goals in one game, finishing second the first season and winning the division in the second - Richards' playing days came to an unlikely end. "I started the second season up front and ended at centre-back. I was one of the tallest players at 5ft 10in and, in my very last game, they made me captain and I scored.

"It was a wonderful experience. Some games were played on sand and, for one in Lisbon, it was that hot that the fire brigade had to hose the pitch before kick-off. In Funchal, the capital, we shared the only grass pitch in Madeira and were allowed to train there once a week for two hours. Once, the groundsman came up and told the manager our time was up. He said: 'Yes, but we've got a practice match to finish.' So the groundsman switched the sprinklers on."

At this point, rain threatens in Pattingham and, with Pam not yet home, Richards is off swiftly to get the washing in. Waiting for the kettle to boil, we trawl his office for photos and memorabilia he's happy to share. Reconvening in the conservatory, we're disturbed by a heavy-duty bumble bee. At least it is wearing the right colours.

In 1994, Richards returned to Wolves as a non-executive director. "I was so proud to be invited by Sir Jack Hayward to keep a link between the board and ex-players," he says. "I was asked to take Billy Wright's place, which was a fantastic honour. I was also told I went on board the same as everyone else, without payment or expenses. Of course, this wasn't an issue. It was nice to be involved again. I'd forgotten how enjoyable it was, going to matches. It was nine years since I'd gone regularly because I'd been working in local government."

Three years later, Sir Jack replaced Jonathan, his son, as chairman, and Richards stepped up to become managing director. "It was felt important to have someone representing the chairman day-to-day. We appointed a head-hunter firm and I was involved in some interviews. Then Sir Jack asked whether I might be interested. It hadn't crossed my mind because I was more than satisfied with my role. I was reluctant to a degree and spoke to many people whose opinion I valued. Pam and I went away for a week to talk it through; I spoke to Richard Skirrow, the secretary, and Mark McGhee, the manager. I could see the potential pitfalls as well as the positives but I knew I'd regret it later if I didn't take on the challenge. I said yes and it was a highly enlightening three years - frustrating but enjoyable. I'm glad I did it."

Richards' brief was to stem losses averaging over £5m a year while helping maintain the push for the Premiership. "It was Sir Jack's club but he was never a dictatorial chairman," he says. "He is one of the nicest people you could wish to meet. He's a gentleman, honest, genuine. If the fact he was not always well advised led to problems, he, to be fair, was always willing to take it on the chin himself." Richards' promotion came the year Sir Jack let loose with his 'golden tit' tirade in the wake of the play-off semi-final defeat by Crystal Palace. The benefactor felt squeezed unfairly for a never-ending supply of funds which still failed to lead Wolves to the top flight. "He speaks his mind, like a fan, and supporters appreciate that. If it hurts him, it frustrates him, then it's his club. Why shouldn't he say as much?'"

The MD enjoyed a good relationship with his managers. "I have a lot of time for Mark. I know a lot of fans say he wound people up but his confidence reflected how he saw things. He had Wolves' interests at heart. I can say the same of Colin Lee. It was disappointing when we didn't do better under Mark but it was part of the brief we had, to curb his spending. I wouldn't do anything differently over the sale of Robbie Keane. We got the best value at that time. Some board members were willing to take significantly less [than £6m]. Colin and myself were fully aware of his value."

Richards never wanted to be a manager and is frustrated when directors intervene in team affairs. "The skills are totally different. It was laughable and annoying - you could see it in the manager's face - if people who knew little about football questioned tactics. People who are on the board because of their wealth or via an invitation might say: 'I'd play 3-4-3' or 'I wouldn't play so-and-so in that position.' If this happened, I'd say: 'We appoint a manager to manage the team. Let him train and manage the players, select and pick a team, then judge him on results.' You can't start interfering with tactics and selection of players. It's hard for people to stop themselves. Everyone's a manager but you'd expect professional people to draw the line.

"Mark and Colin never asked my opinion about how the team played but we would talk about players, if they had personal difficulties, if they were carrying injuries, because all that can affect performances. At least then I was armed if the board asked me questions. I also spoke with the manager about strengthening the team or if we'd had any offers. It was at policy level rather than the actual details."

Nearing the end...a snap-shot taken from the Waterloo Road Stand captures Richards at his 1982 testimonial against Moscow Dynamo.

The club's losses were cut by 50 per cent in Richards' first year but then increased the next as Wolves, after reaching the FA Cup semi-final, gambled again on promotion. In the summer of 2000, Jez Moxey was brought in, a decision that effectively sidelined Richards. Was there a need for change? "Someone on the board obviously felt so," Richards says, "and I wouldn't necessarily say it was Sir Jack. The fact is if you're the MD or the chief executive of an organisation and the board don't think it is as successful as they'd like, you have two alternatives: the board goes or the MD goes.

"I walked out in the June. I don't think I had any alternative. I was MD and they brought in a chief exec. I did not accept the suggestion we could operate together." Was it a diplomatic bid to soften the badly-handled exit of a club great? "It wasn't diplomatic," he says. "I'd been out of my playing days a long time. You always prefer people to be honest and stab you in the front, so to speak. It's fair to say there were many things about my departure that disappointed me."

Pam comes in at this point, bronzed and healthy after her afternoon's sport, says hello, and hands her husband the day's *Express & Star*. Richards hurriedly turns it over to scour for Wolves news. He has been back to Molineux a couple of times in this Premiership season, although he generally keeps a politic distance. But his interest in the club's fortunes has not waned. He is optimistic they can push for an immediate return to the top flight, as they did in his hey-day a quarter of a century ago. He sympathises with Dave Jones' attempts to build a Premiership squad but does not join in the chorus of those asking Sir Jack why more funds weren't forthcoming.

"They had a lot of changes last summer, then, in January, with the addition of players such as Carl Cort. It takes a while for people to settle and I can understand Dave needing numbers in the Premier League. But it's impossible to juggle so many new balls. It takes time to adjust. You can see Dave is putting together the makings of a team. Looking back, the 3-3 draw at Manchester City was telling and the game at Chelsea could have been so different. I think there's enough there to give them a decent chance of automatic promotion."

There has been talk - inflated talk, Jones tells me subsequently - that Wolves will put the £7m 'parachute money' straight into squad strengthening. "If they could, that's pretty big money in the First Division. Dave has done an excellent job. It was difficult with coming late into it, needing numbers in his squad, then, because there was not enough money, needing to compromise on quality. I think Sir Jack was astounded that, despite the club getting up, with all the money from TV, people still went to him for money. It was a blow to him, the day they reached the promised land, the land of milk and honey, that the riches weren't enough to finance a Premiership club. I understand him walking away. We had a bad start to the season and people started slagging him off again. The longer you're in football, the more you realise there are people who are totally impossible to please. It's the Oliver Twist syndrome: more please."

Such are the ways of modern football. Liverpool splash out £100m chasing glory

Peter Lansley and his hero: a snap from the author's own album.

and fourth place isn't enough, Chelsea come in, splash out £200m and *second* place isn't enough. Excuse a moment's nostalgia, if you will, for the times when the soul of the game did not come with a price tag attached, and the random nature of the sport meant anyone could go into a game or a season with the hope of winning. I drove up the Holloway on the way to this interview to see the house we lived in when such was the ethos of football. Wood End looks jaded now, a tired version of the fresh and trendy house that Dad built us three decades ago, and so remarkably small. How did my brothers and I make that little driveway our Molineux?

It is time to move on. My host has a social engagement I'm making him late for; my Mum's got dinner on the table in Bridgnorth, where I'm staying overnight in order to meet Dave Jones in the morning. It has been a long and pleasant haul - four hours to cover 20 years of Richards association with this club. But I get the impression we could have carried on for another four and still not tired of running with Wolves. There are some things you just can't get out of your system, nor want to.

John Richards

Born:	November 9, 1950, in Warrington
Signed:	July, 1969
Wolves appearances:	486
Goals:	194
Left:	August, 1983
International recognition:	1 full England cap

Afterword

LESSONS TO BE LEARNED FROM AN OPPORTUNITY MISSED

May 17, 2004: Wolves' training ground, Newbridge, Tettenhall

The potholed pathway to the huts that pass for changing-rooms is full of puddles. Like a course to safety in the Barclaycard Premiership, it is riven with obstacles. Yet while relegation has been mathematically sealed two days earlier - no 17-0 wins can save Wolves now - there is a positive vibe about the club that refuses to go away. No cigar, but the fire still burns.

Perhaps an incipient acceptance of their impending demotion had hit home earlier, when grand efforts against Chelsea and Liverpool brought exactly the same number of points as capitulation to Aston Villa and Southampton. Maybe now Wolves have left the Premiership with their heads held high, with a few goals flying in, a run of one defeat in six games boding well for next season and boardroom talk of backing Dave Jones for a renewed promotion campaign, supporters have regained some credibility.

"There are a lot of good players here, good pros," Jones says, as Catherine Preece, from the press office, passes teas round in the end hut. "This club has changed in the last three years. I don't honestly think the fans have seen players like this for many years. And they have seen how hard they work. We talk about foundations - they are here, but they do need to be built on."

Jones has heard the right noises from Rick Hayward, his chairman, and believes Wolves will build and can return a stronger club. Training-ground facilities leave a lot to be desired but a £3million renovation is promised. Transfer funds are being made available and Jones has put his list in front of the powers-that-be and asked them to go shopping. If Wolves can bounce back - without taking another 19 years about it - the manager is adamant they should have learned enough lessons to stay put next time.

The big question remains: why did Wolves not invest more ambitiously following promotion? That is not one Jones can answer; he can deal only with player selections within the squad he was allowed to assemble. I could ask why he threw Paul Jones in when Michael Oakes had just found his best form in January; indeed, why start Carl Cort when Steffen Iversen and Kenny Miller had just struck up an understanding? Sure, the squad needed greater depth - understatement or what - but it was after those changes that the stuffing was knocked out of Wolves' revival hopes. It all goes back, though, to the lack of quality signings last summer. I could plough on and ask why

Jody Craddock was given such a long stay of execution when he had hit a run of form so bad that he could not kick the ball out of play when James Beattie was right behind him in the penalty area. But these would be the nit-pickings of a tired and angry fan.

"I don't regret anything because I made a decision and I live by it," Jones says. "It's easy to look back and wonder about doing things differently - but how do you know how it would have panned out? So I'll stand by my decisions or fall by them. There are lots of things you could say I'd like to change. I think we've missed an opportunity to stay in the Premiership; now what we have to do is learn from that and become stronger. This club can be anything it wants to be. We just have to make sure the decisions we make from now on are the right ones.

"In the three full years I've been here, talking about the whole club now, we haven't made many wrong decisions. We might have made them too late, but I don't think we've made the wrong ones. The big question's going to be: why didn't we invest at the start of the season? That's one you'll have to ask the people in charge."

The football world has asked that question enough this past season. Alan Curbishley, who had to build his Charlton Athletic side through bouncing between the top two divisions, is thought to have expected Wolves to throw £20m at strengthening. Chat about where they have faltered to Martin O'Neill, the Celtic manager who repeatedly took promoted Leicester City into the top ten of the Premiership, and the lack of investment is soon cited.

There are other factors. In gaining promotion late, through the play-offs, Wolves were still - understandably - locating the suntan lotion when others were signing the few Premiership players going begging. And, as Kenny Miller played on into June with Scotland, his recuperation from surgery meant a delayed and staggered start from which he never recovered. Mark Kennedy missed the start of the season; Joleon Lescott and Matt Murray, two players I'd have hung my hat on performing decently in the top flight, made a single appearance between them. "I'm absolutely gutted for those two," Lee Naylor says, as we watch Lescott enjoying his light training. "They're two of the main characters who got us into the Premier League and to miss out on the whole experience is gutting. We want to get it back for them. They're big players and we want them to enjoy the Premiership with us next time.

"To get that experience under your belt is a massive thing. Knowing what to expect is really useful. A lot of the players did have that, but many of us didn't, so now everyone's had a taste of it, they want it back badly and, when they do get it back, I'm sure they won't let it go that easy."

A campaign has begun to persuade Henri Camara to stay. The Senegal flags started popping out at St James's Park, where Wolves gave the sort of heroic performance that, if produced in the devastating opening weeks of the season, would surely have given the team a platform to stay up. These concluding sentiments are not supposed to be mere lamentations for a single season that did not finish in glory, however. The bigger picture remains that Wolves are a club not only steeped in grand traditions and great old players, but one with the potential to reclaim them once more. It may take time but the capacity is there.

May 9, 2004: St James's Park, Newcastle

As soon as they played *Hi Ho Silver Lining* at Brassington village disco the night before we went to Newcastle, I knew it was going to be a good day. Wolves fans were sweating and breathless by the time they reached their segment right up at the top, in the corner, of St James's Park. Altitude sickness? We had our sights on 18th place. Emboldened by fish and chips from the Bigg Market and a couple of pints in the Black Bull - told you we were fated for a good afternoon - the gold and black travellers were in fine voice. Simon, initially frustrated at not being allowed to hang down the 'Out of Darkness' banner Sue made him, turned to me after Paul Jones saved Alan Shearer's penalty and yelled: "Happy birthday to me." Seventeen years after we had celebrated my little brother's birthday with a Bully hat-trick against Hartlepool United in Division Four, this felt like progress.

The grass we pinched off the turf at Blundell Park, after we nicked a 1-0 win off Grimsby Town 14 months ago, and that from the Millennium Stadium pitch remains mingled in my wallet, just underneath pictures of Tom and Joe. Get promoted again in 2004-05 and I might just smoke it. By this time next year, there might be another hero making an indelible impression upon the Wolves fraternity. See that spare shirt on the cover? It is waiting to be filled in with a name.

June 11, 2004: Brassington, Derbyshire

England play France on Sunday in Euro 2004 and, as we sit out on our terrace overlooking the village green that has become our sports field, Jacqui, emboldened by her Pimms, takes a risk. She asks the boys if they imagine they will support Wolves all their lives, like Dad and Grandpa. Twelve months to the day since I started writing this book, 24 hours after the new gold and black kit, with a simple collar, has gone on sale, I miss a breath. I don't want to place any unfair burdens on our children, naturally, but then again...

As the house martins and swallows swoop in the field beyond, Tom gnaws on his barbecued burger and says he might have to consider Reading, seeing as he was born there, but he'll see how it pans out; Joe confesses that Manchester United and Wolves share top billing. Their mother points out that Arsenal won the Barclaycard Premiership, if excellence is crucial, and that Derby County and Stoke City are rather more accessible if regional loyalty is a factor. Joe comes to a unilateral decision. "Let's stick with Wolves," he says. Then it's time for the penalty shoot-out.

Subscribers

Scroll of Honour

A

Pete Abbott
Chris Alldritt
Douglas Allsop
Cole Arkinstall
Charlie Arkwright
Matt Ashwood
Martin Astley

B

Adrian Paul Baker
Andrew Baker
Aidan and Aimie Ball
Charlie and Peter Bamforth
Neil and Sheila Barnes
Josef and Jessica Bartl
Paul Bater
Jonathan Bayley
David Bellingham
Mr L F Best
Joseph Grant-Bicknell
Andrew Bill
Malcolm Black
George Blackhall
Laurence Blackhall
Robert Blackhall
Richard Bonner
Gordon Bradshaw
Tim P Brady
Ulf Brennmo
Simon Brown
Tim M Brown
Victor Browning
Mr T J Buckle
Andrew Bullock
Craig W Bunday
Paul Burden
Steve Burroughs
David Paul Burrows

C

Alfred Camilleri
Mick Canning
Don Carman
Robin Carr
Martin James Carroll
Carter family, Codsall
Edward Cartwright
Elizabeth Cartwright
Fran Cartwright
Jonathan Cartwright
Rob Cartwright
Angela J Checketts
Melvyn J Checketts
Lauren Chrimes
E Clark
Ian Clarke
John Clarke
Luke Clarke
Mark Clements
David Cleveland
Dick and Matt Cleverly
Chris Collier
Celine Commenge
Ann Corser
Gareth Corser
Keith Cox
Steven Cox
Graham Cozens
Bob Crockett
Malcolm Crockett
Reg Crook
Gio and James Cura

D

Simon Dale
Stian Dalland
John Dallaway
Ashley and Joe Dallow
Brian N Daniels

Harry Davenhill
Rob Davies
Roy S Davies
Davies family, Leics/Shrops
Eric Deakin
Peter J Deans
Gisela and Harold Degg
Brian and Helen Dennis
Simon Devereux
Alistair Dey
Sharon Dimmer
Carolyne Dix
Tom Dreyer
Keith Dunn

E

Ian Eccles
Lawrence Ellis
Margaret and Terry Emery
Paul Endersby
Steve English
Barrie Evans
Les Evans
Michael Evans
Richard Evans
Matthew William Everiss

F

Carol Faulkner
Trine Fehmerling
Mrs Judith A Fish
Andrew and Maggie Flack
Margaret Fletcher
Nigel Flook
Bryan and Tina Follett
Sally Foster
Rich Frampton
Victoria Frankham
Peter Frohlich
Colin Futrill

G

Nick Gage
Kate Gelsthorpe
Tim Gingell
Jack Giles
Clive Green
Robert H Green
Ken Gregory
Crad Griffiths
Bjorn Gudbjornsson
Stuart A Guest

H

Steve Hale
Alan Hall
Ron Hall
Robert Hands
Nigel Harcourt
Martin Harold
Carl Harper
Matthew Harris
Reg Harris
Alan Harrison
Daniel Harrison
Neil Harrison
Alan J Harvey
John Harvey
Stephen Harvey
Michael Hawkes
Jim Heath
Andrew Hemming
Odin B Henrikssen
Alwyn Hill
Jake Hill
Rod Hill
Robert Holding
Guy Holland
Chris Honeywill
Paul Horton
Gareth John Hughes
Jonathan Hunter

J

Mark S Jackson
Ken and Darren Jaffrey
Gareth Jenkins
Adam Jewkes
Wayne Johnson

Glen Jones
Graham Jones
Peter Jones
Trevor Jones

K

Dalbir Kang
Randhir Kang
John Kedward
David Keeling
Alec Kokinis

L

John Lalley
Gareth Langdon
Sarah and George Lansley
Shawn and Pauline Law
Andy Lewis
Andrew Light
Hannah and Richard Lloyd
John D Lloyd
William Lloyd
Jonathan Lockley
Duncan Lowe
John Lowrey
Roy Lyon
Nina Lucas
Arild Lund
Peter and Ryan Lunn

M

Gwilym Machin
Jackie 'The Wolf' Maddox
Liam Maher
Peter J Marchant
John Marquis
Derek Marriott
Beulah and Eric Mason
David Matthews
The McAtamneys...Kathleen,
Leo, Martin, Kieran, James,
Rory, David and Conor
Maria and Iain McGuinness
Terry McIntyre
Rob McLeod
Paddy McShane, Irish Wolf
Mark Meredith
Royden Meredith

Per Magnar Meyer
Jean Pierre Micallef
Tarcisio Mifsud
Philip Miles Jnr
Mr E J Millington
Brian Millward
Molloy Family, Belfast
James Monks
John Moon
Lee Morgan
Andy Morris
Joe James Morris
Jake Moses
Neil Murray

N

Geoff Narraway
Antony Nicholls
Debbie Nicholls
Doreen Nicholls
Isaac B Nicholls
Mark Nicholls and family
Bob Nicholson
John Nuttall

O

Steve Oates (in memory of
Fred Oates)
Mark O'Connor
Terry Owers

P

Phil Page
Robert W Palmer
Terry Palmer
Stuart Parry
Matt and Tom Partridge
Anthony Paternotte
Ron Peacock
Douglas John Pearl
Richard Pendrell
David Phillips
Mr J Picton
Steve and Nick Polkinghorne
Kevin Ponder
Jason Poole
Michael Poole (1968-2003)
Robert Poulton

Martyn Pritchard
Tommy Purslow

R

Dale Race
Norman Edward Radford
Clifford Arthur Raison
Steven Ralph
Neil Raphael
Mike Redfern
Trevor and Callum Reed
Laura Richards
Paul Richards
Bill Richardson
Mark Roberts
Olwyn Roberts
Phil Roberts
Colin Robertson
Chris Rowsell
Jonathan Russell

S

Chris Salmon
Danny and Roy Sanderson
Brian Sawbridge
Mark Sawbridge
Peter J Schofield
Richard Sharp
Neil Shaw
Ben Sherriff
Ken Sherwood
Max Sidbotham
George Sinagra
Dave Slape
Mike Slater
John Slynn
Adam Smith
Christopher Daniel Smith
Clare Smith
Stew Smith
Svein Solberg
Southport Wolf
Mark Squire
John Stanford
Nigel Steel
Adrian Steele
John G Steventon
Paul D R Stimson FBDO
Dagfinn Stokkenes

T

David K Taylor
Graham Taylor
Mark Thomas
Brian Timmis
D A E Tomlinson
Ross Tuckwood
Glyn Tunney, Emma Evans
Glenn K Turner
Tony Turpin

V

Stig Vangsnes
Petr 'Prague Wolf' Vovisek

W

Roger J Wakeham
Tyrone Walsh
Dennis Walton
Gethin Andrew Webb
Andrew Wedge
David J Welham
Mike and Hazel Westwood
A E White
Fred Whitehouse
Chris Whittall
Nigel Wilcox
David Williams
Joan and Peter Williams
Judith A Williams
Stephen Williams
Steve 'Willi' Williams
Thomas A Williams
David Willis
Darren Winwood
John Raymond Winwood
Don Wolvey
Craig Wood
Harry Woodman
Robin M Woodward
Nicholas Worthington
Andrew L M Wright
Katie Wright
Peter Wright
Michael Wright

Z

Sandra Zebedee

Other Wolves titles by Thomas Publications, all written by David Instone, are:

*The Bully Years (£8.99)
*Wolves: Exclusive! (£6.99)
*Sir Jack (£12.99)
*Forever Wolves (£16.99)

All these books are available by writing to Thomas Publications, P O Box 17, Newport, Shropshire, TF10 7WT, or e-mailing thomaspublications@blueyonder.co.uk

Look out soon for the Thomas Publications website.